From the Front Porch to the Front Page

Number Thirteen:
Presidential Rhetoric Series
Martin J. Medhurst, General Editor

From the Front Porch
to the Front Page

McKinley and Bryan

in the 1896 Presidential Campaign

WILLIAM D. HARPINE

Texas A&M University Press   College Station

Photograph is courtesy of The Wm McKinley Presidential Library and
Museum, Canton, Ohio.

Portions of chapters 1, 2, 3, and 10 appeared in an earlier version as
"Playing to the Press in McKinley's Front Porch Campaign: The Early
Weeks of a Nineteenth-Century Pseudo-Event," *Rhetoric Society Quarterly*
30.3 (2000): 73–90. Used by permission of the Rhetoric Society of
America.

Portions of chapters 1, 2, 4, and 10 appeared in an earlier version as
"Bryan's 'A Cross of Gold': The Rhetoric of Polarization at the 1896
Democratic Convention," *Quarterly Journal of Speech* 87 (2001): 291–304.
Used by permission of the National Communication Association.

LIBRARY OF CONGRESS CATALOGING-IN-PUBLICATION DATA

Harpine, William D. 1951–
    From the front porch to the front page : McKinley and Bryan in the
1896 presidential campaign / William D. Harpine.— 1st ed.
        p. cm. — (Presidential rhetoric series ; no. 13)
    Includes bibliographical references (p.   ) and index.
    ISBN 1-58544-450-2 (cloth : alk. paper)
    ISBN 13: 978-1-58544-559-2 (pbk.)
    ISBN 10: 1-58544-559-2 (pbk.)
    1. Presidents—United States—Election—1896. 2. Political
campaigns—United States—History—19th century. 3. United
States—Politics and government—1893–1897. 4. McKinley, William,
1843–1901. 5. Bryan, William Jennings, 1860–1925. 6. Rhetoric—
Political aspects—United States—History—19th century.
I. Title. II. Series.
E710.H37   2005
324.973'087—dc22   2005000436

To Elaine,

who has not only shared her life with me,

but who has supported and encouraged me

throughout this project.

Oratory sometimes has been laughed at, but, my friends, oratory will be with us as long as the human race endures. Whenever there is a cause that stirs men's hearts there will be orators to present that cause. Eloquence is simply the speech of a person who knows what he is talking about and believes what he says.

From a speech by William J. Bryan
in Des Moines, Iowa, on August 7, 1896

Contents

Acknowledgments

So many people helped me to complete this project that it is impossible to thank all of them. No one is more aware than the author of the limitations of a study like this. Without the help of all of these persons, however, this study's limitations would be far greater.

Research used in this project was gathered at the libraries of the University of Akron, John Carroll University, Youngstown State University, Kent State University, and George Mason University as well as at the Chicago and New York public libraries, the Kent Free Library in Kent, Ohio, the Library of Congress, and the library of the Western Reserve Historical Society. I am grateful to the unfailingly courteous staffs at these institutions for their willing and knowledgeable assistance in finding obscure materials, guiding me in productive directions, and helping with uncooperative microfilm readers.

While working on this study, I presented drafts of many portions of this book as papers at scholarly meetings. A number of professors offered comments about the work, and I have incorporated their suggestions to the best of my abilities. I particularly wish to thank John Hammerback, Delores Tanno, Robert Sullivan, Mary Kahl, and Michael Schliessmann. Bill Balthrop pointed out to me the relevance of Simon's work on social movements.

A number of members of the American Society for the History of Rhetoric offered me encouragement during the early stages of the work. I would especially like to thank Jeffrey Walker, Sean Patrick O'Rourke, Glen McClish, Michael Leff, and Carol Poster for their part in energizing my work. Mari Lee Mifsud made some important suggestions for pursuing certain kinds of historical approaches.

Martin J. Medhurst, Mary Lenn Dixon, and Jennifer Ann Hobson encouraged and advised me throughout this project. Most of all, I express my gratitude to my wife, Elaine Clanton Harpine, who read several drafts of the manuscript and repeatedly offered me encouragement to complete the project.

Introduction

I N THE WANING DAYS of August 1896, still early in his first presidential campaign, William Jennings Bryan of Nebraska stood before an audience at the Music Hall in Cleveland, Ohio, and thundered: "We have the gold standard. It came to us without our desire." He announced that in opposition to the gold standard, "We have begun a war that knows no truce, we ask no quarter, we give no quarter. It is war, war, war."[1]

Indeed it was war, in a fashion, although fought with words rather than bullets. Ohio's former governor William McKinley faced off with the former newspaper editor and former member of Congress from Nebraska, William Jennings Bryan. Nonetheless, the opponents never met on the same battlefield. McKinley refused to accept the monetary standard as the central issue of the campaign. He discussed the money issue frequently, but he presented his own highly successful oratory, founded on his own issues, in his own way, on his own ground.

The year 1896 witnessed one of the hardest-fought, most dramatic presidential campaigns in the history of the United States. Soon after the election, Bryan himself wrote that "the campaign of 1896 was a remarkable one whether we measure it by the magnitude of the issues involved or by the depth of interest aroused."[2] Although some described the 1896 campaign as a campaign of education, oratory played an important part. The candidates, and often the public, characterized the election as a pivotal point in American history. Both candidates employed dramatic, impressively creative campaign devices. Both candidates proved to be capable and energetic public speakers. Both addressed the campaign issues, mostly the gold standard and the protective tariff, in a way that roused public interest in politics to a frenzy. That the campaign's major issues turned out, in the end, to be stunningly inconsequential does not even seem to matter. The 1896 campaign gave the public what was very likely the most dramatic political oratory in the nation's history. From the folksy speeches that McKinley gave from his front porch, the campaign rapidly progressed to Bryan's famous speech "A Cross of Gold" and to vigorous, sophisticated attempts by both candidates to win the public.

McKinley stayed at home in Canton, Ohio, throughout the campaign. Thousands of people rode the train to Canton to hear him present brief speeches from his front porch. Within a few weeks of the campaign's beginning, the front porch speeches became dramatic political spectacles. Well reported in the press, McKinley's more than three hundred speeches repeatedly advocated a small number of political positions. McKinley's Front Porch campaign was not typical of his approach from earlier campaigns. Even McKinley's supporters noted that his earlier campaigns often featured vigorous speaking tours.[3] For McKinley's image, the consequences of this stay-at-home campaign were startling. Even decades later, some otherwise well-informed writers got the impression that McKinley hardly campaigned at all.[4]

Bryan, in the meantime, traveled around large parts of the country by train. He stopped at towns and cities along the way to give speeches, some short and some very long. Bryan gave perhaps twice as many speeches as McKinley, some of them quite dramatic. Bryan also covered a much larger range of issues than did McKinley. Thus, the candidates campaigned in striking but contrasting fashion.

Both candidates in this election have been the victims of widespread misunderstanding. During the campaign, the candidates' various public opponents threw out unjustified personal attacks in quantity. Unfortunately, this kind of political posturing of the candidates' supporters and opponents continues to influence scholarly opinion about these two orators even today. A popular view emerged that McKinley was too boring to study, that he was a dull, stodgy orator who won only because Marcus Hanna, who chaired the Republican Party National Committee, bought the election for him. McKinley's rhetoric was actually far from boring, for he was intelligent, articulate, and quick on his feet. Although he lacked Bryan's ability to strike to the heart of an issue with a single, rapier-like thrust of eloquence, McKinley's speeches are not without expressiveness. He possessed a rare ability to give speeches that were solemn and dignified and yet could convince ordinary Americans that he understood them and had their best interests at heart. When one reads McKinley's speeches in the newspapers, a certain solid, trustworthy folksiness jumps off the page.

Bryan's critics, on the other hand, too frequently dismiss him as a bombastic ignoramus. Although Bryan was often a flashy speaker, and made calculated appeals to the ordinary American, his speeches show considerable evidence of intelligence, knowledge, and insight.

Bryan may be equally well known today for his work assisting the prosecution in the 1925 Scopes evolution trial. No doubt the excellent play *Inherit the Wind,* in which the character of Matthew Harrison Brady obviously takes after Bryan, has encouraged the public to underestimate Bryan's accomplishments.[5] Although many authors criticized his performance in that trial, an argument can be made that his rhetorical skills not only remained sharp, but that he saw the trial as continued advocacy of his liberal social ideals.[6]

Rhetorical scholars have not studied either of the major presidential candidates in the dramatic campaign of 1896 as much as one might have expected, but it is ironic that the loser in this campaign has become more renowned as an orator than the winner.[7] Nonetheless, although Bryan is greatly admired as an orator, even the loser's campaign speaking has received surprisingly little scholarly study.[8]

This book presents the results of an investigation in political rhetoric. To gain a better understanding of political rhetoric of the late nineteenth century seems worthwhile in and of itself, and it is fascinating to discover—contrary to much of what students of political communication seem to believe—how similar the 1896 campaign was in its techniques and strategies to the campaigns of much later. Bryan and McKinley lacked access to the communication technology of radio and television, so central for candidates of a century later, but they accomplished the same purposes with newspapers and the wire services. The differences are instructive.

A hundred years later, politicians came to specialize in the brief sound bite that appeals to a television audience. McKinley and Bryan, however, both devoted greater attention to developing and explaining their positions on the campaign's issues than did the candidates of a hundred years later.

This is, however, not merely a study of politics but of political rhetoric. What does that mean? The root of the word *rhetoric* is the Greek *rhé*, which signifies speech.[9] Rhetoric, in its origins, meant public speaking. Over the years the study of rhetoric has come to include all persuasive communication, including written and nonverbal communication. All the same, speech continues to be central to rhetoric, no matter how broadly one thinks about it. The present book is focused on the candidates' public speaking. This is not to deny the importance of the extensive publications that the machinery of all the major political parties distributed during the campaign.[10] A number of excellent books cover the campaign's organization and issues.[11] The actual public speaking of the candidates has, strangely, been slighted.

Nonetheless, in an election like that of 1896, the effect of the candidates' speaking remains in the back of one's mind. It is difficult, perhaps impossible, to measure the impact of historical speeches. So many factors other than a speech can influence an audience's response. One must be cautious about ascertaining the effects of a speech or even a campaign of speeches.[12] Perhaps the best indication that the candidates' own speaking in this campaign made a difference comes not from external evidence of effect—for that type of evidence is notoriously difficult to find—but from examining the texts and other records of the speeches themselves, viewed in their context within the campaign as a whole. I aim to show that both McKinley and Bryan presented oral rhetoric of power, ingenuity, and interest. In the end, the public speaking of these candidates stands up for itself. The candidates' oratory possibly had its greatest influence in the press reports of the campaign, rather than through the responses of the live audiences, but the oral quality of the events emerged all the same.

Why is the public speaking in this campaign, among the many presidential campaigns of American history, worth our attention today, more than a century later? There are several reasons:

1. The campaign sharply divided American politics into two rival camps. Bryan, nominated by the Democrats but also supported by the more radical Populist and National Silver parties, wrenched the Democratic Party away from its traditional reactionary stance and transformed it into a party of the ordinary worker who resented the wealthy and powerful. Thus Bryan paved the path that the Franklin Roosevelt revolution in the Democratic Party would follow. McKinley, presumably recognizing the need to appeal to traditionally Democratic voters, undertook to make the Republican Party attractive to ordinary working people. McKinley understood, more clearly than did Bryan, the significance of the nation's urbanization and industrialization. Both candidates thus undertook to create new and often controversial coalitions of voters.

2. The campaign of 1896 generated an enormous amount of attention among the public. The losing candidate, Bryan, received more votes than any winning presidential candidate before him. Voter turnout reached about 80 percent.[13] People cared about this election with a deep, almost unfathomable passion.

3. Both candidates were outstanding public speakers, but they employed contrasting approaches. Bryan was energetic and, at his best, remarkably eloquent. He was able to articulate key issues with great precision. Members of the public, even those who opposed him, turned out in huge numbers just to hear him speak. Myron Phillips terms Bryan "one of the greatest orators of modern times."[14] Few would argue with that assessment. McKinley possessed an exceptional ability to make himself seem just like "home folks." His ability to identify naturally and easily with the common citizen deflected the Democrats' charge that he was a stooge of big business. Far less dramatic than Bryan, McKinley may actually have been an even more persuasive public speaker. One does not study a McKinley speech and feel that one has studied great oratory. McKinley did, however, speak very convincingly. Thus, the speeches of both candidates serve as outstanding examples of political public speaking. It could be said

that Bryan at his best excelled at oratory as an art, while McKinley mastered oratory as a means of getting things done. One might respond to a Bryan speech as a great speech about a silly idea; with McKinley one is more likely to respond that the speech was rather dull but the speaker was right.

4. Although the campaign issues seemed like little more than footnotes to the whole business, they symbolized important relationships for American voters. Bryan's central issue, the unlimited coinage of silver money, represented his attack against the big business interests of the Northeast. McKinley's chief issue, the protective tariff, symbolized the importance of economic and industrial development. Thus, although both McKinley and Bryan advocated what many modern economists would consider to be economic absurdities, they did so in a way that conveyed concern for the welfare of the voters.

5. In a thoroughly modern manner, both candidates created what Daniel Boorstin calls *pseudo-events*.[15] That is, they put on a series of spectacular meetings and events designed to gain public attention and staged for the sole purpose of being reported. Despite their ability to captivate live audiences, both candidates constantly produced events that enabled them to speak to the public through the media. Although both candidates were aware of the importance of reporters and newspapers, McKinley's campaign speeches seemed to be more consistently adapted to the newspaper readership.

In a more general way, a closer look by historians of rhetoric at the public speaking of late nineteenth-century presidents and presidential campaigns is long overdue. Although the rhetorical history of the eighteenth and early nineteenth centuries has received careful study, the post–Civil War period of American oratory has been largely neglected. The few studies of this period typically examine Chautauqua-style speaking, relatively obscure public speakers, or obscure speeches by famous people. For example, although some of Bryan's speeches have received scrutiny in the scholarly literature, little critical study has been devoted to the "Cross of Gold" speech he gave during the 1896 platform debate at the Democratic National Convention—the speech that made his career. Nor has any rhetoric or communication journal ever published a study of Bryan's railroad tours during the 1896 campaign. Most observers agree that Bryan's speaking during this campaign was powerful and effective, to the point that it is routinely mentioned as a model of political speaking, but they hold this opinion in the absence of serious scholarly evidence.

McKinley, one of the most successful politicians of his time, has been even more neglected. Only a few studies have examined his public speaking, and there has been little study of the rhetoric of either of his presidential campaigns. There have been some excellent studies of McKinley's Spanish American War rhetoric.[16] Rhetorical historians, when they mention McKinley at all, often dismiss him as a tool of Cleveland, Ohio's big business interests.

Some of Bryan's speaking did much to advance his image as an uninformed, dangerous firebrand. Nonetheless, by and large, the criticisms of Bryan are based on the views of his political enemies, most of whom hated him with a passion rare even in the torrid atmosphere of late nineteenth-century politics. The following chapters present evidence that Bryan knew the issues as well as did most major politicians of his day. Certainly the powers of his mind are often obvious, and the great liberality of his heart sometimes shows as well.

Thus it is impossible for anyone who has studied their speeches to sympathize with the common misimpressions of McKinley and Bryan.

On a broader note, too many rhetorical scholars take the view that there has already been enough historical research about American public speaking, and there is no need for any more. This attitude is insupportable. Although a number of historical studies appeared before 1960, only some of them investigated primary source materials; many relied on previously published historical and biographical studies. As a result, too few rhetorical figures have been investigated at first hand. Important figures in American public address completely escaped scrutiny during that supposed heyday of public address studies.[17] Years later, many important rhetorical events are still unstudied.[18] This is unfortunate, for few of the biographers and historians who have gathered the primary sources about great American orators have taken much interest in the public speaking careers of these individuals. As a result, their studies often do not reflect a sophisticated understanding of public speaking. Consequently, many of the opinions that rhetorical historians have held about public speakers are not the result of careful examination of contemporaneous materials. This is certainly the case with McKinley and Bryan and may be the main motivation behind the bizarre evaluations that persist about both speakers. There is no substitute for studying sources that come close to the actual events.

The reasons for conducting historical studies in public address are many. One is so that we as public speakers can learn from the past. Public speakers often wish to examine models of public speaking to guide their own work. Some of the most frequently cited models, however, are ceremonial speeches that are not typical of the kind of speech most likely to be effective in a political or business setting, for example. Much-studied speeches like Martin Luther King Jr.'s "I Have a Dream" or John F. Kennedy's inaugural address may have been created and delivered more to reinforce basic values than to motivate people to undertake specific and controversial courses of action. There has been far too little study, and therefore too little understanding, of nuts-and-bolts political campaign speaking.

In addition, we as *consumers* of political rhetoric can learn from the past. Was the political rhetoric of the past more issues oriented? How did politicians of the past manipulate public opinion? How did they adapt to their audiences? Can we find the roots of modern political discourse and in so doing better understand the political rhetoric of our own time? To what extent does present-day political oratory reflect the traditions of American public address? Such questions can only be answered by studying the interaction between the speakers and the audiences in detail.

A few words are in order about methodological issues. In this study, both historical and critical in focus, I endeavor to offer insights into McKinley and Bryan's public speaking. Theory is employed with a lighter touch than would be typical in a scholarly communication journal. The book is quite eclectic methodologically. During the course of this study, Burke's concepts of identification and division emerge as a continuing, underlying theme.[19] McKinley, for the most part, put forward a *rhetoric of identification* while Bryan sought to *divide and conquer*. Within this theme, various theories and methodologies of rhetorical criticism shed light on different aspects of the campaign's rhetoric. The book does offer some theoretical innovations, particularly in the analysis of McKinley's speech to the workers of Homestead, which no previous methodology seemed capable of illuminating clearly.

In other words, analysis uses theory to illuminate rhetorical history, not the other way around. The 1896 political campaign featured a unique and complex series of political events. A too vigorous effort to impose a preconceived theoretical model on those events would shroud the significance of much of what happened. The events of this important campaign should not be judged by their ability to illustrate theory. In the end, rigorous theory can arise only from a careful study of events. Furthermore, although this work is light on theoretical refutation, it should become clear that some of the rhetorical criticism apparatus scholars have brought to bear on speeches such as those of 1896 needs to be modified because it has been based on imprecise information about rhetorical practice.

A different critical methodology is employed in each chapter to illuminate a particular feature of the candidates' rhetoric. This process resembles what Donald Campbell calls "triangulation."[20] Different sources and points of view can confirm and clarify one's conclusions. Truth is likely to be complex and subtle. A quantum physicist does not expect a single perspective to explain the entire subatomic world. Scholars of rhetoric cannot expect a single theory to explain all rhetorical accomplishments. Thus different chapters employ theoretical positions based on the work of Kenneth Burke, Jean-Paul Sartre, John Waite Bowers and Donovan Ochs, and various other thinkers.

Although this study is methodologically eclectic, it is theoretically coherent. Presumably, if one placed all of the sages named in the same room at the same time, they would find various issues about which to disagree. As an obvious example, if one were fortunate enough to bring the shades of Jean-Paul Sartre and Kenneth Burke together in one's living room, those two astute spirits might soon get into a lively dispute about Freud's theory of the unconscious. Nonetheless, the study does not employ any concept from one theorist that is inconsistent with concepts employed from other theorists.

One might compare the critical methodologies used with a decorator looking at a table lamp. Viewed from above, the lamp is circular. Viewed from the side, the lamp has a mushroom shape. One perspective leads the decorator to conclude that the lamp is circular; the other perspective leads the decorator to conclude that the lamp is a much different shape. Are these conclusions contradictory? Seemingly they conflict, yet both are correct. Interestingly, all the methodologies employed in this study point toward the same central themes; the conclusions do not even appear contradictory. Rather, they elucidate different aspects of the same group of rhetorical phenomena.

In the case of most of the material about McKinley, the chapter-by-chapter choice of methodology was often arbitrary. Overall, McKinley's rhetoric followed a consistent pattern from the beginning of the campaign to the end. He played the same immensely complex themes repeatedly, and he often addressed the same two issues in similar words in one speech after another after another. His speeches, most of them short, seem at first glance to be remarkably simple. Even so, most of them employ a host of ingenious rhetorical techniques. Thus, for example, McKinley's summer speeches are studied as part of what Boorstin would call a pseudo-event. McKinley's speeches of September, 1896, were not much different from the August speeches, and one could as easily have studied the September campaigning as a series of pseudo-events. Similarly, the theme of rhetorical identification, which comes to the fore in chapter 6, actually emerged in the great majority of McKinley's speeches throughout the campaign. The month-by-month breakdown for McKinley simply helps to organize the study's ideas in a way that illuminates the speeches vis-à-vis each theoretical concept.

Bryan's rhetoric, on the other hand, developed during the campaign. Less experienced and less self-assured than McKinley, Bryan began the campaign as a little-known political insider who raised the roof at the Democratic convention. A month later, he turned briefly to solid respectability to give his acceptance speech. As the campaign progressed from beginning to end, the Democratic candidate became increasingly bitter and defensive. He changed the focus of his speeches and his attitude toward his audiences. By coincidence, the change of the calendar from one month to the next correlated with changes in the tone and content of Bryan's rhetoric, making a month-by-month arrangement convenient.

Most of the chapters offer conclusions based on a study of an entire month's worth of speeches. This gives a clear representation of the campaign as a whole and shows the patterns and trends of the rhetoric that audiences heard in person or read about in the newspapers. This procedure also ensures that the conclusions are founded on an understanding of the campaign as a whole, not just of one or two arbitrarily chosen speeches. Depth, however, seemed to be as important as breadth, and three chapters therefore examine individual speeches in detail. In Bryan's case, the famous "A Cross of Gold," delivered during the platform debate at the Democratic convention, was obligatory. This was the speech that made Bryan's reputation. Bryan's acceptance speech was also a major, widely reported address that may have done nearly as much to undo his oratorical reputation as "A Cross of Gold" did to create it. Furthermore, the rhetorical intricacies of both speeches are extremely interesting.

In contrast to Bryan, no single speech of McKinley's stands out clearly over the others. McKinley's acceptance speech was dull, routine, and safe.[21] Although commotion and ceremony filled the Front Porch campaign, McKinley studiously avoided the kinds of dramatic mass spectacles that became *de rigueur* for Bryan. Indeed, the most striking feature of McKinley's speeches was their day-in, day-out similarity. The speeches varied just enough to keep people interested. The critic's task was therefore not to choose a remarkable speech of McKinley's to study in depth but rather a typical one. His speech to the workers from Homestead thus serves as an example of a kind of rhetoric that was characteristic of McKinley's Front Porch campaign. Although this was one of his better speeches, it does not seem especially noteworthy—at least not until one examines it in depth. Once one studies it in detail, several important features of the speech, and of the campaign in general, become clearer.

For the most part, I have used the texts of speeches as published in the newspapers. Other sorts of texts are occasionally examined due to necessity or expediency. Both candidates published their speeches as campaign documents, but these cheaply printed books and pamphlets were sometimes extensively edited and may not closely reflect what the candidate actually said. In the case of McKinley's published speeches, the typescripts of the campaign documents, apparently prepared for the printer, have been preserved in archives. Comments like "Applause" appear to be penciled into these works in the handwriting of McKinley's private secretary and editor, newspaper reporter Joseph Smith.[22] Shorthand reporters employed by newspapers and wire services did the same, of course, but presumably only when applause actually occurred. Rough drafts of some of the speeches have survived in various archives. They provide insight into the candidates' thoughts and methods of speech preparation, but both McKinley and Bryan often altered their speeches during oral presentation, sometimes considerably.

The newspaper and wire service reports include what usually appear to be transcripts of the speeches based on the work of shorthand reporters. Although shorthand is not always reliable, it probably reflects the candidates' speaking somewhat accurately. Even these texts should be taken with a grain of salt, as customary newspaper practice of the time allowed the speaker to make changes in the texts before they were published. The final, and perhaps conclusive, argument for relying on the versions published in newspapers is that these were the versions most likely to have affected public opinion during the actual campaign. Most newspaper accounts of Bryan's speeches appear to be based on shorthand records.[23] McKinley's speeches were also recorded and reported by shorthand.[24] Overall, despite the hazards of shorthand reporting, newspaper texts of the speeches are presumably more reliable than those that Bryan published in *The First Battle*, which he had the opportunity to edit at leisure, or the edited versions of McKinley's speeches that appeared in various campaign documents.

CHAPTER 1

Why Oratory
Made a Difference
in the 1896 Campaign

WILLIAM J. BRYAN, the great rhetorician from Nebraska, lost the 1896 presidential election. A stodgy Ohio politician, William McKinley, won. One might therefore conclude that the candidates' rhetoric was not relevant to this campaign. One would conclude falsely.

Although Bryan's public speaking in the 1896 campaign has impressed generations of communication scholars, McKinley won the election rather handily.[1] It is ironic that students of rhetoric have slighted the rhetoric that McKinley produced during this campaign. Perhaps, enamored with Bryan and bored with McKinley, they attribute Bryan's defeat entirely to the enormous financial resources that the Republican Party marshaled in 1896. Other authorities, working from charges that Bryan himself set forth after the election, believe that Republican fraud produced McKinley's victory. Many persons may have felt that McKinley was too boring, too prim, and too pedestrian to have been a significant speaker. This drives them to find a non-rhetorical explanation for McKinley's victory. That Bryan and his supporters offered so many excuses for their defeat fuels this endeavor. Bryan develops many such excuses throughout his book *The First Battle*.[2] In any case, despite their admiration for Bryan's rhetoric, few scholars seem ready to admit that either candidate's public speaking made much difference during the campaign.

This prevailing opinion arises from two fundamental mis-assumptions: first, that Bryan lost the election only because the Republicans overwhelmed him with a veritable juggernaut of resources; and second, that Bryan's oratory enabled him, against impossible odds, to achieve a near victory in the election. Neither claim survives serious examination, as this chapter shows.

It is, of course, possible for an election to be determined by factors that have nothing to do with the campaigning of the candidates. Political contests are decided by many factors, of which the candidates' public speaking is only one. An economic calamity may guarantee the incumbent's defeat, as in the presidential election of 1932. An ongoing war can ensure the incumbent's victory, as in 1944. Public scandal or some other factor not related to the rhetoric of the candidates can determine the outcome. If such a contention turned out to be true in 1896, one might indeed conclude that the candidates' speeches made little difference. Since the Depression of 1894 was a major campaign issue in the rhetoric of both candidates, it is entirely possible that the voters in 1896 were reacting to the economic conditions as much as to the candidates' rhetoric. There is, however, more to the matter than that.

First, several authors claim McKinley had so much money behind his campaign that Bryan never stood a chance.[3] Immediately after the election, Bryan himself promoted that belief when he issued a statement that "the friends of bimetallism have not been vanquished; they have simply been overcome." He continued that the silver cause almost triumphed in the face of "the efforts of the administration and its supporters; in spite of the threats of money loaners at home and abroad; in spite of the coercion practiced by corporations and employers; in spite of trusts and syndicates; in spite of an enormous republican [sic] campaign fund, and in spite of the influence of a hostile daily press."[4] In his post-campaign book *The First Battle*, Bryan reviewed evidence that employers had coerced their employees, that banks had bullied their customers, and that businesses had threatened to cancel orders if he were elected. After the election, Bryan said that "if the gold standard continues," then "the time will come when the convictions of the majority will be so deep that neither creditor nor employer can control the result of the election."[5]

Along the same lines, Paolo Coletta states that Republican National Chairman Marcus Hanna "defeated Bryan in every detail of campaign management."[6] Coletta discusses the immensely greater budget of the Republicans for printing literature and hiring speakers. He also repeats the charge that "Hanna brought the people to McKinley, expenses paid."[7] This charge without a doubt exaggerated the degree of support provided for McKinley's pilgrims. Donald Springen does note briefly that Bryan contributed to his own defeat by oversimplifying the issues and by his distrust of easterners.[8] Nonetheless, despite the weight of both popular and scholarly opinion, the evidence does not support an implication that McKinley's supporters bought the election. Let us examine these issues in detail.

Paul Glad comments that the Democratic campaign looked "like a peanut operation" compared to McKinley's.[9] Another scholar claims that "the Republicans spent $7,000,000 to Bryan's paltry $300,000."[10] A major Democratic newspaper offered the preposterously exaggerated complaint that Hanna would spend "the greater part of $10,000,000" by October.[11]

These figures were all overstated; the Republican National Committee's treasurer reported that the committee actually spent about $3.5 million on McKinley's behalf.[12] This amount was still significant—even enormous—by the standards of the time.

Along the same lines, in addition to repeating Bryan's excuses for losing the election, Robert Oliver comments more accurately that "so far as resources were concerned, the presidential campaign was completely one-sided. Mark Hanna raised $3,500,000 on behalf of William McKinley, as contrasted with the $300,000 Bryan was able to get."[13] Neither of these figures includes off-the-books funding sources such as labor union efforts or locally organized campaign events. Coletta states that "Bryan most likely would have won had the election been held before the gold Democrats put their ticket into the field and before the businessmen of the East gave Hanna their millions and Hanna effected his superb organization of intimidation and misrepresentation."[14] *The Cleveland Plain Dealer,* a leading Democratic paper, charged that in September workers were sent to Canton by their employer after having their train fare deducted from their pay.[15] These charges echo Bryan's claim during the campaign that employers were trying to coerce their employees.[16] During the election, such charges reached the point of one Cleveland factory issuing a denial that they were encouraging workers to support McKinley or visit Canton to hear McKinley speak.[17]

To what extent are these views fair and accurate? To be sure, McKinley outspent Bryan's pathetically underfunded campaign, at least at the national level.[18] Much of the money, however, went to organize his public speaking campaign and to distribute copies of various speeches by McKinley and his supporters.[19] Therefore, even granting these critics their due, one must look past the money to the campaign speeches to appreciate fully McKinley's appeal to the voting public. Money talks in a campaign, but the money helped McKinley only if the message was persuasive.

Furthermore, figures relating to the national committees seriously understate the total campaign effort. Bryan (and presumably McKinley) gained support from state party organizations. For example, Bryan met with his erstwhile opponent Senator David Hill in August, apparently in an effort to work out a political compromise and throw the support of New York's Democratic Party Organization to Bryan.[20] The value of this kind of support is difficult or impossible to estimate, but its extent was probably considerable. To the public, Bryan appeared to be running a nationwide campaign. However, only to a limited extent did Bryan and the national Democratic Party control his schedule and finances. Bryan controlled the broad outline of his schedule, but once he entered a state, his speaking schedule, railroad and lodging arrangements, and indeed all other aspects of his campaign fell under the control of the state's Democratic Party Committee. The state committee typically hired a private railroad car for the candidate and arranged the speaking venues. Bryan's campaign often had a thrown-together look, with no central authority supervising the arrangements.

For example, when Bryan traveled through Michigan in October, the state committee provided a train car for him and escorted him through the state.[21] Similarly, the Missouri Democratic Party State Committee organized Bryan's September 12 speeches in St. Louis, at least in the details. Members of that committee arranged to meet the candidate and his party at the train station and take them to dinner, thence to Concordia Park for one speech, then to a large auditorium, and finally to another venue in Sportsman's Park. These arrangements all seem to have been the work of local and state party officials.[22]

Sometimes the state party officials arranged a schedule to which the candidate raised futile objections. As Bryan entered New Jersey, it was announced that the state's Democratic Party Committee "will dictate his movements and Brooklyn will hear him that evening." The Delaware Committee decided at the same time that Bryan should leave early for Dover, thus cutting short his rest.[23] In October, the Indiana Committee scheduled Bryan for nineteen speeches in twenty-four hours.[24] Traveling through Virginia in September, he was at times provided with "an ordinary day coach" instead of his usual private Pullman car.[25] Various incidents of this kind occurred throughout the campaign, as described later.

Arriving in town for his speeches, Bryan usually discovered a platform especially erected for him and often also found Bryan banners on display. Local political clubs and other campaign organizations were ready to greet him with ceremony.[26] Bryan also gained some support by being the nominee of the Populist Party and the National Silver Party. In addition, various Democratic leaders, especially in the West, did go out to campaign for Bryan.[27]

Thus, the difference in funding between the Democratic and Republican national parties in this campaign may have been due in part to the less centralized nature of Bryan's campaign. While McKinley's campaign activities revolved around Canton, Ohio, and the Republican Party's operations were controlled from dual headquarters in Chicago and New York, Bryan's traveling campaign was to a large extent organized state by state. None of the figures that have come to light about campaign finance in 1896 seem to have taken into account spending by state and local parties.

Similarly, Bryan received substantial support from many labor unions.[28] Although Terence Powderly, the former leader of the Knights of Labor, supported McKinley, most labor unions gave their unquestioned support to the nominee of the Democratic Party.[29] Socialist leader Eugene Debs also openly supported Bryan.[30] The American Federation of Labor became publicly active in politics at its 1893 convention, expressing official views on a number of subjects. By 1893 they supported free silver, and they continued to do so through 1898. Despite Samuel Gompers's public call to the American Federation of Labor to stay away from party politics, he surreptitiously worked on behalf of Bryan's candidacy during the 1896 campaign.[31]

The American Labor Union, the United Mine Workers, and the Knights of Labor all supported the Democratic ticket in 1896.[32] The American Railway Union also backed Bryan.[33] When Bryan spoke in Brooklyn near the end of September, 1896, the chair of the local Democratic Party commented that the mass meeting showed "that the organized labor of the country is with our candidate, and that means we will win in the election. In the other large cities of the country we were sure of the labor vote and we were anxious to know what would be the outcome of the Brooklyn meeting."[34] Labor union leaders devoted considerable efforts to convincing their members to line up behind Bryan and the Democratic platform.[35] Much of the contribution made by state parties and labor unions is unquantified, even unquantifiable, because apparently so much occurred behind closed doors. All the same, these contributions were probably significant.

Overall, therefore, while the enormous resources available to McKinley and the Republican Party were without a doubt important, the published dollar figures do not tell the whole story. In addition, Bryan often made his lack of resources a campaign point: "We have not so many daily newspapers through which we can talk and therefore we have to do more talking ourselves," he told a crowd in Traverse City, Michigan, "and we cannot afford to bring all the people to Nebraska. I am going around and seeing the people themselves."[36] Such appeals may have seemed persuasive to the farmers and poor workers to whom Bryan made his plea.

Furthermore, any implication that Bryan's limited material resources prevented him from conveying his message to the public is insupportable. Bryan's railroad tours of the country garnered a tremendous amount of attention. For one thing, they obtained abundant news coverage. On four whistle-stop tours of the nation, Bryan gave by his own estimates about six hundred speeches to several million citizens. The *Review of Reviews* made the more modest estimate of about four hundred speeches that were reported in the newspapers.[37] A swarm of reporters followed Bryan's every move, to the extent that he complained about the lack of privacy. Bryan later listed the names of dozens of reporters who traveled with the campaign.[38] A staff from the Associated Press accompanied Bryan and wired reports of his speeches, often including complete texts taken down by shorthand, to newspapers all over the country.[39] Newspapers often published complete texts or excerpts from Bryan's speeches and described his campaign activities in detail. Many Democratic newspapers, especially in the West and South, endorsed Bryan and covered his campaign.[40] The major Republican and pro-gold papers also generally gave Bryan good, albeit sometimes biased, coverage.[41] Even the obsessively anti-Bryan *New York Times* published texts of or excerpts from many of his speeches.[42] The *Salt Lake Tribune* and the *Rocky Mountain News* were examples of non-Democratic newspapers that endorsed Bryan.[43]

A complete explanation for McKinley's victory must include the nature of the rhetoric, not just the enormous resources that his campaign exploited. Probably the most important difference that the funding made was that Bryan was not able to publish the immense quantities of campaign literature that Marcus Hanna was able to issue on McKinley's behalf. Certainly libraries and archives today have preserved a much larger quantity of Republican campaign literature, such as pamphlets, short books, and published speech texts, than Democratic literature from this campaign. However, contemporaneous copies of Bryan's "A Cross of Gold" have been preserved in abundance.

In addition, the Democrats complained about unethical Republican campaign tactics. For example, in a patently political article, the Democratic, pro-silver *St. Louis Post-Dispatch* accused Hanna of passing out "boodle" to be used "in the different states where voters are to be bought."[44] However, the *Post-Dispatch* offered no evidence of voter fraud. Bryan claimed that factory owners told their workers not to come to work on Wednesday if Bryan won the election on Tuesday. He further asserted that Democratic employees were often intimidated at work.[45] Springen claims that "Bryan won the election, many historians now believe, but was cheated out a victory by widespread voting fraud in several crucial states."[46] Regrettably, Springen does not offer details.

Many of these charges may have been true, although the charge of "boodle" seems to have been unsubstantiated.[47] By 1896, 92 percent of the voters were using the secret ballot, which seriously reduced the opportunity to intimidate workers.[48] Jefferson Myers, an official at Bryan's Chicago headquarters, wrote to the candidate on October 24 to remind him that the secret ballot protected Bryan's supporters from being coerced by their employers.[49] Bryan already knew this, of course, and his actions during the campaign pointed up his conviction that if he campaigned well enough, he could gain the votes he needed for victory. Bryan himself repeatedly pointed out in his speeches that the secret ballot restricted employer intimidation.

Also, one too easily forgets that much institutional corruption favored Bryan. Some of this corruption was so deeply rooted in the traditions of the Democratic Party that it apparently did not even occur to McKinley supporters to complain about it openly.

Bryan had a reputation as an anti-machine politician. Yet he campaigned with support from Democratic machines such as New York's Tammany Hall. Bryan's picture often appeared on the front page of the Tammany newsletter. Electoral fraud was a routine part of the machine's way of doing business.[50] Machine support for Bryan forced McKinley into a battle for the voters of New York. The cities of the East supported Bryan about as well as they had supported Cleveland in 1892, due in part to Tammany Hall's efficient work.[51] This makes it difficult to appreciate such Bryan claims as "I am proud to be the nominee of a convention which represented no machine or bosses, but the unpurchased suffrages of the voters of this country. (Great applause.)"[52]

Perhaps even more important in swaying key states toward Bryan, however, was the denial of voting rights to African Americans. During Reconstruction, African Americans in the South received extensive protection for their voting rights. By 1896 Reconstruction was almost twenty years in the past, and many Southern states were in the midst of a massive effort to recast their voting rights laws to disenfranchise African Americans.[53] Influential southern Democrats spearheaded this movement.[54] For example, residency requirements made it difficult for African-American sharecroppers to vote. The poll tax and literacy tests also restricted voting by African Americans. As Lawson comments:

"By 1890 it was apparent to the Republican party that it would disappear completely in the South unless something were done to protect the Negro voter." However, the voting rights legislation that resulted from this concern failed to pass Congress. By the 1890s, the hard-won voting rights of African Americans in the South had deteriorated.[55]

The African-American vote at that time tended to be heavily Republican, and in the Deep South many of the cities had substantial populations of African-American voters.[56] The movement of the majority of African-American voters to the Democratic Party dates back only to the early twentieth century.[57] Aware of this important political reality, McKinley had lobbied to have the Republican National Convention held in Chicago.[58] He was overruled, and to his consternation African-American delegates were denied accommodations and meals in St. Louis.[59]

Various African-American groups from the North visited McKinley in Canton to hear him speak during his Front Porch campaign. In a speech to one of those groups, Harry C. Smith, an African-American politician and newspaper editor from Cleveland, gave McKinley an assurance.[60] He told the candidate that "you have no more sincere or energetic friends among the many in all this broad land of ours, than are to be found among the Afro-Americans, and that on the third of November next you will have a practical demonstration of this fact such as you have never before had an opportunity to note."[61]

There were reports of African Americans voting en masse for the Democrats under the supervision of their landowners. The Populist movement, which was pro-Bryan, also appealed to many African Americans.[62] Bryan himself commented that "It may . . . be remarked that the colored men who left the Republican party in 1896, did so because of an intelligent understanding of the money question." Bryan claimed that the number of African-American supporters was greater than for any previous Democratic candidate.[63] If true, this could simply have been due to the generally high voter turnout. Overall, however, Bryan probably profited greatly from the gradual impingement on African-American voting in the Deep South.

Another Democratic excuse for losing the election was bossism. Throughout the campaign, the Democrats thundered about

"Boss Hanna," criticizing McKinley for caving in to the political bosses of Cleveland.[64] This accusation is startling, considering that Ohio's political bosses actually gerrymandered McKinley out of his congressional seat and opposed his nomination for the presidency.[65] On January 28 Charles Dawes, who was subsequently elected as treasurer of the Republican Party National Committee, privately worried that "it is McKinley against the field—against the bosses—against everything that the bosses can bring to bear."[66] (Dawes, no mean authority in political matters, eventually became vice president of the United States and won the Nobel Peace Prize.) In March, 1896, McKinley refused to make a deal with the bosses; Dawes commented that "the Governor would not make these concessions, and told me he proposed to take the place, if it came to him, unmortgaged."[67] Hanna became a political power only because he and McKinley ran an effective campaign.

Politics is a curious business. Bryan's campaign was underfunded in any normal sense. Unlike Dawes, Bryan's campaign officials did not routinely come across business magnates ready to hand them unsolicited packets holding thousands of dollars. Political resources, however, come in many guises. To a certain extent, each candidate conducted a campaign geared to the kinds of resources that he had available. McKinley and Hanna had access to colossal amounts of money. They used this money to hire speakers and to print mountains of literature. They inundated the public with information. An article in the *Review of Reviews,* an opinion periodical of the time, noted that "the Republican National Committee has broken all conceivable records for a campaign resting on the basis of educational literature."[68] Bryan did not have millions of dollars to dispose of as he wished. He did, however, have the support of Tammany Hall, state Democratic Party organizations, and most labor unions. These intangible resources should not be taken lightly. Bryan could not raise enough money to finance a nationwide campaign, but he was able to organize what amounted to a series of vigorous statewide campaigns. His campaign was thus disorganized but quite active.

Bryan's supporters and opponents alike painted a picture of the campaigner as the lone voice crying out for the people in the face of irresistible opposition. Early in the campaign, Bryan himself commented in Chicago: "When I see this assemblage to-night and when I remember what the newspapers in the city say (loud and continued hissing) I am reminded of what one of our friends said to me: 'Nobody is on our side except the people.'"[69]

Shortly afterward, the *New York Times* ridiculed Bryan for his alleged use of "the familiar appeal of the demagogue" and his claims that "study and science are of no account; the popular intuition is better than reason, and what the people say 'goes.'"[70] This was a rather jaded misinterpretation of Bryan's contention that politicians should take seriously the citizenry's opinions and desires. Bryan's actual views were more along the lines of his statement in Utica, New York, that "we appeal to a people capable of governing themselves." Similar if somewhat more bellicose was his statement in Chicago that "I look into the faces of these people and remember that our enemies call them a mob and say that they are a menace to free government."[71] In August, Bryan responded to the Republicans' claim that they were running an education campaign: "I am reminded of what a friend in Lincoln said the other day. He said: 'It used to be the newspapers educated the people, but now the people educate the newspaper.'"[72]

Therefore, although the Republican Party certainly brought considerable resources to bear during the 1896 campaign, one must turn to the rhetoric of the candidates to understand the 1896 campaign fully. Showing the even-handedness that distinguished the periodical from other news outlets of the era, the *Review of Reviews'* editors commented that "considering the remarkable expenditures for the dissemination of argument by means of the printed page, the poster, and the cartoon, it might have been supposed that in this campaign oratory would have had but a minor part." They pointed out, however, that both candidates were nominated in large part because of their speaking ability. "Mr. Bryan," they remarked, "set his own pace in his Chicago convention speech," while "Mr. McKinley was known at the start as one of the greatest campaign orators of his time."[73] Shortly after Bryan's "A Cross of Gold," the rabidly anti-Bryan *New York Times* commented of his stage delivery that "Bryan's bearing is graceful; his face is handsome; his utterance is clear and strong, with something of the McKinley sing-song, and his style is free, picturesque, and brilliant."[74] This is certainly an interesting, presumably firsthand, comparison of the candidates' presentations.

A deeper reason leads to the belief that the candidates' rhetoric mattered. Although Bryan was eloquent, it is not clear that his rhetoric was always *effective*. Bryan's oratory gained him the Democratic nomination, not to mention national fame, but his divisiveness and defensiveness may have served him poorly in the long run. The argument about the Republican Party's excellent finances appears to explain McKinley's success, and yet it is obvious to anyone who looks closely at this campaign that the tremendous public response resulted in part from Bryan's exciting rhetoric. This kind of thinking, which underlies all the charges made by Bryan's defenders, misses the point completely. Bryan's rhetoric energized the people, but this energy may not always have helped him.

The principal measure of success in political public speaking is effectiveness, the ability to persuade an audience. Several of the following chapters make it obvious that Bryan's rhetoric had a confrontational quality positively calculated to offend voters of the populous Northeast. In contrast, McKinley's relatively low-key, inoffensive rhetoric was calculated to appeal to as broad a group of the public as possible. Moreover, Bryan frequently wandered away from his main issues, while McKinley stuck more persistently to his own ground for the entire campaign. More generally, the later discussion establishes many points about the candidates' rhetoric, and it becomes apparent that in a number of ways, McKinley may well have been a better political speaker than was Bryan: not a more exciting speaker but a wiser one.

A final, speculative point must be made about the issue of campaign resources. It obviously seemed unfair that McKinley's supporters had more money to spend than they knew what to do with. Nonetheless, Bryan and his sometimes confrontational rhetoric may have aided McKinley's fund-raising more than did any other factor.

Everything in a campaign is related to everything else. McKinley did not start out flush with money. On February 1, well before the convention, Dawes commented that "Hanna is being greatly disappointed in his canvass for funds. The great trouble with our campaign is lack of funds for legitimate expenses."[75] On August 28, two months after McKinley's nomination, Dawes wrote that the outlook for campaign funds "is very poor."[76] The shock of Bryan's nomination soon energized the fund-raising, however. On September 11, Hanna handed Dawes an envelope containing fifty thousand dollars in cash from a railroad company (that sort of thing was legal then). At the same time, Dawes received a similar check from someone else. These turned out to be the largest contributions Dawes received.[77] From that point forward, there was little evidence of concern for adequate campaign funding.

Why did the business community donate so generously to McKinley? The most likely explanation is fear. The nation's industrial interests were not merely concerned about a Bryan presidency; they were terrified. As the following chapters make evident, Bryan's rhetoric did a great deal to terrify them.

CHAPTER 2

Free Silver or Free Trade?

The Campaign's Issues

P RESIDENTIAL CANDIDATES have battled about the economy throughout history. Jackson and Clay went to the wall over the national bank. The Great Depression ruined Hoover's chances for re-election. Clinton and Bush argued about the causes of unemployment and the federal budget deficit. Although McKinley's presidency would center on the Spanish-American War, the 1896 campaign featured two perplexing economic issues: the money standard and the protective tariff. Other than the Great Depression, no economic issue would again capture the public's imagination with the same keenness. The general public, political parties, and business, farming, and industrial interests all seemed to view both these economic questions as matters of history-setting importance.

McKinley and Bryan each offered a solution to the Depression of 1894, a period of hard economic times that continued through the election. Bryan advocated the free coinage of silver at the fixed ratio of sixteen to one with gold. The intention of this plan was to increase the supply of money and permit farmers to pay off in inflated currency the crushing debts that they had accumulated since the Civil War. McKinley's bread-and-butter issue was the protective tariff, which he had favored during his years in Congress.[1]

Probably no economist of the early 21st century would take seriously the arguments of either candidate. As surfaces from time to time in later chapters, the candidates had trouble finding academic economists to take their arguments seriously even in

1896. J. Laurence Laughlin of the University of Chicago, whom Bryan repeatedly quoted to support the free silver cause, wrote in the 1896 edition of his book on the subject: "An example [of National Bimetallism] is the proposal for free silver coinage in the United States, where, although no other country of importance has the same ratio (and although the legal ratio does not correspond with the market value of the two metals), we have a proportion of 1:16. Such a system is not upheld by any economic writer of repute."[2]

The standard argument against the protective tariff is that the economy as a whole benefits from foreign trade. Any serious restriction by the United States against foreign competition would lead foreign nations to retaliate by restricting United States imports into their country, resulting in fewer markets for American goods. The lack of cheap imports leads to higher consumer prices and reduced quality of goods. Economists almost universally believe that free international trade benefits nations.[3] However, government leaders are often reluctant to implement free trade and tend to have other priorities that they consider more important. Furthermore, tariffs are almost certainly not effective methods for improving employment.[4] Bimetallism, Bryan's hallmark issue, succumbs to Gresham's law, which predicts that the public will hoard money made of the more valuable of the two metals, while using only the less valuable currency for the payment of debts. Thus, briefly, neither candidate advocated an economic issue of any real merit.

This does not, however, fully represent the political and rhetorical importance of these issues.

Bryan may have had a valid point, to a degree, that an increase in the money supply might remedy an economic recession. Whether his version of bimetallism would have succeeded in doing this or whether (as his opponents feared) it would have produced runaway inflation is probably still debatable. If one stops to think about it for a moment, it is unlikely that the supply of either gold or silver, or of both combined, would add up to the correct amount of money to finance a nation's economy. There is no reason to think that the quantity of any commodity would exactly correspond with the amount of money that an economy requires. If it occasionally did, this would occur purely by coincidence. Thus it is quite possible that the gold bugs, who felt that silver would be inflationary, and the silverites, who felt that the gold standard was deflationary, were both right (or both wrong, depending on one's point of view).

Nonetheless, during the campaign these issues symbolized fundamental conflicts. Noteworthy was the struggle between the rich and the poor, together with the conflicting interests of the industrial Northeast versus the agricultural West and South. The voters of the Northeast felt that their interests conflicted with those of the West and South, and so the issues of the 1896 campaign quickly came to symbolize those distinctions. The traumas of the Civil War lurked less than thirty years off in the South's past; some western states were newly added to the union. People of the West and South still worked in a largely agricultural economy; the Northeast was rapidly industrializing. Bimetallism became a rallying cry for the West, while the prospect of inflationary money filled many northerners with unreasoning dread. One could question how much the public understood about economic theory, but these issues struck profound symbolic chords in the voters.

Less symbolic but equally important, both candidates were trying to make political profit from the depression's hardships. The conservative Democratic president, Grover Cleveland, was taking the blame for the troubles in the economy. The depression affected the different regions differently. Industrializing areas, particularly in the regions east of the Mississippi and north of the Mason-Dixon Line, were hit by factory closings, bank failures, and layoffs. In the West and South, on the other hand, automatic machinery was revolutionizing farming. Farmers had gone into debt to purchase machinery and to enlarge their farms. The depression cut the prices they received for their produce. Simultaneously, the depression increased the value of the currency in which they were to repay their debts.

To transport cash crops to market, farmers were often at the mercy of railroads, many of which monopolized transportation in local areas. The railroads sometimes charged outrageous transport fees.[5] Moreover, many farmers worked as sharecroppers for large landowners or financed the operation of their small farms by the crop-lien system, which typically put them farther and farther into debt every year.[6] Squeezed from both ends, the farmers felt their situation deteriorate steadily.[7]

An inadequate money supply probably did contribute to the farmers' desperate situation. The value of the dollar had been increasing by about 1.5 percent a year for twenty years prior to the election of 1896.[8] Despite remarkable economic expansion, the money supply had increased too slowly for decades. The inevitable result of having too few dollars chasing more goods was for the dollar to gain value. Further, many conservatives still believed that sound money needed to be tied to a valuable product, such as precious metals.[9] Although by 1896 most of the nation's money existed in the form of paper currency and checking accounts, not in gold or silver, the old way of thinking was slow to die.

Although the depression was moderating by the autumn of 1896, it continued to be a significant issue. For example, on September 12, when McKinley gave a campaign speech to the steelworkers of Homestead, Pennsylvania, and Bryan left Nebraska on a railroad speaking tour, the wire services reported that although the economy was improving, prices remained low. Farmers were failing in their efforts to sell their corn and oats for a profit. The Connellsville Coke plant found its output down from the year before.[10] A mob from Washington County, Kentucky, grew tired of paying turnpike tolls and tore down ten turnpike gates, threatening to lynch the gatekeepers if they returned to their duties.[11] The Commerce Bank of New Orleans suffered a run and closed its doors to regroup. It was the fourth bank in a row to fail.[12]

The depression also reduced the output of factories. Many of the factories that made steel, tinplate, and pottery had cut back production and laid off their employees. Factory workers were beginning to unionize, but unions commonly faced vigorous, sometimes violent opposition from industry and government.[13] The nation would presumably vote eagerly for the candidate they felt could lead the nation back to prosperity.

A number of political movements sought to solve the problems by increasing the supply of money. The Greenback Party, for example, had wanted to discontinue retiring the inflationary paper currency left over from the Civil War. The Greenback Party failed to triumph, however, and their approach became moot when the last greenbacks were withdrawn from circulation.[14]

The free silver movement followed. This movement received a boost as well as a body of doctrine from a popular book entitled *Coin's Financial School,* an entertaining little volume that attributed the depression to the hoarding of gold money by banks and industrialists. The free silver movement proposed to place more money into circulation by allowing anyone to take raw silver to the mint to be coined. By the mid-1890s, the People's Party (Populists) were integrating free silver into their program.[15] The Democratic and Republican parties both developed free silver wings. Nonetheless, many people associated free silver with agrarian reform movements like the Populists, giving those wings the reputation of being radical.

The usual proposal was to coin silver at a ratio of 16 to 1 with gold by weight. This infusion of money, the silverites contended, would stimulate the economy, halt the deflation of currency, increase employment, and relieve the farmers' debt load.[16] Silver was at that time worth only about half that much on the market; however, the free silver groups contended that the demand for silver coins would restore the value of silver to about 16 to 1.[17] Historically, silver had traded for about 16 to 1 during the years prior to its demonetization in 1873; however, by 1896, it was trading at slightly over 30 to 1.[18] By the 1890s, additional discoveries of gold started to relieve the money shortage.[19] Curiously enough, one economic historian argues that bimetallism served as a compromise because it nominally continued the nation on a hard-money standard, as opposed to currency devaluation or other monetary manipulations.[20]

Bryan eventually became the chief advocate of the free coinage of silver, contending that the solution to the economic downturn was to increase the supply of money, thus restoring the dollar to its pre-depression purchasing power.

Industrial and banking interests found free silver to be unsavory. The banks in particular entertained no pressing desire to see debts repaid in devalued currency. Industrial interests worried that the silverites' proposal would be inflationary because of their fear that it would produce an uncontrolled increase in the money supply.[21] Small savers, who gained from deflation, worried that bimetallism would reduce the value of their savings.[22]

Overall, Bryan's principal issue during the 1896 campaign was a radical version of bimetallism. Bryan succinctly stated his fundamental position on free silver in many campaign speeches. In a typical speech at a railroad stop in Ohio, the candidate explained his central thesis: "My friends, we believe that free coinage of silver, the opening of the mints to the free coinage of silver at 16 to 1, without waiting for the aid or consent of any other nation on earth, means the advancement of the interest of the people and of general prosperity."[23]

The ratio of 16 to 1 had been a battle cry of bimetallists starting with the Jackson era. Most economic authorities of Jackson's time recommended a ratio of 15.625 to 1, so 16 to 1 was presumably a round-number compromise.[24] This ratio stood firm in the political rhetoric despite fluctuations in the prices of silver and gold over the decades. In 1873, the law that the bimetallists decried as the "Crime of 1873" ended the practice of unlimited silver coinage. However, the United States had for all practical purposes moved to the gold standard long before 1873. As Angela Redish dryly notes, "since virtually no silver coinage other than the subsidiary coinage on government account had occurred for at least twenty years, and the silver dollar had not been coined since 1836, the impact of the legislation may not have been immediately obvious."[25] Since the time of the Civil War greenbacks, the United States had been on "a paper money standard under which the end of free silver coinage in the United States, the so-called Crime of 1873, was not so noticeable."[26] In other words, since most currency was not made of metal anyway, the silver issue may have diverted attention from real economic issues. The Sherman Act of 1890, which was something of a compromise, required the Treasury to purchase silver at market value.[27] Grover Cleveland had used his influence to obtain the repeal of the Sherman Act during his administration.[28] Nonetheless, Nobel Award economist Milton Friedman has argued that bimetallism would have reduced the "economic upheavals" of Cleveland's last administration and agrees with the silverites' contention that the ratio would have returned to about 16 to 1 had silver been remonetized. He cautions, however, that Bryan's version of bimetallism came much too late to be helpful.[29] In any case, like many significant issues, bimetallism raised complexities far greater than politicians liked to talk about.

Nobody discussed the various positions about currency standards by obviously accurate names. Instead, each side invented what Richard Weaver would later call "god terms" and "devil terms."[30] The Democrats, and their allies the Populist Party and National Silver Party, frequently referred to "free silver," "the money issue," or "the financial issue."[31] The pro-gold forces traditionally spoke of "sound money," "honest dollar," and "honest money" to refer to the gold standard. Sometimes the pro-tariff term reciprocity became a stand-in for the gold standard as well. These artful synonyms, which had been in use for years, serendipitously helped to gloss over the fact that McKinley himself, until the start of the campaign, had advocated a moderate version of bimetallism.[32]

Bryan's years in Congress were marked by strong advocacy of the unlimited coinage of silver. In a remarkable speech of 1893, three years before his "A Cross of Gold," he told Congress: "I denounce that child of ignorance and avarice the gold dollar, under a universal gold standard, as the most dishonest dollar in the world." He attacked head-on the charge that bimetallists were anarchists: "The man who wants the people to destroy the Government is an anarchist, but the man who wants the Government to destroy the people is a patriot." He also complained in this speech that "we have been called cranks and lunatics and idiots because we have warned our fellow-men against the inevitable and intolerable consequences which would follow the adoption of a gold standard by all the world." Bryan supported his argument with statistics and many quotations from economists and public figures. He endorsed the Populist Party's platform, which advocated the coinage of silver at the ratio of 16 to 1 with gold. He quoted the Republican Party's bimetallist platforms of 1888 and 1892. Bryan noted that "the Democratic party has won the greatest success in its history." Concluding, he asked, "Standing upon this victory-crowned summit, will it turn its face to the rising or the setting sun? Will it choose blessings or cursings—life or death—which? Which?"[33]

Even so early in his career, Bryan was discussing currency standards in colorful, overblown language.

Bryan also argued for the free coinage of silver in Chicago in 1895. He explained during that speech that "there never has been and is not now enough gold in the world to do the business of the world. The total amount in existence is less than $4,000,000,000, and amounts to only about $2.50 per capita for the population of the world." He denied the charge that he favored "repudiation, or fifty-cent dollars" and stated that "the natural law of supply and demand" would enable the two metals "to adjust themselves, at a practical equality," as he asserted was the case before 1873. He accused gold of being "dishonest and oppressive" because its value increases, making debtors pay in a currency more valuable than what they borrowed.[34] These earlier speeches offered many themes and phrases that would recur during his 1896 campaign. Like a candidate of a hundred years later, Bryan had been trying out his rhetoric for quite a while before beginning his campaign in earnest.[35]

By the start of the campaign, McKinley had reluctantly endorsed the Republican pro-gold platform.[36] The Republican platform called for bimetallism by international agreement and advocated retaining the gold standard until that time.[37] Conservatives worried about adopting bimetallism independently of other nations because other nations might in that case dump their silver on the United States markets, as Representative Samuel McCall of Massachusetts argued in 1893.[38] In 1890, McKinley had stated on the floor of Congress that bimetallism was "the well-established financial policy of the country." He did warn against "the free and unlimited coinage of the silver of the world," instead suggesting that gold and silver needed to be maintained at parity. He concluded that "whatever dollars we have in this country must be good dollars, as good in the hands of the poor as the rich; equal dollars, equal in inherent merit, equal in purchasing power, whether they be paper dollars, or gold dollars, or silver dollars, or Treasury notes." He stressed further that the various kinds of dollars needed to be equal and interchangeable.[39] Thus McKinley advocated bimetallism in 1890 but in a more moderate form than Bryan's proposal.

McKinley spoke for a similar proposal in 1891. On that occasion, he was launching his campaign for the governorship of Ohio by giving a speech near the high school in his birthplace, Niles. He stated that "I am in favor of the double standard, but I am not in favor of the free and unlimited coinage of silver in the

United States" until the various nations were able to negotiate an agreement about monetary standards.[40] These moderately pro-silver views were not completely consistent with the Republican Party's 1896 pro-gold platform, but they were not as different as his opponents claimed from the principles that McKinley was to advocate from his front porch in 1896. For example, in a September, 1896, campaign speech, McKinley stated: "Nothing is more vital to the standing and progress of a country than that the currency of the country shall be so honest that it can cheat nobody."[41] In October he attacked "the proposition to enter upon the free and unlimited coinage of the silver of the world."[42] A few days later, he spoke for "Republican party, Republican principles, sound money and a protective tariff."[43]

Just before McKinley's nomination, the conservative *Washington Evening Star* remarked that "McKinley is wavering on the [gold plank in the] platform" and that "in the selection of the financial plank of the platform is the only thing where there is any idea that his advice will not be followed." They added, correctly, that McKinley "is not dogmatic on that question."[44] McKinley's turnabout for gold caused some mirth among Democrats, which continued throughout the campaign.[45] Bryan and the Democratic newspapers, however, never seemed to be able to draw any political capital from McKinley's flip-flop.

McKinley's friend and campaign manager Marcus Hanna later excused the switch with the idea that McKinley was not "a doctor of finance," and his earlier pro-silver views "had followed the popular trend of the time."[46] McKinley's earlier bimetallist views embarrassed even his strongest supporter, perhaps unnecessarily.

McKinley put the tariff at the forefront of the campaign. The tariff issue never seemed to arouse the violent emotions of free silver. Nonetheless, the tariff has been one of the greatest ongoing controversies in the oratorical history of the United States. Henry Clay's tariff speech on the "American System" is one of the most widely studied speeches in American public address.[47] In 1896 the United States government still obtained a considerable amount of its revenue from taxing imports. In addition, many American leaders had for the entire century advocated import taxes so high that they would discourage foreign countries from competing with American business and industry. All the same,

McKinley's pro-tariff stand distressed an editorial writer from the farming state of Kansas, who opposed silver but called McKinley's pro-tariff stand "erroneous."[48]

While serving in Congress, McKinley received a great deal of credit for passing the McKinley Tariff of 1890. He co-authored a book advocating the tariff.[49] In 1883, he spoke to Congress about "the benefits of a protective tariff and the evil results of the doctrine of free trade." In that speech, he also said that "we can have the Democratic doctrine of free trade whenever the Democratic party can make slaves of our laboring men, but not until then." In seemingly Bryanesque language, he also stated that "I do not speak for capital. Capital can take care of itself. . . . I speak for the workingmen of my district, the workingmen of Ohio, and of the country."[50] McKinley insisted on the tariff's patriotic merits when he spoke against the Morrison Tariff Bill that proposed to reduce tariffs: "No interest is pressing it. No National necessity demands it. No true American wants it."[51]

In 1890, speaking on behalf of the tariff, McKinley recited numerous figures relating to tariffs, imports, and exports. For example, he stated: "In 1886–87 we built thirty-one boats, with a capacity of 65,750 gross tons, valued at $4,074,000."[52] Near the conclusion of the speech he reiterated a theme of his life in public service: "When merchandise is the cheapest, men are the poorest."[53] In his 1891 speech at Niles, McKinley asserted that "the tariff of 1890 will make its own way. It will achieve," he patriotically asserted, "its own victories for American labor, American enterprise, and American genius, and for the whole American people."[54]

Although the currency question dominated the campaign, McKinley made the tariff into a significant issue, and he spent as much time on it as he did on currency. It was his own issue, independent of Bryan's silver issue. McKinley's personal secretary Joseph Smith noted that Ohio "would at least have been very doubtful had not the tariff question also been an issue. As it was there was a rearrangement and a readjustment of party lines [during the 1896 election] such as had never before been known."[55] Although Bryan's "A Cross of Gold" put the free silver issue at the forefront of public awareness, McKinley never lost sight of the issue that he considered to be his home ground.

The candidates' speeches during the 1896 campaign stressed these issues almost to the exclusion of all others. McKinley rarely strayed to other questions; Bryan did so somewhat more often. In many respects both candidates discussed issues with considerably more insight, depth, and persistence than does the typical presidential candidate of a century later. The issues were, in one sense, the focus of the campaign. Nonetheless, the issues represented larger, deeper, poorly articulated feelings and sectional conflicts. That is, the candidates' speeches brought up many complex, interconnected, sometimes contradictory messages with intricate, highly emotional implications. It is in this context that one must conclude that the candidates' oratory played a central role in this campaign.

CHAPTER 3

The Early Weeks of McKinley's Front Porch Campaign

O N AUGUST 9, 1896, with his presidential crusade just under way, Bryan was campaigning at Davenport, Iowa, when a voice from the crowd asked him, "How about Republicans?" Bryan retorted, "I do not think any Republicans can speak."[1] In early September, a Democratic newspaper cartoon showed McKinley sitting on a tree stump with a bear below. The bear carried the legend, "financial issue." The caption stated, "JUST THE BARE FACTS: McKinley will not go on the stump this Fall. He knows what would happen if he did."[2] The *Cleveland Plain Dealer,* a major pro-Bryan newspaper, wrongly predicted as late as September 4 that McKinley would have to make a campaign tour, which would get "McKinley off his high horse of nonparticipation in the campaign."[3] Even decades later, some writers got the impression that McKinley hardly campaigned at all.[4]

The genius of McKinley's Front Porch campaign was that it did not look like a campaign. The impression could not be avoided that Bryan was stumping desperately for votes while McKinley casually waited at home for the people to endorse him. Nothing, however, could have been farther from the truth: McKinley's energetic, well-organized campaign was not casual. Indeed, texts of more than 250 of his 1896 campaign speeches have survived.[5]

McKinley's Front Porch campaign did not resemble his approach in earlier campaigns. At the time, McKinley's supporters noted that his earlier campaigns had often involved vigorous speaking tours.[6]

Thus, in the summer of 1896, McKinley remained at home while Bryan conducted an energetic railroad campaign. Nonetheless, McKinley was not idle; he was in fact campaigning in a striking manner. Numerous groups from around the country visited McKinley at his home to hear him give brief speeches on behalf of his candidacy. The Front Porch campaign, even in its earliest weeks, consisted of a series of artificial events staged for the media. Furthermore, this feature of the campaign shaped what McKinley said and how he said it, as he created the impression of *identification* between the voters and himself.[7]

Daniel J. Boorstin characterizes what he calls a "pseudo-event" by four criteria: (1) the event "is not spontaneous, but comes about because someone has planned, planted, or incited it"; (2) "it is planted primarily (not always exclusively) for the immediate purpose of being reported or reproduced"; (3) "its relation to the underlying reality of the situation is ambiguous"; and (4) "usually it is intended to be a self-fulfilling prophecy."[8] McKinley's campaign, as we shall see, met all four of these criteria.

Rhetoric constructs identifications among diverse persons, ideas, and events.[9] Out of the awesome mass of visitors, parades, and cheering, staged purely for purposes of the campaign, McKinley somehow created a feeling that he cared about each visitor, that he welcomed each one warmly to his home, that their interests were identified with one another's and with the Republican cause. Thus the pseudo-events of the summer weeks of the campaign, indeed of the entire campaign, created in the news reports and campaign documents the strong impression of a candidate who was dignified, yet warm and caring, and who sought to bring the entire nation together. In contrast, Bryan would soon be divisively calling his opponents "enemies."[10]

Many authorities believe that the pseudo-event is something new. Boorstin seems to assume that pseudo-events originated in the twentieth century and came to prominence only in the age of radio and television.[11] Judith Trent and Robert Friedenberg similarly point out how television and radio have shaped present-day presidential campaigns. As a result, they argue, "candidates no longer had to be dependent on extensive national speaking tours to become well-known to the public."[12] However, even in the age of broadcasting, most candidates for nationwide office embark on a campaign tour. In 1896, long before the advent of broadcasting, McKinley accomplished the same purpose as a modern candidate and did not make a campaign tour.

In this light, McKinley's decision to stay home in 1896 may seem extraordinary. By August, Bryan was obviously conducting an energetic speaking tour. The sense that McKinley was not campaigning at all surely worked to McKinley's advantage by making him seem more dignified and self-assured than his opponent. McKinley's 1896 campaign, however, despite these perceptions, was a remarkable series of seemingly newsworthy, but utterly artificial, events staged in large part to gain attention from the press. McKinley gave his speeches amidst parades, flags, demonstrations, and speeches by visiting dignitaries. By spreading information about these events, the wire services and newspapers served for the Front Porch campaign the same functions that the radio and television would fulfill many years later.

A presidential candidate in 1896 could speak in person only to a small portion of the electorate, but technology could spread the candidate's words across the land in short order, as would become the norm. The 1968 Democratic National Convention, which can be categorized as a pseudo-event, featured activities that existed mostly because they could be reported.[13] Much the same was true in 1896. What developed in Canton during the summer of 1896, indeed during the entire campaign, was a carefully organized series of staged incidents. The parades, the thousands of tiny American flags, the demonstrations, and the speeches all became part of a media circus.

McKinley developed his rhetorical approach in speeches presented as early in the campaign as June, July, and August. Feeling his way through the early stages of the campaign with great ingenuity, he drew together his two seemingly unrelated issues, the gold standard and the protective tariff.

McKinley's rhetorical task was to identify the interests of business with the ordinary industrial workers who made up a large part of the voting population. In doing so, McKinley conveyed a convincing impression that the nation's interests all hung together. During the summer, his New York campaign manager, William Osborne, wrote to McKinley on the money issue that "it is the unanimous opinion of all of us here that our whole attention must be paid to the masses—to the laboring classes. The people who have got property are all right and can take care of themselves."[14]

McKinley may not originally have intended to campaign from his home. His nomination was orchestrated ahead of time and required the candidate to exert little public effort; William J. Bryan himself, who attended the Republican convention as a reporter for the *Omaha World-Herald,* commented later that "some time before the convention convened it became evident that Mr. McKinley would have a majority on the first ballot, and the convention was, therefore, not as exciting as it might have been with a more even contest between the leading candidates."[15] Weeks after his nomination McKinley failed to suppress speculation that he might take to the stump.[16] On July 2, before Bryan's nomination, McKinley told a reporter from the *Washington Evening Star* that "it is hardly likely that I shall leave home at all during the campaign, unless the party leaders deem it best that I should do so." Even more pointedly, McKinley also told the interviewer that "I shall remain at home . . . and take no active part in the campaign."[17]

On July 2, on the occasion of a visit from vice presidential candidate William Hobart, a newspaper reported that neither Hobart nor McKinley was likely to hit the campaign trail.[18] On August 13, a number of Republicans in Washington, D.C., promoted a McKinley campaign tour. They were concerned, among other matters, to have McKinley take the tariff issue to the West Coast.[19] As late as August 16, a Democratic newspaper reported, at the time of a private meeting between McKinley and Hanna, that "the opinion still holds here [Canton] among his friends here that he will probably not address any strictly political gathering during the campaign."[20] This opinion surely surprised anyone following the campaign closely, since McKinley had been doing just that from his front porch for almost two months. On July 23, McKinley delivered three political speeches in nearby Alliance, Ohio.[21] However, he made few other campaign appearances outside Canton.

It is quite possible that given the disastrous state of the economy under President Cleveland, the election of a Democrat seemed so unlikely that McKinley saw no reason to campaign at all. Perhaps he simply fell into the habit of speaking to various groups that visited him. He persisted in this practice even though numerous party officials were attempting to convince him to campaign around the country.[22] When the Democrats nominated the anti-establishment Bryan, however, the Republicans suddenly had a fight on their hands. With his uncompromising agrarian views, Bryan could campaign against the status quo with even more authority than McKinley could.

McKinley may have had in mind to duplicate, but on a larger scale, Garfield's 1880 campaign. Garfield stayed at home to receive visiting delegations because it was not at that time considered proper for a presidential candidate to canvass the people.[23] Julia B. Foraker, wife of the powerful senator Joseph Foraker, wrote that Benjamin Harrison conducted a front porch campaign. In Harrison's campaign, she mentioned, "each delegation was received with a speech that directly appealed to the district it represented and which captivated by its sympathetic, intimate understanding of individual conditions and its mastery of facts."[24] McKinley brought this approach to the height of enthusiasm and organization.

McKinley's friend Myron Herrick quoted him as saying during the summer that "I might just as well put up a trapeze on my front lawn and compete with some professional athlete as go out speaking against Bryan. I have to *think* when I speak."[25] Instead, the Republican National Committee organized trips—"pilgrimages"—to Canton. Newspapers across the United States published stories about and speech texts from the Front Porch campaign. The image could be projected of the candidate remaining at home with his invalid wife, whom the crowds might see peeking from the window, as he delivered heartfelt messages from his porch to audiences that spontaneously arrived on the scene.

Some of the first speeches of the campaign gave little impression of careful advance planning. They do, however, demonstrate a consistent pattern as McKinley rapidly evolved his campaign's procedures. He quickly seized on the notion that the press would report every public act connected with the campaign. While staying at home during almost all of the campaign, McKinley eventually had the assistance of a staff consisting of four secretaries, including James Boyle and Russell Chase, a shorthand reporter.

Joseph Smith, a former newspaper reporter, also advised McKinley on publicity issues. Boyle established a business office for the local campaign in downtown Canton.[26] It should be understood that McKinley's secretaries were not clerical workers but professional people who advised him during the campaign. A large Citizen's Committee and a group of local campaign managers also assisted McKinley's work in Canton. A group of forty-six men formed the mounted, uniformed "McKinley Escort Troop," featured in many parades as various delegations marched from the train stations to McKinley's home.[27]

Since, as was common during that era, McKinley did not attend the Republican convention in person, an assorted group of mostly local supporters met him at his home right after the nomination on June 18. They presented his wife, Ida McKinley, with a bouquet of flowers. McKinley climbed onto a store crate on his porch and, in a brief speech, praised their communities.[28] The use of the crate itself was surely contrived for effect, for the Republicans could doubtless have managed a more distinguished podium. A larger crowd of local citizens gathered at his house. McKinley declared himself to be impressed by the "non-partisan character" of the demonstration, which "forbids political discussion." The candidate promised that nothing honored him more than "to have the regard of his fellow townsmen."[29]

The characteristic pattern of the campaign evolved further as early as June 19, when the McKinley League of New York State arrived in Canton on a chartered train. This league itself had obviously come into existence only to participate in the campaign. The event opened with a speech greeting McKinley by John E. Milholland, a New York newspaper editor. The speeches of greeting, which became part of the campaign's ritual, had several interesting rhetorical qualities. For one thing, these speeches were often full of partisan praise for McKinley. It would surely have been immodest for the candidate to praise himself so profusely. McKinley eventually adopted the practice of requiring speakers to forward advance copies of their speeches.[30] This presumably made it possible for his staff to screen them to ensure that they were free of offensive or divisive content that would look bad in the press. The press routinely printed many of these speeches in part or in their entirety.[31]

Milholland's short speech assured McKinley that he would win in the November election by a large majority. Stating that his group had to return to the train in a few minutes, he apologized that he did not have time for "making a speech" and assured McKinley that the Republicans of New York would support him.[32]

It is no surprise that a delegation from McKinley's boyhood home of Niles, Ohio, a local center of the tin industry, was among the first to visit Canton. Their factory had closed for the day so that workers could pay homage to McKinley.[33] The delegates marched down Market Street carrying homemade tin signs. At first, the candidate awkwardly remarked how few faces he recognized. Then, a familiar face catching his eye, he commented that "I remember that he was kind to every boy—and I like a man who is kind to a boy. (Loud cheering.)"[34]

It is unclear what influence these early, primitive speeches had on McKinley's thinking. The visit from Niles seems to have been more or less spontaneous, and McKinley was to all appearances not well prepared to speak to them on political issues. In any case, the eagerness of groups to visit him and to hear him speak became obvious early, as did the willingness of the press to report these visits in detail.

Within a day after McKinley was nominated, vendors were strolling around Canton selling "campaign badges and fans." A Republican newspaper proudly reported that McKinley's small but well-tended lawn was quickly trampled "as bare and brown as a prairie swept by fire or trampled beneath the feet of a herd of buffalo."[35] Then again, a group of three bicycle tourists dropped by to visit McKinley on June 25. At this early stage of the campaign, the trivial event made the afternoon newspaper.[36] It was becoming apparent that at least to the Republican press, McKinley's every public action became news. The rhetorical task, then, became to manipulate this seemingly natural process to the benefit of the candidate.

The development of the campaign's pseudo-events led to a strange tension between McKinley's instinctive desire to adapt to his immediate audiences, on the one hand, and to reach out to the national audience, on the other. It seemed to be fundamental to his personality to say something personal about each visiting group of voters. McKinley often mentioned that he had visited their town or brought up some sort of information to show that he had researched the economy of their community. Material such as this was typical of McKinley's speaking throughout the campaign. As an opinion magazine of the time noted near the end of the campaign, McKinley's speeches were "prepared in advance, and have been punctuated with statistics and precise statements of fact which a 'whirlwind campaign' from a train platform would not allow."[37]

When it came down to campaign issues, McKinley stood by his bread-and-butter topics. He did not promise to serve the particular needs of the visiting delegation; rather, he assured each one that the protective tariff and sound money would benefit their community's interests. The visiting delegations, no matter who they were, became in McKinley's speeches symbols of the American worker. He could thus seem to adapt to the immediate audience, while his campaign was artfully designed to obtain support from the national audience.

For example, McKinley's early front porch speeches turned bimetallism into a vague conspiracy to deprive the ordinary American worker of fair wages. This approach let McKinley turn the issue toward the factory workers' interests. Speaking to a group from eastern Ohio, he phrased the point to express the depth of his concern for the factory worker: "And, my countrymen, there is another thing the people are determined upon, and that is that a full day's work must be paid in full dollars."[38] By this, he implied that silver money would degrade a factory laborer's earnings.

A delegation from Wheeling, West Virginia, visited McKinley on June 20 (the same day as the Niles group).[39] The West Virginians presented McKinley with a banner made of tin praising him as the "father of the tin plate industry in the United States."[40] After the leader of the delegation lavished praise on McKinley, the candidate said he could receive no higher accolade than to know that he had contributed in any way to helping provide "employment to American labor" or to bringing "comfort to American homes." The West Virginia group thus became, in McKinley's rhetoric, representatives of the American worker.[41]

Of course, no campaign event gains public attention as much as its official beginning. The campaign opened more or less formally on June 27 with a large parade and "ratification" organized by a group from Cleveland.[42] McKinley told the large group of visitors to the Canton area of his advocacy of "honest money, a dollar as sound as the Government, and as untarnished as its flag." Not missing a beat, he then tied sound money to the needs of the ordinary worker: "A dollar that is as good in the hands of the farmer and the workingman, as in the hands of the manufacturer or the capitalist."[43]

The Canton ratification was only the first of a number of events that opened the campaign. More would follow. No event could conceivably be more artificial than these repeated campaign openings (which continued even in the autumn), held and publicized only so that they could be reported. There was no other need for any of them, since the Republican machinery started the campaign promptly after the convention, and no formal launching of any kind was necessary.[44] McKinley launched the campaign again on July 2 when an official Notification Committee of some sixty persons arrived at his home. Senator John Thurston, who had opposed McKinley earlier in his career but who had come over to McKinley's side before the convention, chaired the committee. Thurston spoke first. He commented on the need for "Protection and Reciprocity" and rued in biblical style the actions of those who repealed the McKinley tariff: "They sowed the wind. They reaped the whirlwind." Thurston compared the nation's endorsement of McKinleyism with the faithfulness of the Israelites to the Law of Moses.[45]

After referring to the great honor and solemn responsibility of the nomination, McKinley remarked that the issues in the campaign were serious, that they required "our sober judgment," and that they should be resolved without partisanship or excess emotion. He continued at some length about the tariff, which he argued should be raised to provide better for the government's expenses.[46] McKinley had prepared this speech well in advance and read a draft of it to Dawes on June 26.[47]

The notification was a pseudo-event. Although the notification ceremony was common practice in that era, there was no need for a committee to notify McKinley, who already knew that he had been nominated. The purpose of this event was to provide a newsworthy opportunity for Thurston to express his partisan views and for McKinley to offer a carefully prepared account of the issues, knowing perfectly well that the press would report whatever they said. McKinley's real audience was not the group of Republican leaders who had come to Canton to notify him but the national audience, who would be paying special attention to the event.

At another large rally late June, a large but highly organized crowd showed up at the modest two-story frame house on Market Street, cheered McKinley, and heard him speak. In the midst of parades, drum rolls, and fireworks, the Tippecanoe Club of Cleveland delivered their trademark yell:

Hi-Hi-Hi
O-h-i-o
Tippecanoe, McKinley too.
Cleveland
O-ho[48]

McKinley had progressed beyond seeking a familiar face in the crowd; the Front Porch speeches were rapidly becoming part of a series of manufactured events, full of freshly generated enthusiasm that came into being to stir up ardor for his campaign.

This process continued in the middle of July when a group from the Cleveland Foraker Club dropped by McKinley's home. This group supported Ohio's influential senator. Perhaps they had heard that the campaign was to be dignified. If so, this had little effect on their spectacle. A local committee met them at the train station. A military band escorted the group of more than two hundred men, plus, the newspaper noted, eighteen women, to Market Street. When they reached McKinley's home, Kirk's Military Band performed the "Star Spangled Banner" and cheers for McKinley were heard. D. H. Lucas, the Foraker Club's president, announced to McKinley: "We have followed you, and will put our armor on."[49]

The group then heard a carefully reasoned speech in which McKinley set out his views about sound money and a protective tariff. Bryan had just been nominated on a platform that featured the unlimited coinage of silver money, which aroused a forceful response from McKinley.[50] After his customary warm salutation, and a word of praise for Foraker, McKinley compared the issues of the 1896 campaign with those of the Civil War, of which he himself was a veteran: "Then it was a struggle to preserve the government of the United States. Now it is a struggle to preserve the financial honor of the government of the United States. (Cries of 'yes' and applause.)" In 1861–65 the war preserved the Union; today McKinley campaigned to "save spotless its credit."[51]

Taking advantage of the split between the Gold Democrats and Silver Democrats, McKinley announced that "in this contest patriotism is above party, and national honor is dearer than any party name."[52] McKinley depicted free trade and free silver as a single conspiracy against the ordinary worker: "Not content with the inauguration of the ruinous policy which has brought down the wages of the laborer and the price of farm products, its advocates now offer a new policy which will diminish the value of the money in which wages and products are paid."[53] With minor variations, this argument, phrased more or less in this way, would appear in many subsequent speeches.

On a rainy July 16, a group of women from the Cleveland area arrived on a special train. They paraded toward Market Street, various men joining them as they marched. The crowd gathered at McKinley's home. Ida McKinley was joined by the wife of McKinley's adviser, Joseph Smith, on the front porch to meet the visitors. Mrs. Elroy M. Avery came forward to present the speech of greeting: "We come from Cleveland; Cleveland, the beautiful; Cleveland that still lives; the queen city of the lower-lakes; the great heart of the western reserve that gave Giddings, Wade and Garfield to the nation." She said more about the issues than did the candidate: Cleveland, she said, was "a city of great American industries that are suffering from un-American legislation," by which she presumably meant the Democrats' low tariffs. She mentioned her lack of appreciation for "man-made political platforms." Avery assured McKinley that every woman has an interest in the money issue: "If our husbands earn the money, we spend and intend to spend it."[54]

McKinley then responded with a speech in which he praised the contributions of women and the influence that they have in society. He assured Avery that "it is in the quiet and peaceful walks of life where her power is greatest and most beneficial."

Birdelle Switzer, the society editor of the *Plain Dealer,* the leading Democratic paper of the region, then presented Ida McKinley with a bouquet of flowers. Switzer commented: "We cannot all hope to win presidents for husbands, but your example as a wife is before us." Mary Ellsworth Clark, another member of the delegation, then sang "A Prayer for Our Nation," which had been composed for the occasion. The song began, "Ring out, bells of freedom" and concluded "McKinley, McKinley, our captain shall be." At the conclusion of these ceremonies, the women marched with an equestrian escort to a hall where a group of Presbyterian women served them lunch; they then enjoyed some music and sightseeing.[55]

A few days after the Cleveland women took the train home, a visit by Civil War veterans from Cuyahoga County gave McKinley another opportunity to drive home the relationship between patriotism and sound money. After noting their common experience of the war, McKinley carried the theme of patriotism from the past to the "living present." "The devotion to discipline and duty" that the soldiers practiced during the war remained alive, he said, in 1896. The soldiers "have not faltered and will not falter now." Then in a single brilliant, if astonishing, passage, McKinley announced that "all men who love their country must unite to defeat by their ballots the forces which now assault the Nation's honor." He was proud to announce to their cheers that the soldiers would stand today against any assault on freedom or the flag, including, one presumes, Bryan's assault on the honor of American currency.[56]

The two main issues, the tariff and sound money, still dominated this speech. It was a ticklish task to appeal so shamelessly to the patriotism of Union veterans without offending the South, from whom McKinley may have hoped for (and ultimately received) some support. Hence he concluded the speech with a comment that "honesty, like patriotism, can neither be bounded by state nor sectional lines."[57]

Shortly before lunchtime on August 10, William Jennings Bryan himself whirled through Canton on the Pennsylvania Railroad and gave the large crowd a brief speech from a flatcar about free silver. He promised the "toilers" of the nation that he would make his campaign their own.[58] The two candidates did not meet that day, but McKinley did not, as it would soon turn out, overlook what Bryan had said.

A day or two after Bryan's brief visit, McKinley stepped out again onto his front porch to meet a group of a few hundred citizens from Geurnsey County, Ohio. Many of them were Union army veterans. After hearing a formal greeting from the group's senior retired officer, a Colonel Taylor, McKinley clambered up onto a chair. He spoke of friendship: "I have made many visits to your county in years gone by." He congratulated his visitors on their community's success in the tin-plating industry: "I am glad to know," McKinley stated, "that Republican legislation gives to this country an industry that gives work and wages to American workingmen and brings happiness to American homes. (Great cheering.)" He reviewed the pensions paid by the government, pensions delayed, he said, by the Democratic government's policies. McKinley informed his visitors that the government carried "970,000 pensioners on the honored pension roll" and paid "in pensions over $140,000,000 every year to the soldiers and sailors, the widows and their orphans."[59] In this way, McKinley exhibited what may have seemed like abstruse knowledge of the specific struggles that the veterans faced.

Then came the key point: "Every dollar of that debt must be paid in the best currency and coin of the world. (Great cheering and cries of 'The Republican party will see to that.')" To drive his point home, he pointed to a nearby American flag. He told his visitors that they, his comrades from the Civil War, would no more allow an attack on the integrity of the nation's currency than they would permit an attack on that flag.[60] Thus McKinley moved seamlessly from the simple act of offering his guests a warm greeting to a political issue of national import. He used the seemingly meaningless statistics about the value of Civil War pensions to stress the importance of sound money.

When a group of glass workers came to visit, McKinley responded to Bryan's recent speech in a very subtle way. He continued to equate his cause with patriotism and the will of the American people. McKinley called his visitors "the strong and sturdy men who toil." McKinley said that in his "battle" he would be aided not only by Republicans but also by "thousands of brave patriotic and conscientious political opponents of the past" who now stood together against the tide of repudiation and dishonor.[61] With this surprisingly bold oratory, McKinley implied that Bryan's "toilers" would stand firmly against silver money. Once again, a group of workers heard themselves transformed into representatives of the American worker.

In August, McKinley stressed to an African-American group, the L'Ouverture Rifles of Cleveland, that "we are all political equals here—equal in privilege and opportunity, dependent upon each other."[62] The members of the rifle team had arrived in Canton accompanied by hundreds of African Americans from Cleveland and Akron. Giving the speech of greeting, Harry C. Smith, a noted African-American leader and a member of the Ohio legislature, stated: "The Afro-American has watched with the eye of the American eagle every act of special interest to him of your wonderful career." Smith awarded McKinley honorary membership in the rifle team.[63]

McKinley then took a few moments for a highly upbeat discussion of the Civil War, the importance of equality, and the benefits of racial progress. McKinley called the L'Ouverture Rifles "my countrymen." He turned their attention to the tariff and sound money. In an echo of his speech to the Foraker group, McKinley warned the rifle team that "having reduced the pay of labor, it is now proposed to reduce the value of the money in which labor is paid."[64] McKinley endorsed racial justice but did not champion any issues directly related to racial justice. Instead, he sought to convince them that his policies, the same policies that he advocated with every other group, would bring betterment to them. Thus, once again, the specific concerns of the audience were subsumed under the banner of McKinley's central campaign issues.

Only rarely did McKinley's numerous statistics prove anything, but they were always adapted to the visiting delegation. They were a subtle aspect of the pseudo-event, permitting McKinley to appeal to the delegation while actually speaking through them to the national audience. Yet this human touch had no impact on the heart of McKinley's message. For example, in August McKinley spoke to a group from East Liverpool, Ohio, a center of the pottery industry. He mentioned that before the Democrats took office, the pottery industry had "fifty-five potteries and two hundred and forty-four kilns, twenty-six of which were decorating kilns, with a capital invested of $5,076,000."[65] This established little about the Democrats' policies. It showed that McKinley cared enough about East Liverpool to learn a little bit about their city. It conveyed, however, no hint that he would promote any of their special interests. Once again, the only issues that McKinley discussed were sound money and the tariff.

Also in August, it was time to open the campaign again. McKinley published a carefully prepared written response, his "Letter of Acceptance."[66] Far more printed copies of this document survive in libraries than of any other material connected with the campaign. The party's New York office alone sent out half a million or more copies of the letter in early September.[67] McKinley's letter thanked the committee for the honor of the nomination. The statement reviewed McKinley's positions on a number of the issues of the day: bimetallism versus the gold standard, the protective tariff, immigration, veterans' benefits, civil service reform, and so forth.[68] Dawes mentioned in his journal that McKinley showed him a draft of the document and that Dawes suggested "a few minor changes which he adopted."[69] McKinley had apparently intended to write a short letter but instead prepared a full discussion of the issues at the suggestion of Osborne, who managed the Republican Party's New York campaign office.[70] McKinley ended with an argument entitled "Sectionalism Almost Obliterated." McKinley's letter laid out a moderate, judiciously phrased, comprehensive discussion of the Republican candidate's views on the issues that the 1896 campaign, as fate had it, would never see again. McKinley's speeches in September and October would drop almost all reference to these other issues and zero in on the gold standard and the protective tariff. The Letter of Acceptance established McKinley's mood, but the speeches gave the campaign its emphasis.

Few political speakers have ever mastered to such a high degree the ability to make everyone present feel such personal warmth. Perhaps no one outside McKinley's family and closest friends ever really knew his private thoughts and emotions. When he spoke in public, however, he could convey to the audience with great immediacy a feeling that he knew the working people and understood them, that he cared about them, that he earnestly desired to be their friend. He expressed a strong identification between himself and his audience. The press reports of the campaign often discussed McKinley shaking hands with the crowd and otherwise interacting with the people. His speeches often ended with a warmly phrased promise to shake the hands of everyone in the delegation.

He invariably opened his speeches with charming little pleasantries. McKinley stressed to a delegation of Pittsburgh workers, "I bid you warm and hearty welcome."[71] To a group from Lawrence County, Pennsylvania, he said: "It gives me very great pleasure to welcome the citizens of a neighboring state to my city and to my home."[72] Repeatedly, McKinley reminded his audiences that they were visiting his home. He conveyed the distinct impression that he was welcoming his guests—not an unruly swarm of political supporters whom he had never before seen but rather a group of newly made friends who enjoyed his warmest regard. He told the veterans of his old Civil War regiment that "nothing gives me greater pleasure than to meet at my home my comrades in the Civil War."[73] With only a little variation, he told a group visiting from Cleveland that "it gives me very great pleasure to welcome you to my home city and to my home."[74]

McKinley's Front Porch campaign was a pseudo-event, or series of pseudo-events, in Boorstin's sense, and became so early in the summer. First, the campaign's events occurred because they were carefully planned. Although the speeches often gave the impression of spontaneity, much advance organization went into manufacturing the situations in which McKinley presented them. McKinley's staff screened the speeches of greeting. A committee of local organizers met each visiting delegation and organized them into a parade. The visiting delegations often arrived with drill teams and marching bands. This does not mean that at this early stage the campaign's events were organized like clockwork, which they were not, but rather that they were organized deliberately.

Second, the Front Porch campaign existed for what Boorstin calls the "purpose of being reported or reproduced."[75] Representatives of the press reported almost every speech. McKinley's intentions were made clear, however, by the content of his speeches. Although every speech made some polite reference to the identity of the visiting group, and often cited some fact or figure about the group's home town or state, McKinley almost without exception zeroed in on the sound money and the protective tariff. Thus he could convey the impression that he cared about each group, an impression so vital to McKinley's image as a man who cared about the ordinary worker, while at the same time expounding only on issues of national import. This, more than anything else, shows that the Front Porch campaign existed to be reported in the press. Even the sometimes bizarre speeches of greeting existed to be reported. What other explanation can we have for Avery's speech about "Cleveland, . . . the queen city of the lower-lakes" except her realization that she would, for a few brief moments, bask in the national spotlight?

Boorstin's third criterion for a pseudo-event is that "its relation to the underlying reality of the situation is ambiguous."[76] This may be the most troubling, since the Front Porch speeches were unmistakably a part of the reality of the campaign. Yet, the campaign itself bore a fundamentally ambiguous relationship to reality. The parades up and down Market Street, the brass bands, the cheers, were not to celebrate a holiday; they existed merely because the campaign's organizers wanted them to exist.

Finally, Boorstin specifies that a pseudo-event is by design a "self-fulfilling prophecy."[77] McKinley's supporters created a vision that McKinley was not campaigning but that the Front Porch speeches and the associated hoopla were ceremonial ratifications of McKinley's inevitable election victory. Enormous throngs of voters steamed into the train station and paid homage to their "advance agent of prosperity." The campaign gave birth to powerful sentiments: that McKinley did not even act like a campaigner, that his popularity had achieved such heights that voters gave up their Saturdays to come to him, that the voters did not come to elect him but to ratify him. The people did not come to be persuaded; they came to delight in the greatness of their nation's future leader. They came, as for a holiday, to celebrate by waving flags, blowing whistles, and collecting souvenir spoons and walking canes.[78]

The visiting delegations were not, however, the main audiences. They were, instead, just part of the show. McKinley adapted to these audiences, but in a peculiar way that the critic can understand only by seeing the speeches as part of the artificial events.

McKinley's speeches repeatedly *implied* an argument something along these lines:

> McKinley cares about the ordinary working people of X, Y, and Z delegations.
>
> These ordinary working people are typical of the American population.
>
> Therefore, what benefits them will benefit the public.
>
> Vote for McKinley to obtain these benefits.

This shows what McKinley was really saying in these speeches. Why did he repeatedly cite meaningless statistics about how many kilns a town had, or how many acres of farmland were found in a state, or the dollar value of Civil War pensions? Why did he invariably mention any occasion on which he had visited the town or state from which the delegation hailed? How could it affect national policy to realize that Niles is a center of the tinplate industry or that East Liverpool has a pottery factory? Why did he make a point of welcoming them all to his home? McKinley's rhetorical objective was to show that he cared personally about the members of the delegation and, by implication, that he cared about all of the nation's working people. In this way, he made an implied argument that identified the diverse members of the nation's population. It is a remarkable accomplishment that despite the artificial atmosphere, McKinley imparted such a strong sense of his warmth and his unity with the audience.

Similarly, in discussing the campaign's two principal issues, McKinley did not address the delegations as special interests. At least in public, he never promised that he would perform special acts for them once he took office; instead, he assured them that the actions that he would take about the tariff and the money standard would benefit their special interests. It was an interesting twist, and one that makes sense only in the context of a mass media pseudo-event. To advocate a group's special interests would have implied that the candidate would be blind to the interests of the whole country. McKinley instead appealed to the audience that the main issues on which he focused, national in scope, would benefit them particularly. Especially in contrast to Bryan, who stressed regional and class divisions, McKinley sought in his speeches to integrate the interests of the entire nation.[79]

Thus, as he launched his Front Porch campaign, McKinley adapted to the national audience in a carefully calculated series of media events. The pseudo-event is not a unique creation of twentieth-century political communication. Nor, for that matter, was it McKinley's invention. Building on his long experience in politics and on the example of previous candidates, McKinley made the most of the technology and customs of his time. In his campaign, the railroads could bring large crowds to his home to hear him speak. The wire services and newspapers published accounts of the events and texts of the speeches shortly after they occurred. In this respect, his campaign oratory differed from the televised speeches of a century later mostly because print technology, not television, brought the campaign into the voters' homes. McKinley created the impression that in the fashion of pre–Civil War candidates, he was waiting casually at home for the people to elect him. Yet during the summer of 1896, McKinley initiated a vigorous, carefully crafted campaign that employed all the resources available to him to reach and persuade the national voting public.

Although the speeches that McKinley delivered during the summer of 1896 were just a tentative beginning to the campaign, all of the major elements that would mark the Front Porch campaign were already present. There was something folksy about campaigning so casually from a modest, middle-class home. When the throngs of voters stepped off the train in Canton, they discovered that McKinley was to all appearances one of them. It was in large part this quality, the ability to project a warm personality through these groups to the press, that led to the Front Porch campaign's success.

CHAPTER 4

Bryan's "A Cross of Gold"

HIS ARMS REACHING OUT, William Jennings Bryan thundered at the cheering crowd that filled the Chicago Coliseum: "You shall not press down upon the brow of labor this crown of thorns. You shall not crucify mankind upon a cross of gold."[1] Bryan's speech of July 9, 1896, which he gave during the platform debate at the Democratic convention, has received over the years more discussion than any other speech in late nineteenth-century American public address. Substantial evidence is consistent with the view that this speech had a powerful influence on the convention delegates; nonetheless, "A Cross of Gold," which featured techniques more typical of radical rhetoric, was a divisive speech that was poorly adapted to the national audience.

Many scholars believe that it was at least in part because of this speech that the dark-horse candidate Bryan was able to gain the Democratic Party's nomination to be president of the United States. Ronald Reid, for example, terms the speech a "rhetorical triumph." One noted scholar of American public speaking writes that "what can be ascribed to his speech is that . . . the 'silver-tongued orator' was nominated."[2] The most thorough book about Bryan's rhetoric calls this speech "a masterpiece of its type."[3] James Andrews and David Zarefsky assert that the concluding lines of the speech contributed to Bryan's nomination.[4] Another rhetorical historian comments that this speech "won Bryan the nomination."[5] Bryan's chief biographer writes that "Bryan had won men's hearts, diverted their passions and preferences, obscured every other presidential aspirant, and wrecked the plans of skillful managers."[6] Margaret Leech states in her biography of McKinley that "Bryan's impassioned periods had electrified the convention, and made him its presidential candidate."[7] Another rhetorical scholar expresses doubts about whether "A Cross of Gold" earned Bryan the nomination, although she does call his speech "the highlight of the convention."[8]

Kenneth Burke points out that "identification implies division." Burke comments further that the rhetoric entails "matters of socialization and faction." He remarks on the "wavering line between peace and conflict, since identification is got by property, which is ambivalently a motive of both morality and strife." Pointedly, Burke continues that "inasmuch as the ultimate of conflict is war or murder, we considered how such imagery can figure as a terminology of reidentification."[9] Imagery of war figures prominently in "A Cross of Gold" and indeed in most of Bryan's 1896 campaign rhetoric.

A number of rhetorical scholars have written insightfully about other speeches of Bryan's.[10] However, studies of "A Cross of Gold," his most famous speech, have mostly been brief and often discuss "A Cross of Gold" only as part of a larger review of Bryan's speaking.[11] Historians have scrutinized the text of the speech and have demonstrated its impact on the convention and on the national consciousness.[12] This study goes beyond their work by examining the speech as an act of rhetoric.

"A Cross of Gold" deserves a careful look for three reasons. First, the speech has been much discussed and widely anthologized. Bryan's speech certainly captured the public's imagination.[13] Second, the prevailing judgments about Bryan's speech are in large part based on claims about the immediate audience response to the event, ignoring the speech's larger implications. This speech differed from most of Bryan's campaign oratory, but it was very likely the most significant speech of his career. Third, "A Cross of Gold" was far and away the most prominent speech of the 1896 campaign.

To achieve the presidency, Bryan had to manage two different audiences, who expected and needed different kinds of persuasion: the delegates to the Democratic convention, and the general voting public. The prevailing view that "A Cross of Gold" won Bryan the nomination may well be correct. Nonetheless, Bryan faced an awkward, if not an impossible task in seeking to adapt his rhetoric to both audiences.

Bryan arrived at the Democratic convention trailing Richard Bland in popularity among the delegates.[14] Indeed, at the opening of the convention, it was not absolutely certain that Bryan would be credentialed as a delegate.[15] To gain the nomination would require all of the resources and skills that Bryan could marshal. McKinley knew that he would be nominated before the Republican convention in St. Louis even began.[16] The *New York Times* commented that McKinley had so much support among the delegates that it would be pointless for another candidate to compete.[17] McKinley could aim all of his efforts at winning in November. Bryan lacked that luxury. As the ensuing argument shows, his speech was adapted so specifically to the silverites who dominated the convention that Bryan either neglected to adapt, or could not adapt, to the national audience at the same time.

In "A Cross of Gold," Bryan used the *forms* of radical rhetoric, casting the issues into the framework of a contest between the haves and the have-nots. Superficially, bimetallism may appear to be a mysterious economic issue. Bryan transformed this issue into a symbol of the struggle of the ordinary working American.

The fundamental point of most radical rhetoric is to advocate a shift in power toward less-favored groups. Radical speakers sometimes reject compromise because it might perpetuate the inequalities against which they protest.[18] Or they may be committed to the absolute truth of their views.[19] Furthermore, radical rhetoric may generalize about the "enemy" to unite less-favored groups in opposition to a common oppressor.[20]

Bryan's thesis in "A Cross of Gold" was that the nation should undertake the free, unlimited coinage of silver to use as money in addition to the gold-backed currency already in circulation. As we have seen, this continued a theme that Bryan had advocated for several years previously.

The free coinage of silver, however, was a footnote to the broader quality of Bryan's speech. The essence of "A Cross of Gold" was what Bowers, Ochs, and Jensen term *polarization*.[21] A polarization strategy goads the audience to abandon the middle course and to place themselves on one side or the other. Polarization is the obverse of unity and compromise. Such confrontational rhetoric, however, can easily drive away persons who were previously undecided.[22] In "A Cross of Gold," Bryan indeed seemed to set himself against large segments of potential voters. This strategy turned around McKinley's strategy of unity and identification.

One key tactic in polarization is the *flag issue*. A flag issue is one that is especially vulnerable to the agitator's attack. The flag issue is not necessarily the most important point under dispute but rather as a target that symbolizes larger issues. The rhetoric undertakes to create such strong emotions concerning the flag issue that the audience will lash out in anger.[23] This can be effective because an audience has trouble becoming aroused against an abstraction, such as the nation's economic system, whereas they can more easily focus their attention on a narrow but more vivid question.

The gold standard served as a flag issue in Bryan's speech and thus took on significance far transcending currency standards. The convention delegates focused their energies on free silver. Nonetheless, Bryan's speech, and the convention delegates' response to it, reflected more than just the currency standard. Monetary standards were merely symbols for more fundamental issues. In Bryan's rhetoric, the gold standard became a symbol of the mighty eastern financiers' assault on the American worker. Thus, Bryan did not depict a conflict between gold and silver but between the rich magnates of the East on the one side and the farmers and workers of the nation's heartland on the other side.

A related polarizing tactic is the *flag individual*. Like a flag issue, a flag individual functions as a target of attack symbolizing a larger question.[24] In "A Cross of Gold," Bryan made McKinley into a flag individual who represented the nation's wealthy interests.

The rhetoric of polarization is familiar to radical leaders. The twentieth-century radical organizer Saul Alinsky says in his *Rules for Radicals* that in a complex society, it can be difficult to find someone to blame for a social injustice. As a result, it becomes ever more difficult to identify "the enemy." One cannot become angry at an abstraction. For that reason, Alinsky urges radicals to use "personification" and to "freeze the target." He concludes that "with this focus comes a polarization."[25] Indeed, he contends that "life seems to lack rhyme or reason or even a shadow of order unless we approach it with the key of converses." It is by seeing the world in terms of opposites, such as good and evil, that Alinsky hopes to gain some understanding of a society.[26] As Bryan demonstrated in "A Cross of Gold," these radical tactics of polarization predated its modern vocabulary.

Yet a difficulty facing Bryan in making his rhetorical choices is that he was not really advocating a revolution. He sought to rise to power within the American political system, a system in which he firmly believed. His announced intention was to use the political system to bring economic reform to the rural elements and other working-class Americans. Thus Bryan ran squarely into what Jonathan Lange calls the "radical's paradox." Lange points out that radical rhetoric is either "dismissed as 'too radical,' 'unrealistic,' 'impossible to achieve,' or it is subsumed within the larger context, re-enforcing the current set of practices" (emphasis in the original).[27] Bryan, doubling the paradox, undertook to polarize the nation and to integrate his economic reforms into its political system at the same time.

The Democrats did not know whom they would nominate when they met in Chicago in July 1896. There was no question, however, that their candidate would be pro-silver.[28] Several silver candidates were being promoted. Bryan, at the time known as a young newspaper editor and former member of Congress, was frequently mentioned as a dark-horse candidate.[29] The *Washington Evening Star,* certainly not a pro-Bryan newspaper, commented that the Nebraskan was "a formidable dark horse."[30] Together with his substantial entourage, Bryan arrived in Chicago confident that he would be the nominee.[31] Bryan had already started work on a text of a speech, presumably believing that it would gain him the nomination if he got a chance to present it.[32] The *Wall Street Journal* tentatively predicted Bryan's nomination even before he delivered "A Cross of Gold."[33] Bryan's good friend, Republican leader Charles Dawes, was also in Chicago. Dawes, familiar with Bryan's speaking ability, predicted in his private journal that if Bryan got a chance to speak, the nomination could not escape him.[34] At the convention, once Bryan was scheduled to give the concluding speech at the platform debate, silver advocate Clarke Howell sent Bryan a note: "This is a great opportunity." Bryan replied, "You will not be disappointed."[35] The Coliseum in Chicago, where the convention met, was an enormous building, measuring 727 feet by 300 feet. The delegates congregated on the floor; others in the audience seem to have been confined to the bleachers on the sides.[36]

The first major order of business at the convention was to discuss the platform. Although the platform dealt with several issues, only silver seemed to concern the delegates much.[37] The predominance of silverites at the convention guaranteed an uncompromising free-silver plank.[38] Bryan worked his way onto an influential committee and arranged to give the concluding speech during the platform debate.[39] By luck and perhaps by design, he had avoided appearing for a speech earlier in the convention.[40] Various demonstrations had called for him earlier.[41] Certain that the silver plank would be adopted no matter what he said, Bryan set out to make a sufficient impression to gain the convention's attention.

Bryan's speech cast out a net for the true believers: but only for the true believers. He argued that the old guard, represented by the Gold Democrats and the Republicans, stood against ordinary working people, the "toiling masses," as he called them. Near the beginning of the speech, in language reminiscent of the Civil War, Bryan asserted: "In this contest brother has been arrayed against brother and father against son."[42]

Nor was Bryan unaware of the conflict that the money issue created in the East. Indeed, part of his method was to build upon the conflict. Despite his assurance that he would avoid sectionalism, Bryan depicted his region to be locked in economic conflict with the East.[43] Responding to the previous speech by William Russell of Massachusetts, Bryan began "A Cross of Gold" by reassuring the delegations that "not one person in all this convention entertains the least hostility of [sic] the state of Massachusetts. But we stand here for people who are the equals of the state of Massachusetts."[44]

Certainly a westerner such as Bryan would praise his own region. He was dressed in what was considered western fashion, in "a short alpaca jacket, a low cut vest, a white lawn tie."[45] Bryan implied that the silver issue pitted the interests of the East against those of the equally deserving West: the pioneers, "who braved all the dangers of the wilderness, who have made the desert to blossom as a rose," and so forth, "are as deserving of the consideration of this party as any people in this country." Continuing with his military metaphors, Bryan stressed that "we do not come as aggressors," but nonetheless "we are fighting in the defense of our homes, of our families and our posterity."[46]

Not only did Bryan try to polarize the East and the West; he also pitted the rich against the poor. He blamed the wealthy for the nation's woes: "What we need is an Andrew Jackson to stand as Jackson stood against the encroachments of aggrandized wealth. (Applause.)" Bryan ridiculed the notion that the prosperity of the rich "will leak through on those below."[47]

To further this point, Bryan commented to his audience concerning the argument that free silver was harmful to business: "We say to you that you have made too limited in its application the definition of business man." Bryan then argued that the farmer, the storeowner, the laborer were businesspeople just as were the eastern tycoons.[48] This passage, which Bryan later claimed to have written the night before, tied free silver to the interests of the ordinary American.[49] At the same time, the passage addressed the claim that free silver would harm business.

It is entirely unclear that free silver *per se* would have been a great benefit to the storeowner, much less to the factory laborer. Free silver would nominally improve the lot of the debtor classes. In Bryan's speech, however, free silver functioned as a flag issue. Calling attention to the economic contributions of ordinary citizens, Bryan emphasized that he stood on their side. He used free silver to show that he stood for the poor, the downtrodden, and the rural. Margaret Wood points out that Bryan did not prove a "causal relationship" between free silver and economic improvement.[50] In this speech, however, Bryan did not place economic cause and effect arguments at the center of his rhetoric. This is one of the many features of this speech in which he varied from the approach that he would use in the months to come.

Bryan also attempted to polarize the farmer from the city dweller. The gold delegates had argued that the large cities all favored the gold standard. Bryan retorted: "I tell you the great cities rest upon these broad and fertile prairies. Burn down your cities," Bryan boasted, "and leave our farms and your cities will spring up again as if by magic. But destroy our farms and the grass will grow in the streets of every city in this country. (Loud applause.)"[51] With such rhetoric, Bryan accented the conflicts within the nation, not its unity.

Successful radical movements often follow a logical sequence of increasing protest. An audience might consider a speaker churlish who *begins* a movement with confrontation.[52] Confrontation may become more credible when milder discourse has failed. In the classic form of protest rhetoric, Bryan stressed that the silverites had already attempted to gain their way by petition and persuasion. Having failed, they were now ready to escalate. "We have petitioned," Bryan said, "and our petitions have been scorned. We have entreated, and our entreaties have been disregarded. We have begged, and they have mocked, and our calamity came." Bryan now moved to a higher challenge: "We beg no longer; we entreat no more; we petition no more. We defy them."[53] This passage was not an attempt at compromise. It was a call to action, made necessary, Bryan implied, by the failure of rational means of persuasion. Bryan's rhetoric admitted no common ground. This is the typical approach of the radical, polarizing speaker.

"A Cross of Gold" did not portray the decision between the silver plank and the gold plank as a simple disagreement between reasonable persons. On the contrary, to Bryan, the advocates of gold were the "enemy": "We go forward confident that we shall win. Why? Because on the paramount issue in this campaign there is not a spot of ground upon which the *enemy* will dare to challenge battle" (emphasis added). In his peroration, Bryan continued to characterize the advocates of gold as enemies: "If they dare to come out and in the open defend the gold standard as a good thing, we shall fight them to the uttermost."[54] This, again, is the language of confrontation.

Bryan struck out at his opponent in personal terms. In this speech, and in this speech alone, he employed the polarizing tactic of attacking a flag individual. In his subsequent campaign speeches, Bryan often spoke about McKinley with respect. In *The First Battle*, Bryan denied that the campaign had been personal.[55] Indeed, he proudly remarked that "I look back with much satisfaction to the fact that the four political contests through which I have passed, two successfully and two unsuccessfully, have been free from personalities."[56] In "A Cross of Gold," however, Bryan said that McKinley, who had compared himself to Napoleon, "shudders today when he thinks he was nominated on the anniversary of Waterloo." After a pause for lengthy cheering by the silver delegates, Bryan continued that McKinley heard "the sound of the waves as they beat upon the lonely shores of St. Helena."[57]

Near the end of the speech, Bryan tied together the constituencies upon which he would base his campaign—"having behind us the commercial interests and the laboring interests and all the toiling masses"—thus claiming unity with those who supported him.[58] To support free silver was, symbolically, to express loyalty to these groups. Yet he also implied his opposition to other constituencies. During the entire speech before this point Bryan had gone out of his way to deny his appeal to industrial interests, and to the East, and to the cities.

The convention voted on its nomination a day after "A Cross of Gold." Support for Bland began to disintegrate after the second ballot, leading to Bryan's nomination on the fifth ballot.[59] Seemingly only the editors of The Wall Street Journal, flip-flopping from their previous forecast, missed out on predicting Bryan's nomination after his speech. They claimed that "Bryan has had his day."[60]

The statements of various witnesses are consistent with the prevailing scholarly opinion that attributes Bryan's nomination, in whole or part, to "A Cross of Gold."[61] The pro-silver press generally attributed Bryan's nomination largely to his brilliant speaking, while the pro-gold press credited the nomination to Bryan's demagoguery. The pro-silver Cleveland Plain Dealer called his speech "an eloquent, stirring, and manly appeal," concluding that the speech "gave William Jennings Bryan the Democratic nomination for President of this great republic."[62] Another free-silver paper, the St. Louis Post-Dispatch, commented that Bryan "just about immortalized himself" with the speech.[63] The Post-Dispatch did note that, although the speech led to Bryan's nomination, Bryan had long been working for free silver.[64] A story in a Charleston, South Carolina, newspaper termed Bryan's speech a "great rhetorical effort."[65]

The Democratic but anti-silver New York Times agreed: "With fine elocution and honeyed Populist phrases he aroused the silverites again and again and stirred them to tumult almost beyond the power of the Chairman to restrain." The Times editors disparaged Bryan as "the gifted blatherskite from Nebraska."[66] A day later, they commented that "Bryan's nomination was not a surprise to anyone who was in the convention Thursday."[67] The *Akron Beacon and Republican*, obviously not a pro-Bryan paper, agreed that "never probably has a national convention been swayed or influenced by a single speech as was the national Democratic convention at Chicago yesterday by W. J. Bryan, of Nebraska."[68] Similarly, the pro-gold, Republican *Pittsburg [sic] Press*, although very critical of the Democratic platform, agreed that "the nomination of Bryan was doubtless assured from the moment when he delivered his oration."[69] Former Senator Patrick Walsh of Georgia stated that "Mr. Bryan's speech secured his nomination."[70] Even the pro-gold *Chicago Tribune* commented that "with the masterful oratory for which he has become famous [he] soon wrought up the crowd to a spirit of the wildest enthusiasm."[71]

After the convention, many political conservatives and moderates expressed deep consternation about the results. The pro-business *Wall Street Journal* warned that free silver would make prices unstable in international trade.[72] The *Akron Beacon and Republican* asserted that Bryan's "smooth and ready tongue" did not qualify him to be president.[73] Cleveland business magnate Myron Herrick reported that after Bryan's nomination the financier J. P. Morgan shut his rolltop desk and announced, "There is not going to be any more business in this office . . . until the election is over."[74] Morgan's reaction does not represent the opinions of easterners in general but appears to reflect Bryan's polarization. Similarly, the stockbrokers in St. Louis, alarmed by free silver, considered curtailing stock trading procedures until after the election.[75]

Bryan was not merely a candidate to oppose; he became a candidate to fear. His admirers have admired him passionately. His opponents have despised him with remarkable intensity. This is the predictable result of polarization.

Many opponents of free silver immediately perceived a radical slant to Bryan and the silver plank. The *New York Times* immediately termed Bryan a "radical."[76] Citing unnamed bankers, *The Wall Street Journal* remained optimistic about the economy on the curious ground that "the Chicago platform and nomination meant revolution, and therefore would be bound to fail."[77] Following "A Cross of Gold" and the adoption of the silver plank, Senator David Hill commented that "I am a Democrat, but I am not a revolutionist."[78] Bryan's nomination a day later left Hill even more shocked: "I was a Democrat before the Convention and am a Democrat still—very still."[79] The pro-Bryan *Cleveland Plain Dealer* commented with approval that "it has well been said that this convention is revolutionary in practice as well as tendencies."[80] The *Washington Evening Star* termed the convention "The Triumph of Populism" and pronounced Bryan to be a Populist.[81] On the other hand, Charleston's anti-silver *News and Courier* called Bryan "a man of high character, of considerable experience in public affairs, of undoubted ability." The *News and Courier* editors also noted his remarkable speaking ability. They nonetheless worried that free silver "would plunge the country in overwhelming financial ruin."[82] McKinley's advisors were sufficiently alarmed that they briefly considered sending him on a speaking tour to the West.[83]

Interestingly enough, on July 14 the conservative Republican newspaper the *Washington Evening Star* quoted at length the remarks of J. H. Turner, a Populist Party leader, in support of the convention's turn to silver. Turner commented that "the result of the late national democratic convention at Chicago is undoubtedly the triumph of populism" and continued that "the democratic party at Chicago simply purged itself, reorganized itself and came out for true democracy, and, to all intents and purposes, substituted the populist platform for the old platforms that the party has been using for years."[84] This predated Bryan's actual nomination as the Populist Party candidate for president. One cannot help suspecting that the *Star* published Turner's remarks to stress how radical Bryan was.

Bryan's polarizing style of rhetoric did not escape notice: The *New York Times* complained about his "cheap and shallow references to McKinley."[85] In an editorial endorsing Bryan, the *St. Louis Post-Dispatch* noted that "no voter, on either side, can fail to know how he is voting. The straddle has been effectively eliminated."[86] This implied that Bryan's speech had forced undecided voters to choose sides, a typical result of polarization.

After the convention, Bryan suffered from an embarrassment when a Republican newspaper reported that several phrases in "A Cross of Gold's" had been plagiarized from Secretary of the Treasury Carlisle and Congressman McCall. A chagrined Democratic Party leadership quickly reprinted the speech with certain questioned passages in quotation marks.[87]

A diligent search of relevant speeches has not proven all of these charges, but one might note the biblical tone in the conclusion of Samuel Walker McCall's excellent congressional speech about the tariff on January 26, 1894: "Do you regard your bill with reference to labor? Ready as you have ever been to betray it with a kiss, you scourge it to the very quick, and *press a crown of thorns upon its brow*" (emphasis added).[88]

Bryan represented Nebraska in Congress at the time and may have heard McCall's speech. After the election, a cagey Bryan admitted only that "the concluding sentence of my speech was criticised [sic] both favorably and unfavorably. I had used the idea in substantially the same form in a speech in Congress, but did not recall the fact when I used it in the convention."[89] The accusation about Carlisle was a bit unfair; Bryan did credit Carlisle while presenting his speech, but apparently some early printed copies failed to put the quotations in quotation marks.

Bryan's speech probably contributed to his nomination by a deadlocked convention as the Democratic candidate for president. Perhaps no less dramatic a speech could have helped Bryan to accomplish this. Nonetheless, by appealing in so uncompromising a way to the agrarian elements and to the West, Bryan neglected the national audience who would vote in the November election.

Bryan's audience at the convention consisted almost entirely of Democrats, the majority of whom strongly favored silver from the outset. Russell, the pro-gold speaker who addressed the convention just before Bryan, admitted in a rueful tone that "the time for debate is past. I am conscious . . . painfully conscious that the mind of this convention is not and has not been Open to Argument."[90] For Bryan to persuade such an audience depended, in part, on demonstrating to them that he was the party's most committed and effective advocate of free silver. "A Cross of Gold" seems particularly designed to achieve this goal. The national audience, on the other hand, inevitably represented greater diversity in composition and opinion, and the rhetorical strategies that Bryan employed at the convention may not have been the ones best calculated to persuade the nation as a whole. Polarization is more often a strategy for energizing true believers; it is not a technique to persuade the masses. By pursuing a strategy of polarization, Bryan made himself the darling of the silverites but failed to adapt his speech to the national audience. He identified, in Burke's sense, with the common people of the West and South but divided himself from other large groups of the population.

Thus Bryan left the 1896 Democratic convention, having attacked the nation's economic institutions in his famous "Cross of Gold" speech. This impassioned speech forever shaped Bryan's reputation as a dramatic orator. Perhaps it also sealed his fate in the general election.

CHAPTER 5

"Unmade by One Speech?"

Bryan's Trip to Madison Square Garden

MONTH AFTER THE CONVENTION, on August 12, Bryan accepted the Democratic nomination in a speech at Madison Square Garden. This speech, much different from "A Cross of Gold," produced much different responses. Looking at the events before, during, and after the Madison Square Garden speech shows that Bryan created tension between radicalism and tradition. The real but unspoken issue in this speech was the *character of the candidate*. Bryan set out to present a speech that would be thorough, thoughtful, almost scholarly. He realized he needed to reassure the public that the man who had presented "A Cross of Gold" was not a divisive fanatic. His acceptance speech merely led to uncertainty, however, because in the way he campaigned before and after it, Bryan continued to bring into question his own character as a moderate, responsible politician.

Ethos is the quality of a speaker to persuade by force of the speaker's character. It is also called credibility. Rhetoricians have struggled with this problem for centuries: is credibility a preexisting quality of the speaker, or is it something that the speaker establishes during the speech? Or both?

Concerning a speaker's character, Aristotle writes that "there are three things we trust other than logical demonstrations. These are practical wisdom [*phronésis*] and virtue [*areté*] and good will [*eunoia*]" (bracketed expressions are the translator's). A speaker who possessed all three of these qualities would be a convincing speaker in Aristotle's view. This is because the lack of one of these is the only reason for which a speaker will say something wrong.[1]

Aristotle did not entirely focus on credibility as an inherent trait of the speaker. In a famous passage in Book I of *On Rhetoric,* he also talked about credibility as a line of argument. He explained that there are three kinds of proof that a speaker can give during a speech: those that address the speaker's character, those that affect the disposition of the audience, and those that make reasoned arguments.[2] In his translation of Aristotle's *On Rhetoric,* Kennedy explains that other than in this passage, ethos means to Aristotle "'character,' esp. 'moral character.'"[3] Kennedy has also explained that the most vital sort of ethos to Aristotle is the speaker's ability to exhibit "moral character." This is what leads an audience to count on a speaker.[4] However, there is in Aristotle's *On Rhetoric* (1355b) a relationship between these distinctions and Aristotle's distinction between "invented" and "situated" proofs.[5] Invented proofs are those that a speaker discovers or develops. Invented proof would find its way into the speech itself, whereas situated credibility exists before the speech.

One Aristotelian scholar tries to reconcile the two different conceptions of credibility, concluding that Aristotle's idea of ethos comes from the speaker's character as presented in the speech, "exhibiting fair-mindedness and adapted to the character of the audience."[6] This view may or may not straighten out the ambiguity in Aristotle's work, but it is of no help to Bryan, for as the ensuing argument shows, Bryan's campaigning in August of 1896 made too little effort to adapt to the national audience in any case.

The distinction between situated and invented credibility is the unspoken issue in Bryan's Madison Square Garden speech, which he crafted in large part to demonstrate his character.

Bryan may have focused so strongly, if implicitly, on credibility to resolve "the radical's paradox."[7] The very nature of radical rhetoric produces this paradox, which is the conflict between being dismissed as unrealistic and being absorbed into establishment institutions. A radical with wild ideas seems to be an impractical visionary. However, when a radical's ideas are implemented, they are no longer radical.

Radical speech often seems to contradict or even to undo itself. Speakers simplify complex issues, or they personalize wrongs that lie deep in society. Radical speakers often attack the same authorities that they hope to persuade.[8] Similarly, the leaders of radical movements often face inconsistent requirements. The conflicting demands of a radical movement shape its rhetoric in complex ways.[9]

These are the kinds of rhetorical dilemmas that Bryan had failed to confront in "A Cross of Gold." A radical rhetor must, on the one hand, object to established authorities, who are alleged to cause the social ills against which the radical speaks. However, on the other hand, an effective rhetor must at some point incorporate the movement's teachings into the social order. This requires the radical to accommodate to established authority or even to become the established authority. This may be what leads James Darsey to point out in his discussion of the prophetic theme of American radicalism that "it is the flight from chaos that provides the fundamental conservatism in American radicalism."[10] Consequently, the very nature of the radical enterprise handicaps the radical's attempts to establish credibility.

Bryan seemed keenly aware of these tensions. He may never have been as radical as his rhetoric sounded. Free silver was no longer a distinctly populist idea. Many established authorities advocated free silver, and beyond a certain amount of inflation, the practical significance of changing the money standard was never clear anyway. Nonetheless, throughout the campaign, Bryan attacked the nation's large businesses and influential leaders. He tenaciously advocated economic reform intended to benefit the common people. Even so, he responded to the nomination by attempting to place himself under the umbrella of the Democratic Party, with all of the advantages that such a thoroughly respectable association could provide. Toward that end, his Acceptance Speech offered arguments from authority and tradition, employed defensive strategies, and introduced a number of researched economic arguments. All of these strategies were calculated to enhance Bryan's respectability as a candidate.

The sparse scholarly opinion about Bryan's Acceptance Speech at Madison Square Garden is mostly unfavorable. In a brief discussion, for example, one rhetorical historian comments that the speech was "poorly organized" and "tiresome." He also states that much of the crowd left before Bryan's speech was over, and that the press responded poorly to Bryan's presentation.[11] Donald Springen complains that Bryan read from a manuscript, that the audience was "appalled," and that many in the audience left early. He does, however, state that the press praised the speech as "thoughtful" and adds that Bryan overcame the occasion to gain a rhetorical triumph.[12] An essay about Bryan summarizes Bryan's 1896 Acceptance Speech very briefly, noting only that Bryan tried to bring unity to his campaign among the different sections of the nation.[13] A well-known review of Bryan's speaking career does not mention the 1896 Acceptance Speech at all.[14] In his book about the 1896 campaign, Jones terms Bryan's presentation "undramatic" and notes that many of the crowd, "sensing that no brilliant display of oratory was likely," left early.[15] Kurt Ritter and James Andrews point out that Bryan's 1900 Acceptance Speech, which attacked American imperialism, "constituted a comprehensive and forceful rejection of imperialism; it could not be ignored."[16] Bryan's 1896 Acceptance Speech, however, seems to have had much less impact.

Yet, considering Bryan's purposes, it is hard to maintain that Bryan was completely unsuccessful at Madison Square Garden. Bryan indeed failed—"refused" would be more accurate—to reenact the emotional kind of oratory that won him the nomination. However, to put on a display was not his objective. His objective was to establish his credibility as a presidential candidate, and he might have succeeded if not for his oratory before and after the Acceptance Speech.

Bryan had gained the nomination as an advocate of the ordinary American farmer and worker, an advocate who challenged the nation's economic system. His views were quickly denounced, even by fellow Democrats, even by some more moderate advocates of bimetallism, as radical or revolutionary.[17]

Once nominated, Bryan found, suddenly, that he was no longer a political outsider. At Madison Square Garden, Bryan tried to place himself squarely within the traditions of the Democratic Party. He undertook to present an acceptance speech that would be thorough, dignified, and, most of all, safe. In addition, Bryan presumably sought to convince Easterners that he bore no hostility toward them. The radical's paradox thus burdened Bryan very early in the campaign.

As a means of accomplishing these aims, Bryan's Acceptance Speech was the climax—or anticlimax—of a series of events. The speeches he gave during his railroad journey from his home in Nebraska to New York City, the defensive rhetorical strategies he employed during his Acceptance Speech, and the brief speech he gave immediately after his Acceptance Speech all contributed to the impression that Bryan created of his own character.

To understand the uncertainty that the Acceptance Speech provoked, it is necessary to join Bryan on his pugnacious journey from Nebraska to New York. He left Nebraska on a special car attached to a regularly scheduled train. At many of the stops, he stepped out of his car to give a brief speech.[18] Various Democratic dignitaries accompanied Bryan during all or part of the trip.[19] Brass bands and fireworks often greeted him at railway stations.[20]

The trip in general gave an impression of inexperience and disorganization. As Bryan passed through a small town in Iowa, he waved to a group of twenty supporters but had no time for a speech, as the train was a scheduled local. In Colfax, Iowa, the train pulled away from the station while Bryan was still speaking.[21] In Iowa City, he competed with the noise of switching freight trains.[22]

The speeches during this trip were mostly short and pointed, and sometimes they brimmed over with regional animosity. For example, at Iowa City he asserted: "Our party tried an experiment which no great national party has ever tried before, I believe, that is, they nominated a candidate for President who has to pass through Iowa before he can get to the White House."[23]

Thus, although the Acceptance Speech itself would have a more public-spirited quality, during his trip to New York Bryan impressed on the nation that he was still a fundamentally divisive, regional candidate. He routinely referred to pro-gold forces and easterners alike as "the enemy." Upon leaving his home in Nebraska, he commented that "I expressed the desire to be notified in New York, in order that our cause might be presented first in the heart of what now seems to be the enemy's country."[24] At Rock Island, Bryan promised that "there is not a State which we are willing to concede to the enemy." In Moline, Illinois, he left the train to speak from a platform, where he called for "free and unlimited coinage of gold and silver at the present ratio of 16 to 1, without waiting for the aid or consent of any other nation on earth."[25] Such statements typify radical rhetoric that makes uncompromising, personalized attacks against established authorities. This stood out against McKinley's strategy of identification and unity.

Arriving in Chicago by August 9, Bryan almost collapsed, exhausted, after giving a few speeches.[26] His train then whirled through several towns in Indiana and Ohio. With a continued lack of organization at this early stage of the campaign, Bryan slept through a demonstration in Valparaiso at 1:40 A.M. In Fort Wayne, he protested his need to safeguard his failing voice for his New York speech.[27]

When he arrived at Van Wert, Ohio, Bryan's car was no longer at the rear of the train and the crowds had difficulty finding a good vantage point to hear or see him.[28] When the train reached Massillon in northeastern Ohio, Bryan stood on the steps between two railroad cars to deliver a brief speech.[29] Overall, from this early part of the speaking tour one catches the impression of a candidate who was relentless and uncompromising but already overstressed.

The stifling heat continued when Bryan arrived in McKinley's home town of Canton, Ohio.[30] Temperatures in northeastern Ohio reached 98°F.[31] Speaking from a flatcar, Bryan discussed the "European financial policy" that afflicted the nation, meaning the gold standard. He did pause, however, to praise his opponent's "high character and personal worth."[32]

The charge that he was a radical clearly troubled Bryan. He remarked to a small-town crowd that someone had said "when one person saw a thing he was a fanatic; when a great many saw it he became an enthusiast, when everybody saw it he became a hero."[33] The tone of these remarks suggests that Bryan would rather have been considered a hero than a fanatic. The remarks did, however, call attention to his reputation as a fanatic.

When Bryan pulled into Pittsburgh later on August 10, the train could hardly progress because of the groups of voters pressing to catch a glimpse of the famous orator.[34] Bryan continued to speak in a bellicose tone. He told a crowd in Pittsburgh that "when I left home I told them that I was coming to open the campaign in what was now considered to be the enemy's country, but which we hoped would be our country before the campaign was over." Echoing "A Cross of Gold," Bryan remarked that the campaign brought up the issue of 1776 again "and that in this campaign, as in that, the line will be drawn between the patriot and the Tory." Despite Bryan's expressed wish not to be thought a fanatic, such comments continued to express an inflexible, polarizing position. His voice was sounding tired and husky.[35] A crowd estimated at about a thousand people greeted Bryan at the station in Jersey City. Unfortunately, he had by this time given too many speeches at too frantic a pace, and on the eve of his Acceptance Speech, his voice completely failed.[36] One cannot question Bryan's dedication, but his failure to prepare himself physically for the challenge of speaking at Madison Square Garden added to the general impression of his being overanxious and inexperienced. Apparently Mary Bryan had warned him that he would lose his voice due to overuse, and indeed he did.[37]

On the positive side, the long train trip, interrupted by many brief speeches, was well reported and thus helped to build excitement for the speechmaking in New York.[38] Leading newspapers, Democratic and Republican alike, covered Bryan's speeches and incidents thoroughly. A group of more than thirty newspaper and wire service reporters, armed with typewriters and teams of stenographers, accompanied Bryan on the train. At each station telegraph agents met the train to take the reporters' typewritten dispatches and transmit them to the papers.[39] In Fort Wayne Bryan met an early morning group of about twenty-five hundred supporters, but he refused to deliver a formal speech to them because the newspaper reporters were not awake yet, and Bryan had promised not to speak without them![40] Even the implacably anti-silver *New York Times* felt the need to comment at length on August 11 that Bryan's railroad tour was uninspiring, which at least shows the degree of attention that he had gained.[41]

Thus Bryan arrived in New York well heralded, but he was also tired and hoarse—and worse, the weather was unbearably hot. The usually sympathetic *St. Louis Post-Dispatch* noted that the candidate "looked tired and sleepy."[42] Bryan consulted a physician, who diagnosed laryngitis and advised the candidate to rest.[43] Bryan's whistle-stop speeches had created the impression that he had come to New York to do battle. Yet, just as the circumstances at the Chicago convention a few weeks earlier had been favorable for a dramatic speech, the situation in New York was beginning to look inauspicious.

Indeed, few speeches have been ruined by a setting as badly as was Bryan's speech at Madison Square Garden. It could not have helped that Bryan found New York City bedecked with huge McKinley and Hobart banners.[44]

If McKinley's summer campaign consisted of a series of highly artificial pseudo-events, no less could be said of Bryan's work. The notification, like McKinley's notification, was in any literal sense unnecessary. Bryan already knew that he was the Democratic candidate. The party already knew he would accept the nomination he had so eagerly pursued. The whole event existed to focus public excitement on the campaign, while providing an eminently newsworthy forum for Bryan to express his views and to demonstrate his character.

The announced procedure for the notification and acceptance ceremony had some rather cumbersome results. The large Committee on Notification would attend the meeting. The Democratic Party's Tammany Hall organization reserved about five thousand seats.[45] Prize box seats were saved for Tammany's senior leaders.[46] The majority of the New York Democratic Party's leadership, however, did not attend.[47] Admission to the Garden would be by ticket only, and certain entrances were designated for the audience to enter the arena. Governor William Stone of Missouri would present the notification speech, formally advising Bryan of his nomination. Richard Bland was also scheduled to appear, presumably to establish by his presence on the platform the solidarity of the Democratic Party's two leading advocates of free silver.[48] Bryan's Acceptance Speech would follow.

The Garden was so arranged that a small platform for the speakers would be against one of the longer walls, with the press directly in front of the platform. Members of the audience crammed themselves into floor seats and box seats.[49] Over fifty thousand tickets were requested, far more than the Garden could accommodate. The organizers removed seats to accommodate as many people as possible. Tickets were sold for up to ten dollars each, a hefty sum for the time, and hawkers resold them for up to fifteen dollars.[50] Before the meeting, Bryan announced his plan to speak from a manuscript. He promised that he would "try to follow it absolutely."[51] On the eve of the speech a reporter for the pro-silver *St. Louis Post-Dispatch,* seemingly having received some inside information, explained that Bryan intended "to merge his reputation as an orator into that of a statesman to-night." Bryan apparently had written the speech before he left Nebraska. The report continued that Bryan would be more concerned about the newspaper readership than about the live audience.[52] Furthermore, speaking in mundane fashion from a manuscript would prevent Bryan from sounding anything like the deranged fanatic that his opponents depicted him to be. Thus the Acceptance Speech was to take a much different tone from the emotional, sometimes belligerent speeches that Bryan had given from the train.

With the heat wave continuing from Chicago to New York, temperatures exceeding 90°F in New York City had resulted in more than a hundred deaths.[53] People in the Garden were allowed to smoke, adding to the suffocating atmosphere.[54] Bryan was doomed to deliver his Acceptance Speech in a stifling, overcrowded hall.

As the crowd gathered at Madison Square Garden, a band played in the gallery. The small speaker's platform was draped with American flags. Mary and William Jennings Bryan entered the hall separately, each greeted by cheers.[55] In the speech of notification, Stone explained at prodigious length that Bryan's nomination resulted from the support of ordinary Americans.[56]

Eventually the candidate got his turn. Bryan spoke at 8:00 P.M. The Garden had been full with a crowd of more than twenty thousand, about double its usual capacity, since 5:00. Those who managed to endure the entire evening heard Bryan speak for almost two hours in a building described as "a fiery furnace."[57]

Bryan's rhetorical strategies were directed, at least implicitly, to the task of improving his credibility. He relied in this speech on an appeal to tradition. Bryan undertook to establish that his views on silver and the Democratic platform positions on other issues were neither new nor radical. This would also imply Bryan's character as a respectable candidate. A reasonable way to prove such a point was to find the proposed Democratic policies and their accompanying arguments in the past. If the Democratic position was not new, then it would seem that it was not radical either.

Similarly, the appeal to authority is by its very nature a conservative type of argument. A creative social reformer analyzes the economic and political realities of the time, studies their causes and effects, and reaches a conclusion about how to improve society. The social reformer expresses the wisdom of the future. Authorities in general, however, and historical authorities in particular, presumably tend to embody established wisdom. In this speech, Bryan employed both kinds of argument. He used the argument from authority to ground his candidacy in the nation's culture. Nothing is either unusual or remarkable about a political candidate quoting public officials of the past. However, in the context of the campaign, and given the criticisms that had afflicted Bryan, this practice took on higher significance. As with many other radical speakers before and since, Bryan's solution to the radical's paradox was to ground his arguments in tradition.

Bryan had briefly mentioned Andrew Jackson, the quintessential people's Democrat, in "A Cross of Gold."[58] Bryan's Acceptance Speech contained several lengthy quotations from Democratic and Republican leaders of the past. Thus, early in the speech, Bryan again quoted Jackson. The quotation he chose, however, was a curious one. Since Bryan was under attack as being too much a commoner, he stressed early in the speech that he understood all persons to be equal before the law, but naturally they were unequal in their accomplishments. He quoted Jackson to say that government could not make people equal in ability or in material possessions. Thus Bryan seemed to retreat somewhat from his position as a candidate of the ordinary people and quoted no less an authority than Jackson to prove that he could retreat in this way and yet remain a true Democrat.[59] He was perhaps already dealing with the radical's paradox. Having shown that a Democratic authority could support inequality, he next showed that a Republican authority could support the common person. Bryan cited Lincoln to the effect that the judgment of the common people was to be trusted above the judgment of all others. Bryan then cited Jackson again to establish that government should not grant special titles or favors, and from there he made a transition to explain that those who opposed him were indeed seeking government favors. Later in the speech, Bryan cited Thomas Jefferson's opinion that it was the government's duty to prevent citizens from harming one another.[60]

Bryan's revolution had come full circle. Turning to an academician for another authority, he referred to Professor Laughlin of the University of Chicago, whom Bryan identified as a leading advocate of the gold standard.[61] Laughlin's quotation supported Bryan's point that gold is not of permanently fixed value.

In addition, Bryan presented lengthy, somewhat dull quotations from Senators John Sherman and James Blaine. The Sherman quotation pointed out the harms that result from deflation, while Blaine, quoted from an 1878 speech, discussed the harms that result from the gold standard. Bryan quoted Sherman again near the end of the speech.[62] Again, although the content of these quotations was surely relevant to Bryan's point, the real thrust of his message was that he could identify respected authorities to buttress his views. The fact that he could do so tacitly helped to discount the charge that he was a radical.

Bryan's work at the Democratic convention had focused exclusively on the money question, and free silver was the only issue that he discussed at any length in "A Cross of Gold." The Democratic platform did, however, introduce a number of proposals.[63] In addition to the free coinage of silver, these included statements opposing both government bonds and a national bank, as well as planks in favor of immigration restrictions, justice for the Cubans, low taxes, the income tax, reduced federal authority, Civil War pensions, the admission of New Mexico, Oklahoma, and Arizona to the union, a moderate form of civil service, and the improvement of waterways. Of these, the income tax eventually proved to be the most controversial.

Now that he was the nominee, Bryan felt a need to endorse the entire platform. He stressed that the money issue "overshadows all other questions" but responded to attacks on the income tax plank by stating that the income tax was "not new." His evidence for this, curious in light of his unsympathetic attitude toward international bimetallism, was that several European nations had already adopted the income tax and that the tax had not harmed the wealthy.[64] As an appeal to tradition, this argument was rather strained, but nonetheless it seemed to be part of Bryan's plan to establish that his ideas were neither novel nor dangerous.

Radical speakers often tie themselves to the past. They do so by arguing that the radical movement is, in fact, a return to the nation's traditional values. They relate their ideas to timeless ideals. James Darsey contends that "conservatism in this sense is not a simple reactionary impulse. The American prophetic tradition is not a retreat into an idealized world in the past. American radicals . . . sought to preserve some agreement on goals."[65] For example, in his analysis of Eugene Debs's rhetoric, Darsey points out that Debs and similar radicals were, at least in a sense, opponents of progress. Their desire was "to restore the values that had characterized America's past." At the same time, these same radicals supported such American liberal ideals as individual autonomy and egalitarianism.[66]

Bryan's rhetoric at Madison Square Garden fits neatly, if restlessly, into this framework. At times he sounded almost desperate to establish that he was in fact a traditionalist who stood shoulder to shoulder with great American leaders of the past. Nonetheless, that he went to such lengths not only to assert but also to prove his traditional ideological lineage suggests that he held a defensive attitude.

One gets the impression that Bryan cited tradition not so much to support the validity of his ideas but more to defend himself against criticism. He started the speech by offering a defense of himself and his policies. At the Democratic convention, Bryan had been on the attack, labeling his opponents "enemies" and promising to resist them "to the uttermost."[67] He had continued that approach during the railroad trip to New York. However, at Madison Square Garden, Bryan responded to the sting of criticism. He had heard himself called a radical, an anarchist, and a revolutionary. The vehemence of the attacks against Bryan's character may have unsettled the young Nebraskan.

In his introduction, after two sentences of polite preliminaries, Bryan had assured his sweltering listeners that he was aware of the "forces arrayed against us" but stated: "We shall defend with all possible vigor the positions taken by our party." He expressed dismay that "some of our opponents, in the absence of better argument, resort to abusive epithets." He moved to discuss the charge that the Democratic platform was an attack on property rights and the civic order. He then assured the audience that the Democrats were "prepared to make known and to defend" their motivations and goals. Bryan reminded his audience that "the commandment, 'Thou shalt not steal,' thundered from Sinai" applies to the rich as well as the poor. He complained that his opponents labeled "Anarchist" anyone who supported the income tax plank. He then defended the legality of the income tax plank.[68]

This would have to be considered weak as a debating strategy, for Bryan began this crucial speech by defending the Democratic platform and candidate against attack. Only later in the lengthy speech did he begin to discuss his own constructive positions. Due to some combination of the heat and the dullness of the speechmaking, many of the crowd left during Bryan's speech.[69] Thus, the audience's first impression—and the only impression of those who left early and who neglected to read the long speech in the newspapers—was that Bryan felt his character and the wisdom of his ideas to be under attack and was interested, first and foremost, in fending off assaults. Thus his foremost argument was not so much "the silver plank is *good,* for it fulfills our traditions," as "the silver plank is *not bad,* for it is consistent with our traditions."

Interestingly, Bryan closed the speech with an appeal for unity: "Citizens of New York," he pleaded, "I have traveled from the centre of the continent to the seaboard that I might, in the very beginning of the campaign, bring you greeting from the people of the West and South, and assure you that their desire is not to destroy, but to build up."[70] It is perhaps curious that Bryan even felt a need to assure easterners he did not wish to destroy them.

Still, Bryan did not rely wholly on tradition. While the arguments from tradition and authority tie a speaker to the wisdom of those who have come before, cause and effect arguments can establish the wisdom of future policy changes. By examining antecedent conditions and predicting their results, the speaker can try to demonstrate that a proposed new policy is a good one. That Bryan could make such arguments, which sometimes became quite technical, also seemed to demonstrate that he possessed serious knowledge of the issues.

After a discussion of the errors of his opponents and his quick look at the income tax, Bryan turned to his main campaign issue, bimetallism. He argued that the gold standard depended entirely on "the money-owning and the money-changing classes" for its support. He then responded to the Republicans' claim that gold was "honest money." "What is the test of honesty in money?"

Bryan asked. He responded that "an absolutely honest dollar would not vary in its general purchasing power." He argued that a deflationary currency was as dishonest as one that was inflationary. He brought up the plight of the farmers, who had to repay debts with money that was now much harder to get.[71]

In another example of economic focus, in trying to identify the causes of the nation's economic problems Bryan argued that the supply of money had fallen too low: "Any legislation which lessens the world's stock of standard money increases the exchangeable value of the dollar; therefore the crusade against silver must inevitably raise the purchasing power of money and lower the money value of all other forms of property."[72] This is not a stirring argument but rather a textbooklike statement of the causes of deflation.

Part of Bryan's purpose in coming to New York was to appeal beyond the farmer. Thus, for a further economic argument, he brought up the dilemma of the wage earner. "Wage earners," Bryan argued, "know that, although a gold standard raises the purchasing power of the dollar, it also makes it more difficult to obtain possession of the dollar." He went on to discuss the impact of bimetallism on life and fire insurance policies and bank savings accounts.[73]

For still another economic argument, Bryan claimed that "the gold standard encourages the hoarding of money because money is rising." He offered this point to refute those persons who, citing Gresham's law, claimed that bimetallism would drive gold money out of circulation. Turning the tables on that line of attack, Bryan offered bimetallism as a cure for hoarding.[74]

Bryan stuck to bimetallism, his main issue, for a considerable period. He responded to the chief criticisms that had been raised against bimetallism. He attempted to show that the wage earner and small saver needed bimetallism just as much as did the farmers. The great bulk of his Madison Square Garden speech was given over to material of this same character.

It seems unlikely that any such arguments would stir the crowd to a frenzy. Bryan's opponents had attacked him as an ignoramus, a hothead, a fanatic, a revolutionary, a wild-eyed orator who could convince uneducated people to believe ideas that Bryan himself did not understand very well.[75] Bryan obviously felt a need to counter these slanderous charges. The tone of the speech may have helped to build Bryan's credibility. His critics could henceforth attack this speech as dull or listless, but they could no longer plausibly claim that he had not studied the issues. The quotations from politicians and experts and the economic arguments established that Bryan thoroughly understood the bimetallists' body of doctrine.

Bryan's delivery at Madison Square Garden engendered much comment. The delivery was calculated to enhance his credibility. Anti-silver newspapers made much of Bryan's decision to use a manuscript for his Acceptance Speech.[76] Bryan apparently had two reasons for reading the speech. The first was to ensure that he would be quoted accurately. Aware that most of the New York press was unfriendly to him, feeling that he was now in "the enemy's country," Bryan was concerned that if he spoke extemporaneously, published texts of his speech would be based entirely on the notes of unsympathetic shorthand reporters.[77] Second, the Democratic Party leadership already had it in mind to distribute copies of the speech as a campaign document; indeed, the press received copies of the speech in advance of its delivery.[78]

Bryan's delivery may not have been as dreadful as some have supposed, even though hoarseness and exhaustion surely took their toll. The best firsthand account of his delivery that night comes from a generally negative article in the *New York Times*. Although the reporter claimed that Bryan's voice sounded "worn," Bryan could nonetheless be understood well enough. The reporter noted Bryan's habit of saying "eighteen and sixty-nine" instead of "eighteen sixty-nine," "Mount Sin-e-i" instead of "Mount Sinai," and the like.[79] This suggests that Bryan did not forsake his taste for the dramatic. It should be kept in mind, however, that members of the press had a better vantage point than did the bulk of the crowd, and the fact that the reporter heard the speech does not prove that listeners on the far side of the building could hear it easily.[80]

Another newspaper account of the speech commented that Bryan's voice had suffered from his speaking trip. The reporter felt that Bryan could be heard everywhere in the building except "in the galleries in the rear of the Garden." The article also stated that the peroration was more effective because Bryan looked away from his manuscript.[81]

After his Acceptance Speech, wishing to accommodate the throngs who were not able to gain entrance to Madison Square Garden, Bryan went across the street to a balcony at the Hotel Bartholdt. From that vantage he spoke much more briefly to a second large crowd.[82] This appearance had been announced in advance.[83] At this point Bryan immediately reverted to his more typical form: militant, divisive, and entertaining. In the seemingly extemporaneous address, he nervously remarked that Nebraskans had been worried about sending him to "the enemy's country." He expressed his desire to convert New York to the silver cause. Bryan attacked the New York financiers, announcing that financiers should abandon the gold standard in favor of the golden rule. Bryan also continued his military metaphors from "A Cross of Gold," announcing to the crowd in the street that "I commission you all soldiers to fight and missionaries to preach wherever you go from now until election." Bryan expressed no concern about the gold Democrats' plan to form their own splinter party, stating that "you will search in vain to find a battle ever won by an army of generals. (Great applause and laughter.) They have not a private in their whole ranks. (Laughter and cheers.)"[84]

After that speech, Bryan planned to stay quiet for several days while he answered correspondence and worked on his Letter of Acceptance.[85]

The expectations of the crowd attending the speech were not fulfilled. Presumably many people, including various otherwise ill-disposed New York reporters, came to Madison Square Garden to hear a flashy demonstration of rhetorical brilliance. For example, the anti-Bryan *Washington Post* speculated: "New York was discussing for weeks the master stroke of oratory by which the Nebraskan inspired the tidal waves of enthusiasm that swept him into the highest place in the gift of his party." The *Post* continued that "curiosity was rife whether the candidate was equal to a second speech that might aid in winning for him the foremost office in the gift of his country."[86] However, Bryan did not come to the Garden to put on a stage show. He came to achieve persuasive purposes, and first among those purposes, it seems, was a desire to appear dignified and competent.

The oft-cited fact that so many in the audience left does not prove that they were unhappy with the speech.[87] They were the victims of tremendous "physical discomfort." It is not certain that everyone could hear the speakers, especially the hoarse candidate. The audience was surely restless after Stone's introductory speech. They knew that they could read Bryan's speech in the morning newspaper.[88] The Garden was overcrowded. New York was beset by a heat wave. Air conditioning awaited the future, as did electronic sound amplification. It is no surprise that many people were unable to endure the lengthy proceedings.[89]

Bryan's supporters were not easily discouraged. Immediately after the speech, copies were printed and distributed as campaign documents. Democratic leaders claimed that about three hundred thousand copies of the speech promptly went to San Francisco alone.[90] Many newspapers, Democratic and Republican alike, published either a complete text of Bryan's speech or excerpts from it.[91] Thus, the speech led to widespread distribution of Bryan's views on the economic effects of bimetallism.[92] Perhaps alluding to the Democratic Party's poor funding, Senator Faulkner said that the speech "is a document which circulates itself and does not need a frank, for the press of the entire country prints it."[93]

Bryan professed himself pleased with the results of the speech. He commented shortly afterward: "I did not expect to overcome all the prejudice at one blow. Neither did I expect to set the North river on fire with oratory. It was not a time for oratorical flights, but for serious and argumentative discussion. I am pleased with my reception."[94]

The press evaluated the speech along party lines. The pro-gold press was, as one might expect, hostile toward Bryan's speech. The *Akron Beacon and Republican* made a point of quoting several comments from an English newspaper critical of Bryan.[95] The Democratic but anti-silver *New York Times* called Bryan's Acceptance Speech "prosy" and "barren of catching sentences." They noted, correctly enough, that Bryan was ready "for a pamphlet rather than for an audience."[96] The Republican *Pittsburg Press* editorialized that the speech "emptied the hall in which it was delivered" and that "there is not one voter in 100 who could be induced to read the entire text." To prove their point, they quoted some especially esoteric passages.[97] Charleston's anti-silver *News and Courier* grudgingly admitted that Bryan "made a great speech in New York on Wednesday night" and that "it was argument, not invective; argument, not abuse." The editors did express alarm at Bryan's support from populist and socialist elements.[98]

On the other hand, the Democratic *St. Louis Post-Dispatch* found the speech "to be an able, masterly effort, clear, logical, pungent and powerful." The *Post-Dispatch* reporter acknowledged that the auditors had hoped for a more enthusiastic speech and that they responded fervently on the several occasions when Bryan "rose to a climax."[99] An editorial in the moderately pro-gold *Chicago Journal* complained that "unfriendly critics of Mr. Bryan began by calling him a boy orator. This morning they are displeased because he is not a boy orator." The *Journal* said that "A Cross of Gold" was designed "to capture an impressionable convention" but that by any other standard it was "immeasurably inferior to" the Madison Square Garden speech.[100] In a front-page editorial cartoon published several days later, the usually dignified *Washington Post* criticized third-party, pro-Bryan vice presidential candidate Watson as "A Georgia Cracker" and described Bryan as "Little Billee" and a "Dimopop." A Dimopop, one presumes, was a Populist in Democratic garb. This indicated, not for the last time, that rational dialogue was not the universal method of campaign discourse.[101]

Political reactions also fell along party lines. After railing against various Populists, Ohio's Republican Senator Joseph Foraker sarcastically commented on August 15 that Bryan could be justly called "the boy orator of the Platte" because that river was "a thousand miles long and only six inches deep." In a much-quoted remark, Foraker also claimed that "Mr. Bryan made himself by one speech, and now he has unmade himself by one speech."[102] The *Washington Star* quoted "Ex-Representative [John Mercer] Langston of Virginia" as saying that "the trouble about Bryan, as shown by this speech, and all others he has delivered in this campaign, is that he is a moral tramp. You know what I mean. He runs with the tramp element."[103] This, also, was presumably targeted at Bryan's populist supporters.

More favorably, Democratic former representative Poindexter Dunn of Arkansas commented that Bryan "had purposely stripped his speech of what was merely oratorical, . . . appealing to reason rather than to emotion." Dunn continued that the speech "entitles

Bryan to rank with the greatest of men" and added that Bryan had proven himself "to be a master of the entire subject."[104] Dunn also commented: "The speech . . . shows him to be a master of the science of government, a philosopher and statesman of the highest rank."

Bryan presumably chose to speak in New York to broaden his support beyond the West and South. Yet his references before and after the Acceptance Speech to the Northeast as the "enemy's country" could not have endeared him to the East. Although the Madison Square Garden speech itself was remarkably devoid of regionalism, Bryan openly acknowledged his suspicions about the East both before and after the Acceptance Speech. This may have replaced with mistrust any impression of reasonableness that he might otherwise have created at the Garden. Instead of proving himself a well-informed guardian of the traditions of the Democratic Party, Bryan may have created the impression that he was still a divisive, regional candidate who knew how to behave himself for a few hours every now and then. This was a failure, perhaps inevitable under the circumstances, to deal efficiently with the radical's paradox.

Thus, there was an ambiguity about Bryan's credibility that night. On the one hand, Bryan wanted to tie himself clearly to the traditions of the Democratic Party. On the other hand, he eschewed the support of the rich and powerful, tying himself instead to the interests and needs of the common people. He expressed that view repeatedly and in uncompromising language. Was it possible to accomplish both goals and yet still be consistent? A major party candidate requires the support of the party machinery; Bryan's pursuit of Tammany Hall's endorsement was only one indication that he realized this.[105] All the same, Bryan's rapidly developing image as the Great Commoner impelled him to reject many of the established authorities of the nation, especially of the industrialized eastern seaboard.

The speech from the Hotel Bartholdt was more like what the public expected to hear from him, and perhaps Bryan's attempt in Madison Square Garden to moderate his image was doomed to failure before he began. If so, it was not doomed because the speech was faulty but because under the circumstances no speech could have convinced the Nebraska orator's opponents that he was a traditionalist. Since Bryan himself had created those circumstances, he had no one else to blame. In one sense, with his open advocacy of the ordinary working American, Bryan is an example of the kind of orator whom Darsey describes as failing "in significant ways" to accomplish their purposes.[106] That is, Bryan's failure embodied a notable attempt to reform the nation's economic system. In another sense, he fell short by his tendency to focus too intensely on what seems like a self-conscious defense of his own character. This, indeed, might in the general case be a good reason for the radical speaker's typical reliance on appeals to tradition: to defuse the common fear that the radical's ideas are untested and dangerous.

The speech may have been of more value than Bryan's critics realized, and its inadequacies, although real, turn out upon careful examination to be more complex than they first seem. Neither a straightforward success nor an ignoble failure, the Madison Square Garden speech was an enigmatic tapestry woven from rhetorical care, misjudgment, and bad luck. The speech reflected tension in Bryan's desire to satisfy simultaneously the pro-silver voters of the West and the more conservative voters of the industrial Northeast. It created further tension because of his goal of convincing his listeners that he was at once both a committed advocate of free silver and a responsible, traditional Democrat.

At the end of his trip to New York, Bryan had presented himself to the national audience as a complex, not entirely consistent candidate for the presidency. As a result, he still failed to solve the radical's paradox. He never quite seemed to let the audience know whether he was a true social reformer or a traditionally minded member of the establishment.

Such conflicts are typical of radical rhetoric. That Bryan was nominated by the Democratic Party so early in his career, and thus had almost immediately gained the endorsement of that venerable organization, heightened the difficulties he faced. An advocate of free silver was likely to view Bryan's nomination with pride—pride that a devotee of the movement had come so close to political power. To a nondevotee of free silver, Bryan's rhetoric would seem self-defeating and inconsistent. The Madison Square Garden speech in itself was what Bryan hoped it would be:

dignified and thoughtful. The speeches he gave before and after it, however, seemed combative and sometimes angry. A speaker taking a rhetorical approach like Bryan's could not realistically hope to gain a consensus from the public. In contrast, to gain such a consensus was precisely the paramount objective of Bryan's opponent.

CHAPTER 6

McKinley's Front Porch Oratory in September, 1896

A CANDIDATE WHO WANTS to sound like a president must unify, while challengers are more of a mind to create controversy. Neither McKinley nor Bryan had yet taken the White House, but McKinley sounded more like a president. McKinley's unifying rhetorical strategies in 1896 remained remarkably similar from the first day of the campaign to the last. Those strategies included McKinley's stress on what Kenneth Burke calls rhetoric of *identification*. McKinley identified the Republican cause with patriotism, law and order, and the flag. He identified himself with the working people of the United States. He identified the tariff and sound monetary policy with the interests of the workers. He lumped together free silver and free trade as twin components of a conspiracy against the American worker. He hardly ever offered significant argumentation on behalf of these identifications, instead making his identifications with simple stylistic devices such as parallel sentence structure and unadorned juxtaposition. McKinley used such speaking devices throughout the campaign. This chapter looks at the September speeches from the Front Porch campaign to show in detail how McKinley developed his identifications.

Voters were still coming to Canton to see McKinley, and in ever-increasing numbers. His campaign continued to feature large numbers of pseudo-events. McKinley created an impression of himself as warm, casual, and welcoming, even spontaneous, yet dignified. The campaign events were carefully staged to create just such an impression. This impression in turn became one of the major tools that McKinley used to create his complex web of identifications.

McKinley continued to campaign in September, and with increasing vigor. He presented almost sixty speeches in that month, all of them in his hometown of Canton, Ohio, most of them from his front porch or from a stand in the street in front of his house, to ever larger and more numerous delegations that came from near and far. This averaged almost two speeches a day, although since a disproportionate number of speeches were on Saturdays, some days became very busy indeed. The bunching of speeches on Saturdays accommodated workers who traveled on their day off and provided extensive copy for the Sunday newspapers, which tended to be larger than the daily editions. The railroads, which generally supported McKinley, often advertised to take travelers to Canton for about half the usual rates, often on special trains.[1] On occasion, recent immigrants heard various speakers advocate the Republican cause in Canton in their native languages.[2]

Kenneth Burke's concept of identification implies that seemingly unlike entities or concepts are rhetorically connected. It occurs when the interests of two individuals "are joined" or when they are persuaded to believe that their interests are joined.[3] Identification between persons implies that two ostensibly distinct individuals appear to be "consubstantial" in having "common sensations, concepts, images, ideas, attitudes."[4]

Burke frequently talks about identification purely in terms of people, with person A finding an identification with person B. Yet, in Burke's work, identification is a richly textured concept, and he notes that people also identify various things, concepts, or subjects with one another.[5] This becomes important in McKinley's rhetoric, as the Republican candidate created a network of interlocking associations.

Some authorities believe that identification is essential if persuasion is to occur.[6] Rhetorically speaking, Burke comments that "you persuade a man only insofar as you can talk his language by speech, gesture, tonality, order, image, attitude, idea, *identifying* your ways with his."[7] Freud influenced Burke's concept, so that identification can occur because people perceive similarity or because people make associations. Perceived similarity refers to an impression that two persons are similar; a process of association creates identification where it did not exist before.[8] In a 1984 Idaho political campaign, congressional candidate George Hansen was able to achieve identification with his audience. However, by virtue of Hansen's implausibly extreme attack against his perceived enemies, the audience may not have shared his interpretation of reality fully.[9] This was a rhetoric of association, albeit an unsuccessful one. This was a kind of mistake that McKinley most emphatically did not make.

In his campaign speeches, McKinley implied that all Americans shared a common interest that made sound money and the tariff to their benefit. Unlike division, identification is an affirmative rhetorical approach. Thus McKinley's astute political oratory during this campaign was affirmative, whereas Bryan's was often negative or even belligerent. Curiously, McKinley often accomplished this in a style that was just as appealing, or more appealing, to the ordinary voter as that of Bryan, the "Great Commoner." Not an unusually eloquent speaker, McKinley nonetheless demonstrated in his September speeches, and in fact throughout the campaign, a gift for relating warmly, clearly, and effectively to ordinary people.

Although McKinley continued to argue forcefully against free silver, he did not rely exclusively on refutation of Bryan's position on the currency issue. He also played up his own constructive argument about the tariff. The September speeches were among McKinley's best; in August, he was still feeling his way to a rhetorical strategy; by October, the campaign became so busy that more of the speeches seemed hastily prepared.

An interesting feature of the Front Porch campaign is that the different audiences who traveled to Canton tended to be specialized, as each delegation came from a particular region, industry, or what have you, and McKinley could use each delegation to symbolize a larger group. As the campaign closed several weeks later, the *Review of Reviews* would correctly note this feature of McKinley's rhetoric: "Mr. McKinley . . . thanks to the marvelous methods of the modern newspaper, has in speaking to a deputation of iron workers, for example, been able to address men of that class everywhere."[10]

With the campaign now running in high gear, the typical ritual of a campaign event began with the arrival of a trainload of McKinley supporters at a Canton train station. The delegation, which might contain hundreds or even thousands of persons, paraded down Market Street toward McKinley's home, often accompanied by mounted escorts, bands, rifle teams, and the like. A leader of the delegation presented a speech greeting McKinley, with McKinley's speech cast as a response. A shorthand reporter from the Associated Press sat at a table on the porch and took down the speeches as they were delivered.[11] Newspaper and wire services distributed and printed them, together with accounts of the day's campaign events.

A selection of the September speeches illustrates how McKinley executed these rhetorical strategies. For the most part, speeches analyzed in this chapter are those that seemed to be the best reported. The best reported speeches would be most likely to affect public opinion in the campaign. A number of other speeches also receive attention so as to portray some flavor of the campaign in general.

McKinley's campaign by this time was running with clocklike efficiency, especially in comparison to Bryan's haphazard, often ill-planned efforts.[12] This does not mean that all of the delegations' visits were arranged in advance but rather that McKinley's staff had matters so well in hand as to be able to cope smoothly even with the arrival of unannounced delegations.

The month got off to a rousing start with a visit on September 2 from the Republican Press Association of West Virginia. This was one of several groups of editors of Republican newspapers who came to Canton not to cover the election but to take part in the campaign. P. W. Morris, the president of the association, began the proceedings with a speech of several hundred words praising McKinley. He passed on some remarks about the bounties of his home state and greeted McKinley "as the coming President of the United States."[13] So much for the objective press.

McKinley opened his response with the assurance that "it affords me sincere pleasure to bid you welcome to my State, my city and my home." He then presented a brief discussion of the main campaign issues, stressing the importance of sound money and a protective tariff: "Nothing is more vital to the standing and progress of a country than the preservation of its credit and financial honor. (Applause and cries of 'that's right.') Nothing is more vital to the standing and progress of a country than that the currency of the country shall be so honest that it can cheat nobody. (Great cheering.) Nothing is of greater moment to the welfare of the country than the adoption of a policy which will give to labor and capital constant employment with fair returns. (Applause and cries of 'good.')."[14]

This was not Bryan-level eloquence, but McKinley made his point well enough by describing an identification between labor and capital. He accomplished this identification in large part just by mentioning labor and capital together in the same sentence, stating their common economic interest. The parallel sentence structure ("Nothing is more . . .") implied identifications among campaign issues that might otherwise seem utterly unrelated.

From that point, McKinley's speech to the editors stressed the vital role of the press. Not only does this illustrate how, as was his habit, McKinley acknowledged his audience's specific qualities, but it also shows how clearly he grasped the importance of the press in a political campaign: "As editors and publishers . . . you help to make public sentiment, and a right public sentiment is what is most needed at this juncture of our national affairs." Driving the point home, McKinley told the editors: "Never did the Republican cause have such mighty support from the newspapers of the United States as it has today."

McKinley then recited various statistics about his audience's home, noting how many tons of coke West Virginia had produced and so forth. These statistics gave no evidence for or against the tariff or bimetallism or any other campaign issue but did show, just as in the summer speeches, that McKinley was thoughtful enough to look up some information about his visitors' home. He concluded by claiming that with "honest dollars" and "honest work at home," there would "not be an idle man beneath our flag."[15] Thus McKinley again implied a link between sound money and the tariff. No logical proof established this link; instead, the link came from his astute phrasing. McKinley accomplished identification by association.

This first speech of the month set the tone for many to follow. The speech appeared to have been thoughtfully prepared in that

McKinley's comments were adapted to the audience, were carefully phrased, and showed at least some signs of research.

Behind the scenes the Republicans were becoming increasingly aware that they had a fight on their hands to beat Bryan. William Osborne, who ran the New York Republican campaign office, wrote to McKinley on September 7 that free silver was catching on with Ohio farmers. He recommended an increase in persuasive efforts "to talk them out of the free silver notion."[16] Several of McKinley's subsequent speeches attempted to do just that. A few days earlier, the Republican *Akron Evening Journal* refuted the common charge that the railroads were giving McKinley's supporters free rides to Canton. They claimed that the main lines were charging their usual rates to Canton, while local companies were giving discounts. They pointed out that some organizers bought blocks of tickets and sold them to McKinley's pilgrims at a loss.

Contrary to Bryan, McKinley denied in his speeches that there was such a thing as classes in the United States at all, or when not in the mood to do that, he suggested that it was immoral to play on class distinctions for political purposes.[17] A speech that he gave on Labor Day, which was held on Saturday, September 5, illustrated this approach. McKinley had begun the day by speaking to a series of groups from Pennsylvania.[18] Sitting down for lunch with his wife and mother, he received word that an unexpected delegation of over a thousand people from Pittsburgh, organized by the *Pittsburg Leader,* was on its way. The trains began to arrive in the middle of the afternoon. McKinley's efficient organization went to work. A marching group and a rather specialized campaign organization called "The ex-Pennsylvanians' Escort Club of Canton" met the trains at the station and quickly organized a parade to McKinley's home.[19] In his speech to them, McKinley took time to discuss the importance of Labor Day. He mentioned that the huge delegation represented the American laborer in general. McKinley denounced the view that there are classes in the United States.[20] A society that included both working-class and upper-class persons would, one would think, seem not to be identified. McKinley sought to bring all of the people together without distinction under the Republican cause.

Continuing, McKinley railed against cheap money, meaning silver money, and spoke for the tariff. He claimed that there was nothing wrong with the money in which workers were paid, provided that they could get good work at decent wages. In an attempt at humor, McKinley mentioned that "they [workers] are satisfied with the present dollar bill, but they are not satisfied with the present tariff bill."[21] The parallel structure in this phrase once again implied a relationship between unlike issues. Raising the campaign against Bryan to a moral level, McKinley assured the audience that preserving the value of the dollar was "indispensable to our national honor."[22] This was nothing like inspiring oratory, but it was well considered for political effect. McKinley appropriated one of Bryan's chief constituencies, the wage laborer, claiming that the people who toil would get their best advantage from a Republican administration. He said nothing that could give offense to any group of voters. Once again, he attacked the free coinage of silver and advocated the tariff as a solution to the nation's economic problems.

A few days later, a group of Ohio Republican editors came to Canton for their annual meeting. When they finished their business, they walked to Market Street to see McKinley.[23] McKinley explained to them that he welcomed the support of Democrats. This made political sense in light of the bolt of the gold Democrats from the Bryan camp.[24] It also continued the theme of unity and identification. McKinley continued that "we must not drive anybody out of camp, but welcome everybody in."[25] This stood out against a strategy of polarization or division. Even the Democratic reporter W. S. Lloyd, whose dispatches usually took an anti-McKinley slant, admitted that the Republican candidate presented this speech "in his most winning and urbane manner."[26]

Although most visitors came from Ohio and nearby parts of Pennsylvania, enough delegations arrived from more distant places to convey the perception of a national campaign. Thus the arrival of a large delegation from Vermont had special significance. Their train arrived early on the morning of September 11, the train cars festooned with pictures of McKinley and Hobart. The delegation included a number of leading Vermont Republican officials and former governors. The visitors wore identical badges that depicted the Republican candidates surrounded by little American flags. McKinley welcomed them in his characteristically warm manner: "I bid you welcome, hearty welcome, from an overflowing heart, to my State, my city, and my home." He praised the heroism of Vermont soldiers in the Revolution and the Civil War. McKinley waxed into a Bryanesque phrase about free trade: "the question of protection as against free trade is a question of humanity, the voice of labor pleading for its own."[27]

Having co-opted Bryan's premise, McKinley claimed Bryan's major constituency: McKinley made it clear that he was interested in the agricultural sector of the nation. He told his auditors that "Vermont is an agricultural State, but her keen, sagacious and honest farmers know full well the value of protection and her twin sister reciprocity." *Reciprocity* was a code word implying that the gold standard should be abandoned only by international treaty. McKinley made sound money and the tariff into "twin sisters." His approach implied that the nation held a common interest. He did not bring up a unique agricultural issue for this audience but instead suggested that they should believe—in fact, assumed they already believed—that they as agriculturalists would gain from the tariff and sound money. Following the speechmaking, an octet from the Green Mountain State added to the celebratory quality of the event by singing a song of five stanzas entitled "We Want Yer, McKinley, Yes, We Do."[28] The same day, a group of nearly a thousand pro-McKinley Democrats from Chicago visited McKinley to hear him speak, joined by a milling crowd of other visitors.[29] A Republican newspaper boasted: "Pandemonium reigns throughout the city. The visitors are regardless of the intense heat and their cheers and hurrahs are incessant."[30]

Also on September 11, Mark Hanna finally put to rest speculation that McKinley would make a campaign tour.[31] Late on September 12, an apparently unannounced group from McKeesport, Pennsylvania, arrived at McKinley's home, accompanied by a marching band. McKinley was no doubt exhausted after giving several speeches to enormous crowds that had started to arrive early in the morning.[32] He came out rather reluctantly and gave a brief speech in which he advocated putting people to work and paying them in good money, following which the candidate shook hands with the visitors.[33]

Following that brief visit, he had a longer exchange with a group of woolgrowers. Mounted greeters from the Canton Troop as well as a committee met the delegation at the train station.

A parade quickly formed and the woolgrowers marched toward Market Street to the music of two bands.[34]

The formal proceedings began with a speech of greeting by D. A. Hollingsworth, the former attorney general of Ohio. Hollingsworth took aim at Bryan's claim that only the money issue mattered, sarcastically reviewing the loss to sheep growers under free trade: "This is one of the object lessons which Mr. Bryan in his Letter of Acceptance says it is not necessary to discuss." McKinley advised the delegation that free trade had hurt them, the farmers, and that free silver would hurt them even more: "you have the same money in circulation now that you had four years ago, but you wool growers haven't got as much of it as you had then."[35] Rain forced McKinley to leave his front porch for another speech on September 12. He instead spoke at a local auditorium.[36]

On September 15, McKinley again stressed the unity of the nation as a delegation of local Civil War veterans came to see him. He noted in his speech to them that many Union and Confederate veterans had come to Canton during the campaign. McKinley claimed that since the end of the war, "Thank God, all sectional lines have been obliterated (applause) and men from all parts of our common country are to-day, though having differed in the past, marching under one banner, upon which is inscribed national honor, the maintenance of law and order and public and private honesty."[37] Thus, out of the nation's strife, McKinley's campaign had discovered an underlying identification among the voters. This differed greatly from Bryan's talk about "the enemy's country." By this time, McKinley was so busy campaigning from his home that he was unable to take a planned recreational trip to the nearby picturesque village of Zoar.[38]

Apparently September 15 had been billed as yet another opening for the local Republican campaign, continuing the seemingly endless series of pseudo-event campaign openings.[39] Due to a change in plans, the Stark County campaign actually opened on September 18. The crowds appeared once again, although the Democratic *Plain Dealer* found the event rather dull. The paper may have been right; after all, how many times can a campaign open? The newspaper did comment on the impressive use of electric lights.[40] Senator Thurston, Governor Hastings, and various other officials appeared and spoke from a reviewing stand that was now set up in front of McKinley's home. McKinley had apparently not planned to take part in the proceedings but appeared on his porch to give a quick speech.[41]

McKinley adapted to his audiences in such a way as to make them feel welcome and understood but invariably gave the campaign speeches a twist to appeal to the national audience. While constantly stressing the identification of various elements of the nation, he studiously avoided regional or insular leanings. The visit of one delegation made this exceptionally clear. On September 16, Joseph Black of Cleveland wrote to McKinley on behalf of the Republican Hungarian-American National Committee. He announced that "the Hungarians of Cleveland" planned to visit McKinley on September 19. He mentioned that McKinley "may possibly desire to refer to their native land" and gave McKinley some basic information about Hungary, including the dramatic fact that Hungarians were celebrating "the millennium of their existence as a nation." He gave the names and pronunciations of several important Hungarian figures.[42] Surely mentioning such details would have appealed to the delegation.

Nonetheless, when the Hungarian Americans arrived a few days later, their Hungarian origins were almost completely forgotten. McKinley's political instincts told him to stress his visitors' unity with their new country, not their fondness for the old. He made no use of Black's information whatsoever. As they arrived in Canton on the Cleveland, Canton and Southern Railway, each of McKinley's visitors carried a small United States flag.[43] McKinley thanked them for their visit. He mentioned that "those of you who were born in a foreign country come here because you love our free institutions." Noting the American flags in their hands, he told them that "you are carrying the right flag." Proceeding to the inevitable issues of sound money and the tariff, McKinley continued that "you want your wages good (cheers) . . . and then when you are paid you want your wages paid in dollars worth one hundred cents each and good everywhere in the world."[44]

He adapted to his audience but never to the point of singling them out; instead, he identified their common substance (in Burke's sense) as Americans.[45] The fundamental issues of the speech continued to be the tariff and sound money. McKinley appealed to the voting public as a whole, not to the particular group of immigrants who stood before him. He sounded friendly, encouraging, and supportive but stuck to his central themes.

Like the many other delegations that paraded through Canton on September 19, the Hungarian Americans of Cleveland found Market Street lined with thousands of Japanese lanterns and were entertained by displays of fireworks.[46] They became just one of the immense delegations to whom McKinley spoke that day, one after the other, as "Major McKinley gave a continuous performance."[47]

Many delegations came with excellent notice and preparation. When a group of the Pittsburgh Commercial Travelers came to Canton, the newspaper announced their arrival a few days ahead of time, together with plans that the Canton traveling salesmen would meet them and that "the ladies will have carriages."[48] A group came from Somerset County in Pennsylvania the same day; McKinley was able to tell them that they had traveled 250 miles to see him (as if they had no other way to know) and that he had visited their community in the past. These were typical of the homely details that encouraged the delegations to feel that the candidate took a personal interest in them and that helped to establish a sense of identification. McKinley's speech to them discussed the tariff, sound money, and Civil War pensions.[49]

A group of railroad workers heard McKinley present one of the more thoughtful speeches of the month. His comments to this group are especially interesting because of Bryan's divisive attempt to court the railway workers' vote by, for example, criticizing the "blankety-blank-blank-blank" railroads.[50] The delegation of about five thousand people filled several trains.[51] McKinley's speech to this group of railroaders simply took the same path that he had trodden with editors, veterans, cyclists, and woolgrowers. He did, however, adapt his arguments to them with exceptional clarity.

McKinley stated his assumption that the visitors supported "protection, reciprocity and sound money." He recited a list of seemingly pointless statistics about the railroad industry, mentioning that railroads "employ one million of men," that thirty thousand locomotives rode the nation's rails, and so forth. He complimented the audience, mentioning that "the railroad men are cool and collected, brave and vigilant in the discharge of their duties." He then explained how the Republican platform would benefit them: "A 50-cent dollar, employes [*sic*] of the railroad companies, will no more add to your earnings than the railroads would add to their traffic by diminishing the size of their cars." This clever analogy illustrated the harms of free silver in terms that the audience might find familiar. He mentioned that the railroad employees "are interested, too, in good money (cheers) and they are in favor of law and order." Not actually repeating the common charge that Bryan was an anarchist, McKinley blithely assumed that no one who supported law and order would vote for anyone but McKinley. Without missing a beat, he turned during the same speech to a nearby delegation of telegraph workers, praised them for the importance of their work, told them that the telegraph companies operate "800,000 miles of wire," and expressed gratitude that they were "enlisted in the great cause as against public repudiation [*sic*]."[52]

Thus, McKinley's criticism of Bryan and the Democratic platform was all carefully implicit. McKinley never mentioned Bryan by name, nor the Democratic Party, nor the Populist or National Silver parties. He never gave an explicit argument as to why free silver meant "repudiation," nor for why supporting Bryan implied disrespect for law and order. The reasons for these controversial claims were left unspoken. They were linked only by being juxtaposed in McKinley's speech. Such pithy matters could be left to the newspapers or to other Republican officials.

Furthermore, although the young and controversial Bryan constantly had to establish his credentials as a knowledgeable and responsible candidate, McKinley, the candidate of respectability incarnate, apparently felt no such need. His approach in this and in many of the other Front Porch speeches was to explain why the Republican position was important for the ordinary Americans who visited him. The real point, however, is that instead of seeking votes by trading on workers' alienation from their employers, McKinley depicted the interests of the workers and the companies as equivalent, thus identifying the workers' needs with those of their employers.

Along these same lines, a group of steelworkers from the Edgar Thomas Steel Works in Pennsylvania heard McKinley present another attack on free silver and free trade. McKinley again used his visitors to symbolize the wage laborers throughout the nation. He cited figures that the average monthly wage in certain factories had dropped from $34.50 to $31.00 during the Cleveland administration. He attributed this to free trade: "Nor do I think that it is economy to buy goods cheaply abroad if thereby it enforces idleness at home." This continued his strategy of identification. McKinley did not tell his audience that he would support their unique interests. Instead, he told them that they shared a common interest with all working people and that his policies would benefit all working people.

McKinley quoted silver advocate James G. Blaine to support a point. He then represented free silver and free trade to be a combined attack against the wage laborer: "But, my countrymen, as if the business conditions were not bad enough and hard enough to bear, we have thrust upon us . . . a proposition to debase the currency of the country and undermine the public credit. . . . We do not propose now to inaugurate a currency system that will cheat labor in its pay."[53]

Contrary to Bryan's portrayal of him, McKinley's argument in this speech was not that the rich would benefit from his platform or that riches would trickle down on the worker from above. His contention was that the Democratic platform was a conspiracy to drive wage laborers deeper into poverty. McKinley ended this speech with a startlingly blunt attack against the Democrats, although still not mentioning either them or their candidate by name: "It is gratifying to me to be assured . . . that the voice of labor here to-day declares that no party which degrades the honor of the nation, no party which stands opposed to law and order, or which seeks to array the masses against the classes, shall receive its vote and support."[54] Thus he criticized the Democrats for their anti-unity approach. McKinley must, however, have slipped when he discussed the "masses against the classes," for a few days later he remembered in another speech that "we . . . spurn the suggestion that there are classes in the United States."[55]

A large delegation from Jamestown, New York, arrived in Canton during the last week of September.[56] The group included two marching bands. One of the delegates, A. C. Wade, presented a long speech greeting McKinley; in the course of it he boasted of the prosperity of Jamestown and complained of the Democrats' plans "to surrender our National honor."[57]

McKinley began his speech by thanking the group for coming to see him "on such an inclement day." He advised them how many acres of farmland New York plowed, mentioning that the state's agriculture annually produced $178,000,000 worth of crops.[58] Once again, these figures demonstrated McKinley's interest in and concern for his audience, even though they established nothing of importance about free silver or the tariff.

Central among McKinley's aims that day was to criticize Bryan for regionalism. Regionalism would conflict with the identification of citizens all over the nation. Never mentioning his opponent by name, McKinley stated: "The attempt to inflame the passions of the west and south against the east is, therefore, but a mischievous and unpatriotic effort to arouse prejudice and hatred against men of their own calling." McKinley then averred that "I have no sympathy, my fellow citizens, with a cause based upon mere hate and passion." McKinley added that he was grateful that regional animosity "receives no encouragement from the sturdy citizens of New York."[59] Once again, he assumed that his audience had indicated their agreement with him simply by their presence. He obviously also treated this delegation as representative of the entire state.

McKinley took time in this speech to describe free silver as "discreditable and dangerous" and "perilous." He glibly identified the issues of the tariff and free silver: "Free silver means free trade. . . . My fellow citizens, do not be deluded." The word free established an identification between these two outwardly unrelated economic issues. McKinley did, however, cite statements from Alexander Hamilton (a New Yorker, like his audience), President Cleveland, and the Sherman law of 1890 to give his claims more authority. Continuing, McKinley turned Bryan's neo-Populist approach on its head: "The capitalist can wait on his dividends, but the working man cannot wait on his dinner." After McKinley's speech, the crowd contributed to the overall enthusiasm by giving the "Chautauqua salute and the Cattaraugus cheer."[60]

The same themes continued in McKinley's speeches for the rest of September. Speaking to a group of tin workers, he accused the Democrats of "dishonor." He stated that "in this contest all the banner we want is the American flag." Bryan had not actually ever spoken of any other banner; nonetheless, McKinley's point was that all true Americans were united under the flag. Celebrating their vocation, the workers applauded by beating on their tin cups.[61]

September 24 found McKinley speaking to a group of oil workers from Pennsylvania, who erected a twelve-foot-high flower display for the candidate.[62] On Friday, September 25, McKinley spoke to one delegation before breakfast and two more before noon.[63] He told a group from an Ohio farming community that "I am glad to be advised that in this audience there are many men who have heretofore been associated with another and different party than that to which we are devoted. I am especially glad to welcome them here to-day." He assured them that "I know all about your county."[64]

Saturday, September 26, was one of the busiest days of the campaign to date, as McKinley delivered eleven speeches to numerous delegations (he gave some speeches to two delegations at a time). A total estimated at more than twenty thousand people heard McKinley speak that day.[65] By this time, McKinley's staff was becoming concerned about the condition of the front porch. Crowds had piled onto the porch to the point that repairs had been necessary and there was some danger of a collapse. McKinley did not wish to leave the porch for his speeches and wanted to give a warm welcome to everyone who came, but he had found it necessary to set up railings to protect himself and his house from the press of the throngs. The railings, unfortunately, were of little use, as the delegations simply tore them away to get closer to their candidate.[66]

The first group to reach Market Street was the Traveling Men's Republican Club of Peoria, Illinois, a group of traveling salespeople. Carrying patriotic red, white, and blue plumes, the group paraded accompanied by the Canton Troop and the Grand Army Band. The short procession reached McKinley's home by 9:20 A.M.

Stressing the identification of labor and capital with great fervor, McKinley spoke to this group against the class system. After praising the great leaders of Illinois history, McKinley railed with uncharacteristic invective against the unnamed forces "who mislead and delude" the people. He criticized those who say that to get ahead, poor people must "form a class of your own." He said that the employee must ask, "Will I be benefited by despoiling my employer? Will it give me more employment and better wages to strike down those whose money is invested in productive enterprises, which give me work and wages?" McKinley recalled that "Four years ago it was said that the manufacturer was making too much money . . . but that cannot be said now." McKinley sarcastically inveighed against those who had repealed "the robber tariff." He concluded that, sadly, "you can not injure the manufacturer without injuring the laborer." McKinley further stated: "I pray God that the burdens of class may never be imposed upon American manhood (applause) and American womanhood. (Renewed applause.)" Thus McKinley identified a common interest between labor and capital. He then offered to meet each member of the group personally.[67]

Another group to which McKinley spoke on that day was a women's suffrage group from Cleveland. The group arrived on a train bedecked "with flags and bunting." The women marched to McKinley's home in a light rain with a trumpet and drum corps and a men's drill corps.[68] McKinley told them that they were "the fifteenth delegation that I have received at my home today." He mentioned the presence in Canton of delegations "of all races and nationalities." That point brought home to the audience, and to the newspaper readers, that McKinley was continuing his attack against Bryan's appeals to class divisions. McKinley assured the suffrage group that "no audience" could offer a better objection to "the false and un-American doctrine of classes against the masses." He said he could have "no sympathy with those who would seek to create inequalities, promote antagonism . . . in conflict with the spirit of our institutions."[69]

The ever-loyal Mrs. Avery returned to Canton on September 26, together with the Elroy M. Avery Drill Corps, to celebrate again her support for McKinley. The usually hostile *Cleveland Plain Dealer* expressed admiration for the quality of the appearance and performance of Mrs. Avery's group. The *Plain Dealer* did complain that many of the delegates had been docked for the fare and shipped to Canton by their employers.[70]

Anxious to offend no one, McKinley discussed the importance of suffrage and of the ballot but did not actually endorse suffrage for women. The speech went easy on the tariff and free silver issues, concentrating instead on the value of good citizenship.

Also on September 26, McKinley warned a group from Duquesne, Pennsylvania, of the "those twin delusions and evils—free trade and free silver."[71] This by now well-tried type of phrasing reinforced the identification between the tariff and sound money. The same day, a group of businesspeople heard McKinley state that "there was never such a cause to fight for since the days of the war."[72]

By the last week of September, the strain of receiving such enormous delegations in Canton had surely become a trial for the McKinleys (not to mention for the small city), and Ida McKinley's physician wrote to the candidate to warn of the strain that the visitors were putting on her.[73] McKinley nonetheless campaigned with increasing vigor, although the papers mentioned the role of his chronically ill wife in the campaign less frequently.

McKinley's September speeches thus expounded several common themes. The great majority of them attacked free silver and free trade, usually (although not always) ignoring other issues such as the income tax. Almost all the speeches expressed a point that was uniquely adapted to the immediate crowd: statistics about the group's industry or home state or a brief, bland discussion of a social issue that the group represented. Almost all of those points, however, were somehow slipped over to the money and tariff issues. If the audience wanted work, support the tariff. If the audience had work, let them be paid in money measured by a high standard. If they desired social reform, let them be aware that free silver would rob them of the fruits of their reform. McKinley changed his emphasis with each speech, according to the nature of the delegation, but did not in any way change his issues to promise something to the particular group. Rather, he claimed to each group that sound money and the protective tariff would benefit them. The matter of unity came to the forefront. Since all of the people of the nation shared a common interest, a common substance, the same issues would appear to benefit any one of McKinley's audiences. In turn, the simple fact that McKinley stayed at home during the campaign contributed to the impression that the countless thousands of people who came to see him represented a united nation spontaneously rallying around him.

McKinley added little new to the issues during September or indeed during the balance of the campaign. What he did was to keep those issues in the news by repeatedly speaking to various crowds, doing so in a way that appeared to demonstrate growing enthusiasm for his candidacy among the voting public. The highly partisan Republican press reported McKinley's speeches thoroughly, and even Democratic, pro-silver papers published accounts of his speeches that were often fairly complete, to the extent of including full or partial texts.[74]

McKinley's campaign created a mass of interwoven identifications. He expressed that he and his audiences were identified, that the tariff and sound money were identified, that business and labor shared a common interest, that the tariff and sound money were identified with the American flag, that his audiences were identified with the American flag, that everybody who came to Canton was welcome to his home, that everybody in the nation was welcome under the Republican cause.

Identification can be a conscious stratagem of the speaker, or instead the audience create identification themselves.[75] Although it would be hard to deny that McKinley followed a deliberate speaking strategy, it would be equally hard to deny that the audiences became part of the identification. McKinley did not create that part of the process, but he did guide it. Their seemingly spontaneous (but often carefully organized) pilgrimages and demonstrations added to the impression that the nation shared a common substance with McKinley and his party. McKinley combined the concept of identification as perceived similarity, for his rhetoric conveyed the impression that all Americans share common interests, and the concept of identification as association, for the constant references to the flag showed the entire nation united under a common symbol. Thus McKinley identified a number of issues, symbols, and moral stances with one another and identified himself and his audience as advocates of those issues that were good. This contrasted with Bryan's characterizing the East as "the enemy's country."

Bryan's political analysis may have been correct; most of his votes in the November election were to come from the West, the South, and the very poor.[76] McKinley's rhetorical strategy, however, proved to be more successful. An astute politician, McKinley surely knew that he would not carry such states as South Carolina, Georgia, and Kansas.[77] Nonetheless, he took care to exclude no one. He advocated the interests of the worker and the manufacturer, the farmer, the salesperson, the veteran. He assured all groups that they would benefit from the common prosperity that the protective tariff would provide. He advised them that they wanted to receive the fruits of that prosperity in sound money.

The very nature of the Front Porch campaign encouraged this identification. Supporters of his opponent were not likely to spend money and time to come to Canton. Unlike Bryan, who often spoke to hostile crowds during his railroad speaking tours, McKinley faced audiences who were already committed to him.[78] McKinley could thus repeatedly allude to the audience's opinions as being the same as his own, simply because for the most part they were the same as his own, and he could create an impression of identification between himself and the visiting delegations. Therefore, McKinley's principal tactic for establishing identification among disparate issues was to phrase them as if they were linked and not to make many logical appeals to establish the unity. He identified himself with the delegations by speaking to them in a warm manner, welcoming them to his home, and assuming simply by their presence that they shared his views and values.

The point that became clear during the September campaigning is that McKinley, at least for the public record, did not intend to concede any of Bryan's target audience. He courted the urban and eastern populations; he courted wage laborers; he even courted the farmers when he got the chance, and he made a point of welcoming every visitor to his home and recognized every constituency under the American flag.

Although McKinley was not divisive, he did distinguish himself from his opponent. This was no inconsistency when he distinguished his supporters from those who supported free trade and free silver, for, as Burke points out, "identification implies division."[79] For people to identify with other people means to create factions.[80] McKinley delicately portrayed his opponent to be identified with those issues that were bad. Still, McKinley welcomed everyone to come into the fold that he defined. Thus his rhetoric soft-pedaled factionalism.

McKinley's criticism of Bryan was always implicit; he never mentioned his opponent's name, nor the names of the Democratic, Populist, or National Silver parties that had nominated Bryan. He never engaged in personal invective against any group. He stressed his own ground, never allowing Bryan's articulate pro-silver rhetoric to divert the public's attention from the protective tariff. Instead, by clever phrasing, he united the tariff and sound money as if they were different sides of the same issue.

In one form of identification, the speaker makes a deliberate effort to express ideas that are associated with the audience's views.[81] McKinley, in a sense, identified with his audience in the obverse manner. Instead of aligning his views with those of his audience—something that he consistently resisted doing—McKinley steadfastly assumed that his audience's views were aligned with his, as if it would be unthinkable for his hordes of visitors to believe otherwise than he did.

Furthermore, McKinley's September speeches, like all of his campaign speeches, took a harmonizing, unifying stand. He stressed his identification with the ordinary people who made up most of the delegations. He focused on his understanding of their needs and interests. While Bryan attempted to win the election by splitting the nation into factions, McKinley tried to maintain a unity, a sense of national identification, among the entire nation. The only real villains in McKinley's speeches were the foreign industries trying to rob Americans of business and employment, against whom the tariff would offer a defense, and the unnamed forces of free silver who wanted to pay the American worker in devalued currency. McKinley often managed to provide for each audience a few facts about their home town, state, or industry, thus conveying the impression that he knew and cared enough about each of them to look up a few pieces of information about them. Oddly enough, considering Bryan's reputation as the "Great Commoner," McKinley in many ways did a better job of appearing to be a candidate of the people. He did so in large part by conveying a simple, down-home impression, by speaking in a way that ordinary people could understand, and by repeatedly stressing both in words and by actions that he supported and welcomed the people of the entire nation. The highly artificial atmosphere of the Front Porch campaign became a tool for creating identifications.

McKinley did not directly refute Bryan's charge that the Republican platform favored the rich; instead, he spoke in a way that robbed Bryan's charge of its effect.

CHAPTER 7

McKinley's Speech
to the Homestead Workers

THE MORNING SUN pelted down on Canton, Ohio on September 12, 1896. The late summer heat wave refused to let up.[1] In one of McKinley's speeches that day, presented to a group from Homestead, Pennsylvania, what McKinley did not say is more interesting than what he did say. While Bryan was just that day leaving Nebraska to start another of his whirlwind railroad tours, speaking at every whistle stop along the way, his Republican opponent continued to spend the campaign at home in Canton with his wife and mother.[2]

One of several speeches that McKinley gave that day was to a group of steelworkers from Homestead, Pennsylvania. The little suburb of Homestead nestled near Pittsburgh among the crowded mountains of western Pennsylvania. The huge Carnegie steel plant dominated the community. Only four years earlier, in the summer of 1892, a lockout at the factory led to a pitched gun battle. Thousands of workers, many of them Hungarian immigrants, had yearned for a better life. The union members confronted a group of about three hundred armed Pinkerton agents who arrived by river barge. Shots were fired and people on both sides lost their lives. The Pinkerton agents, who apparently had climbed on the barge with no idea where they were going or what their mission was to be, eventually surrendered. The angry crowd then beat some of the agents to death. The state militia came in and restored order. The upshot of the labor action was that the union collapsed and Andrew Carnegie regained control of the factory on his own terms.[3]

The name Homestead became a national symbol for the labor movement. Yet in 1896 the Homestead workers cheered as McKinley promised better times for business, blithely ignoring any question of labor strife. Management had won the conflict, but the resulting acrimony lingered for years. Nonetheless, this was not in any way a labor speech—and therein lies its interest.

The Homesteaders' trip to Canton, like many of the events of the Front Porch campaign, was carefully planned and organized. What is most noteworthy about McKinley's speech to this group is that despite some resentful comments in the Democratic press, the event was much like many of the others of McKinley's campaign. McKinley was silent about his audience's presumably most important characteristic. This silence signifies his attitude toward his audience, his purpose as a campaign speaker, and his rhetorical approach to the campaign. The silence was figurative, not literal, since McKinley had a great deal to say about and to the Homestead group.

McKinley's failure to mention the Homestead lockout cannot have been an accident. It drives home two key features of this speech: (1) McKinley was interested in unity, not division, and (2) he saw past the immediate crowd, who for him became symbols of American laborers in general, to the national audience. His campaign speeches were something like "the local address," in which presidents speak as if they are the audience's friends. Such a speech creates an unusual problem for a president: the speaker needs to be the leader of all Americans equally yet also needs to acknowledge the local characteristics of a particular group.[4] Few presidents or presidential candidates worked through this dilemma more skillfully than McKinley.

This speech deserves careful study to appreciate in depth how a typical Front Porch speech was conceived and organized. McKinley's supporters organized the campaign events to help the candidate put his message across. The Homestead speech was, for the most part, indistinguishable from the hundreds of speeches that McKinley presented during the 1896 campaign. It is not being examined here because it was different from the others, but because it was *similar* to them. While Bryan's campaign was marked by a handful of dramatic orations interspersed with hundreds of whistle-stop speeches, McKinley's campaign consisted of a large number of speeches that differed just enough from one another to acknowledge his unique audiences and to attract continuing interest in the press. The Homestead speech itself was not remarkable or especially significant; the significance lay in the hundreds of similar speeches that McKinley gave, taken as a totality.

A more subtle reason to study this speech is to explore how McKinley subsumed the Homesteaders' unique, powerful, and poignant interests under the larger national issues of his campaign. In effect he ignored the obvious. The very organization of the event contributed to this strange sort of reticence. No argument can be made that this maneuver was in any way different in this speech than in hundreds of others. More exactly, the candidate's single-minded focus on his key issues and goals was so strong that he declined to vary from them even in the extreme case of Homestead.

Again, McKinley was not silent about Homestead in any literal sense. The September 12 event in Canton was full of noise, and McKinley had plenty to say to the group, and his speech to them was specifically, even charmingly, adapted to them. Nor was McKinley under any kind of external constraint: neither any powerful forces nor any quietly oppressive influence prevented him from talking about Homestead's defining moment. McKinley instead made what was presumably a deliberate choice to ignore what seemingly could never be ignored, as part of a deceptively simple but in fact quite sophisticated rhetorical strategy. He was silent on an issue on which people might have expected him to speak. The workers followed suit. It is curious that in all their marching and cheering, as far as the records show, there was no mention of Homestead's famous trauma.

On Friday, September 11, McKinley spoke to a series of groups totaling approximately three thousand visitors, including three governors, who stood in the hot sun to hear him. Some had come on the train from as far as Vermont.[5] Saturday, the day of the Homestead speech, was even busier. Earlier on September 12, McKinley had already spoken to a carefully orchestrated delegation of Chicago men.[6] He would expound in speech after speech to thousands of visitors who sweltered in the heat on that stormy Saturday.

The existing literature on the rhetoric of silence argues for two distinct conceptions of silence. In this chapter I discuss how silence can be a strategy, a sort of nonverbal line of argument; another equally interesting but distinct interpretation views silence as the consequence of disempowerment.

The rhetoric of silence has intrigued a number of theorists. One approach finds a relationship between silence and the rhetorical situation. Silence means that something is missing, which in turn implies the existence of potential. One noted scholar points out that "since silence is a sort of absence of something, it suggests a potential, and in potentials lie urgencies."[7] Silence, another theorist suggests, is a rhetorical strategy on occasions "when talk is expected." Thus the failure of a public figure to speak about an issue can be important.[8] It has been suggested that in a ceremonial speech, the speaker may refrain from discussing issues on which the audience and speaker have reached some prior understanding. The prior understanding eliminates the need for discussion.[9] Martin Medhurst highlights the potential dangers of silence as he shows how Harry Truman's longstanding silence about the menace of the Soviet Union's aggressive policies allowed the issues to pass to hands other than the president's. When he finally spoke out, Truman had to react to events rather than to control them.[10] In an interesting twist on the rhetoric of silence, the very starkness of the Vietnam Veterans Memorial in Washington, D.C., appears as a sort of rhetorical quality, leaving the viewer free to define the monument's meaning.[11]

This last point reveals an important idea. Of the many important lessons from this literature on silence, the most noteworthy is that silence is ambiguous. Silence may mean this, or it may mean that. It may serve as a rhetorical strategy; it may represent the suppression of a rhetorical strategy. It can be effective; it can be ineffective. Always, however, the absence of rhetoric that a member of the audience expects carries a meaning for that audience member. That meaning requires interpretation, no matter how uncertain the interpretation may become. In this sense, any rhetoric has the potential for ambiguous silence. Suppose, for example, that Ronald Reagan had spoken at the Normandy beach in 1984 without mentioning the 1944 invasion.[12] One might well take notice.

Edwin Black notes that "there are also times when silence is contemptuous, when words must be spoken."[13] That is, one can be silent because one's interlocutor is deemed unworthy of speech. This second, highly political interpretation of silence is not directly relevant to this study. Already a powerful person by 1896, McKinley was surely in a position to say what he pleased. A careful study of his speeches, including the speech to Homestead, shows no sign that McKinley held his audiences in contempt; indeed, it suggests much the opposite.

Jean-Paul Sartre has written insightfully about nothingness from an existentialist perspective. Silence is a kind of nothingness. Silence is the absence of speech. Silence consists of saying nothing. Those who study communication should feel comfortable with Jean-Paul Sartre's central distinction between the aware subject and the being outside of the mind. In *Being and Nothingness*, Sartre distinguishes between the being-in-itself and the being-for-itself. The being-for-itself is the conscious being; its activities and awareness are in and for itself. Any description of the in-itself is an interpretation by a conscious mind.[14]

Negations include such qualities as "absence, distance, regret."[15] Negation, to Sartre, is entirely a function of the for-itself. Negation creates nothingness. There is, to make a pun of it, no such thing as nothing in the world outside the mind. Nothingness means that the knowing mind, the for-itself, is aware of the failure to perceive what it expects to perceive.[16] In Sartre's example one goes to a café, looking for Pierre. The café is full of people and activity; there is no emptiness in it, but Pierre is nowhere to be seen. One perceives that Pierre is not in the café, even though the café is not empty, because one does not perceive what one is looking for.[17] "This does not mean," writes Sartre, "that I discover his absence in some precise spot in the establishment. In fact Pierre is absent from the *whole café*."[18] Thus, "nothing" does not mean the same as "not anything."[19]

An existentialist teenager, looking for cheese, could stare at a refrigerator full of milk, meat, fruit, and vegetables, and comment that there is "nothing" in the refrigerator. McKinley said nothing about a matter that one might anticipate he would discuss. Perhaps most conspicuous is the absence of the rhetoric that McKinley's *opponents* might have expected, for his supporters seemed to be troubled not at all. It is difficult to imagine Bryan, who enjoyed strong labor union support, visiting Homestead and ignoring the lockout. Given his purposes, McKinley's silence about the lockout does not surprise, but it gets one's attention.

A second, quite distinct perspective on the rhetoric of silence considers the use of power to silence individuals who are thus deprived of their voice. Silence then speaks out in a sort of cultural-historical context, the silenced group's dilemma becoming known not because of their speech but because of the absence of speech. Silence may result from social oppression or from cultural taboos.[20] A society in which some people are privileged will create silence.[21] This second interpretation of silence does not explain McKinley's reticence in the Homestead speech, although it does eventually tie in, albeit in a paradoxical way.

McKinley's task was to unify the interests of business with those of the ordinary industrial workers who made up a large part of the voting population. Perhaps the Homestead group did not seem amenable to being part of such a unity, but that is how matters developed. Perhaps remembering once again Osborne's counsel that "our whole attention must be paid to the masses—to the laboring classes," McKinley continued to depict free silver as a dangerous experiment with the nation's currency.[22] He also continued to stand for the protective tariff. With these positions, the same positions that he took with hundreds of other delegations during the campaign, McKinley undertook to persuade workers of Homestead. To obtain unity, McKinley sought to negate that which would produce division. He did so not by refuting it but by saying nothing about it.

Chaim Perelman and Lucie Olbrechts-Tyteca define the audience as "the ensemble of those whom the speaker wishes to influence."[23] This definition suggests that the audience *exists only as a conception of the speaker* and is not necessarily the same as the group of people who actually hear the speech in person. Thus, the real audience, to Perelman and Olbrechts-Tyteca's way of thinking, would be the audience that McKinley conceived.

The absence of any mention of Homestead's labor strife from McKinley's speech means as much as what he did mention, for McKinley could not win the national audience by appealing to the local concerns of one small community. He could not afford to court organized labor at the expense of management. Nonetheless, in sharp irony, McKinley made the Homestead workers into symbols of the American factory worker. The ghosts of Homestead slept quietly in their graves on September 12.

The preparations that McKinley's audience made were as important, and as nearly as newsworthy, as the speech itself. The group was not taking a sedate little trip to hear a political speaker. The Homestead workers came for a well-planned celebration.

The night before the Homestead speech, the *Pittsburg Press* reported that dozens of railroad cars waited on the siding next to Carnegie's Homestead steel plant. Decorators festooned the waiting trains with banners. When morning came, the cheers of a large crowd and a speech from a local dignitary sent the steel workers on their way.[24] They steamed away on thirty railroad cars divided into three trains at 9:00 A.M. on Saturday, September 12.[25]

The workers arrived in Canton a few hours later. The event started long before McKinley's speech, as the group's organizers presumably set up a carefully planned frenzy to obtain press coverage. The journey of the large delegation from Homestead attracted detailed coverage in the Pittsburgh area. Readers who did not make the trip could still experience the excitement, however vicariously, by reading about it in the newspaper.

McKinley's customarily efficient local officials met the group of two thousand or more workers as they arrived.[26] Each Homestead worker wore a McKinley button on his lapel.[27] McKinley's agents quickly organized a parade. A group of equestrians led the way. The Homestead Band and others played for the marchers while the Homestead police escorted their townspeople to McKinley's house on Market Street. The workers paraded in step more than half a mile to the modest two-story house. The first of the marchers almost reached McKinley's home before the last of them set out from the train platform. Local townspeople who came to hear their famous neighbor speak joined the Homesteaders.[28] The parade was arranged in order by factory departments. The accounting department came first after the musical groups, followed by the technical department, the mechanical department, another band, and so forth.[29]

A crowd of local residents pursued the marching bands down the street. They stopped to sing on McKinley's street and in front of the office of the *Canton Repository.* Numerous impromptu concerts played throughout Canton.[30] After the day's throngs roamed and sang all over town, a Republican newspaper in nearby Akron boasted that "pandemonium reigns throughout the business section of the city" and that Canton's activities were "given over entirely to the demonstration."[31]

Thus, the speech itself made up only a part of the afternoon's events. Like the preparations a day earlier, the parade, the songs, and the demonstration were also newsworthy and were reported in, for example, Akron, New York, and Pittsburgh.[32] Furthermore, these reports conveyed something that the published text of the speech itself could not, which was a feeling of excitement about McKinley's candidacy, some of the same sense of excitement that in a later era would be communicated by television. In this setting, the tragic events of 1892 were unlikely to surface.

After the steelworkers reached McKinley's home, they had to wait for him to come out of his house. The crowd occupied their time listening to the Homestead Glee Club sing Republican campaign songs. McKinley eventually stepped out onto his front porch. The chief marshal of the Homestead delegation was one Mr. Schwab, but J. M. Molanthy, described by the Republican press as "a workman in the mill" and by the Democratic press as "a rather dangerous commodity," was the group's chief speaker.[33]

The speeches of greeting, which were presented throughout the campaign, had by this point become a noteworthy ritual. Molanthy could give a speech that had a sharper bite than one given by the always tactful McKinley.[34] The national press could then report Molanthy's politically inspired praise as news.

Joining McKinley on the porch, Molanthy boasted that the Homestead steel plant "employs over 5,000 men and turns out from 75,000 to 190,000 tons of finished material per month." He asserted that they could double their production if the McKinley tariff were reinstituted. Molanthy offered a snide remark about Coxey's Army, the group of unemployed Populists who had demonstrated in Washington, D.C., a few years earlier. Finally, Molanthy invoked the names of "Washington, Lincoln and Garfield" and assured McKinley that his wise economic policies would bring blessings from "the women and children who are now living on black coffee and bread."[35] A reporter for a Democratic newspaper felt that McKinley looked alarmed during Molanthy's speech.[36]

Following Molanthy's speech of greeting, McKinley climbed on a chair to speak.[37] Given the considerable funds that the Republicans had raised, McKinley's aides could surely have erected a more dignified rostrum. A store crate in the summer might have been marginally understandable; the use of a chair in the middle of September cannot have been an accident. The chair was a stroke of political image making. It certainly sounded folksy in the press. McKinley began his speech by forging a link between himself and his visitors: "I am glad to have at my home and to give welcome to the workingmen of Homestead." Punning on the name of the city, he mentioned that "The Republican party has always believed in 'homesteads.'" He continued that the Republican President Lincoln had signed the Homestead Act, "and from that hour until the present the Republican party has been engaged in advocating a policy that would give a Homestead to every man who works." He complimented Molanthy for his eloquence.[38]

These introductory comments gave a personal touch to the speech. McKinley established that he was thinking of the Homesteaders; he tried to create a feeling that he was addressing their speech particularly to them. None of this, however, addressed any issue of the campaign. Nor did it say anything of substance about the community. McKinley's introduction was a homey greeting, an expression of concern and affection for the group who stood before him. It was an introduction that could offend no one and that established the candidate's human warmth and kindness. Thus McKinley was not silent about Homestead itself. Nor, as the speech continued, did he ignore the labor issues *per se*.

Hoping to counter Bryan in the industrial Northeast, McKinley faced Bryan's free silver issue head-on. Warning that free silver was a "hazardous experiment," McKinley managed to mention the flag by the second paragraph. Bryan had charged in his "Cross of Gold" speech that the gold standard injured the business interests of the ordinary worker.[39] McKinley responded with a sober, fact-filled evaluation of the economic issues. As he did so, he presented a speech that could read as well in a New York newspaper as it would in Canton or Pittsburgh.

McKinley reviewed the state of the economy. He stated that a product would bring a better price if demand for it were high. He related this principle to the workers: "The more people who want your labor, the better wages you will receive (Applause)."[40] Turning the tables on Bryan's advocacy of coining silver at sixteen to one with gold, McKinley commented that: "If there is one day's labor for sixteen workingmen, you would not get as good wages as though there were sixteen days' work for one working man. (Laughter and continued applause)."[41]

It is at this point that the struggle of organized labor would seem most directly relevant to McKinley's discussion. The violent confrontation at Homestead had pitted organized labor against management. McKinley was not literally silent. He was willing to speak to the Homesteaders, and in a sympathetic tone at that. Thus he reaffirmed a relationship, contending that his presidency would bring prosperity to labor and management alike. He did not deny a political relationship; rather, he redefined it by ignoring the Homestead lockout.

Bryan had asserted that behind the silverites were "the commercial interests and the laboring interests and all the toiling masses."[42] McKinley did not pit the interests of Bryan's agrarian and wage-earning supporters against the thriving classes.[43] Almost mocking Bryan, McKinley told the Homesteaders that the workers paid in good money "are the toiling masses who were the most prosperous in 1892 of any working people in the world, and more prosperous than they had ever been before."[44] This was entirely appropriate for the Homestead steelworkers but equally important for persuading working people all over the country. Bryan courted the agricultural communities, the working people of the East, and the general population of the growing West. McKinley courted everybody, including Bryan's toiling masses.[45]

The needs of the worker, the threat posed by competition from Europe, and the hazards of free silver came together in McKinley's view of America's needs. "In the United States," McKinley said, "everything has been cheapened but man." In the free silver nations of Latin America, however, "man alone has been cheapened." In the United States, "with the gold basis and the protective tariff," American workers had enjoyed more employment and financial stability; "they never before were paid in better money," and their money bought more of the goods they desired.[46] By this point in the speech, the workers from Homestead had become representatives of working people everywhere. As a conception in McKinley's mind, the audience had metamorphosed from a few thousand Pennsylvania steelworkers into workers and toilers all over the land. McKinley was not silent about American workers, who were indeed the main subject of his speech, but he was silent about the Homestead crisis and its implications for his specific audience.

McKinley did offer some brief argumentation about the gold standard. "With a given number of consumers and an increased production," he said, "with more competitors and no more consumers, the cheaper will be the products." He continued with various statistics, for example that "in 1889 the number of employes [sic] in the manufacturing establishments of the United States, man and youth, was 2,732,000," and so forth, which he used to establish that "the gold basis has not injured labor."[47]

John G. Carlisle, President Cleveland's secretary of the treasury, had recently spoken in Chicago against free silver. McKinley pounced on this division in the Democratic ranks. He quoted at length from Carlisle's speech, praised the secretary's distinguished career, and commented that Carlisle's speech contained "words of truth and soberness and I commend them to the workingmen of Homestead."[48] McKinley thus drove a wedge between the Democrats, pointed out the error of free silver, and managed to mention the Homestead group in the process. He mentioned Homestead, however, in a way that was once again symbolic: McKinley also seemed to commend Carlisle's words to everyone. He gave no reason that the Homestead workers in particular, as opposed to workers in general, should think about Carlisle's comments.

Although more than half of the Homestead speech discussed the gold standard, McKinley returned to his bread-and-butter issue, the protective tariff. Bryan repeatedly focused attention on the money question.[49] McKinley would not allow Bryan's issue to be the only one in the voters' minds. McKinley pronounced, "Gentlemen, I have always been, as you know, in favor of a protective tariff. (Loud and continuous applause.)" McKinley continued that the same "great principle" led him to "protect the laboring man of the United States against a degraded currency."[50]

How could McKinley impose unity on a campaign that traded on two unrelated issues? His answer was simple. Not only did the "great principle" of protecting the American worker unite these issues, but a series of cleverly phrased parallel sentences also connected them: "I am opposed to free trade because it degrades American labor. I am opposed to free silver because it degrades American money."[51]

Finally, with his customary politeness, McKinley thanked his visitors as if they were his personal houseguests. As he did so, he called them "the men who toil." He assured them that their support was "a source of strength and comfort" to him. McKinley promised them that "if possible," he wished to shake their hands and greet each of them personally.[52]

McKinley had uttered not one word about labor strife. Had his goal had been to woo the Homestead workers, and them alone, the lockout would surely have come to the fore in his speech. No one could have forgotten the tragic events that have ever since defined the small Pennsylvania community. The Democratic press had certainly not forgotten.[53] The Homesteaders would surely be happy to know that their plight was not forgotten. McKinley's goal, however, was to give a speech that would appeal to the nation as a whole. He promised the Homestead delegation nothing about labor union laws or government policy toward labor actions. He did not commiserate about the hardships of the lockout. He simply argued to them that the ordinary worker would benefit from economic policies that stimulated and stabilized the economy. The Homestead speech offered no special interest pleading whatsoever—while facing a group whose passionate special interests were exceeded by those of few others.

McKinley also said nothing about Puerto Rico, the income tax, or indeed many other issues of the day. The absence of such matters from the speech might or might not trouble an individual auditor. To talk about Homestead without discussing the lockout could seem, to some auditors, significant.

At the time of the Homestead speech, Hugh J. O'Donnell, who had been indicted in connection with the Homestead lockout, commented that "I don't think the workingmen of Homestead have forgotten July 2, '92, nor the cause which produced it." He continued to predict that Homestead would vote for Bryan in the election. He asserted, probably correctly, that the trip to Canton "was gotten up by the superintendents and bosses." O'Donnell also claimed that with the mill partially closed and a train ticket provided by the company, there was no question about getting a large crowd together.[54] Needless to say, O'Donnell is not an objective source on the topic, any more than was Molanthy. Nonetheless, what seemed like a perfect and whole speech to McKinley's cheering supporters obviously distressed O'Donnell. He perceived nothingness, in the sense that he noticed the absence of a certain kind of rhetoric and the existence of another.

McKinley talked about Homestead very personably, but he could continue to address the same issues in the same way to every delegation that came to see him. Thus he told a group from Pittsburgh: "Now, my fellow citizens, we not only want good work and good wages but we want good money."[55] In October he told a delegation from Syracuse, New York: "If the free trade policy of the Democratic Congress merited, as I think justly, the condemnation you gave it, how much greater must be your vote of protest and disapproval when it is coupled with the proposition to enter upon the free and unlimited coinage of the silver of the world."[56] He told visitors from West Virginia: "We believe neither in free trade nor free silver. . . . The one debases labor and the other the currency of the country."[57]

By saying pretty much the same things to one group after another, yet with speeches that were each distinct and personal, McKinley kept these issues in the newspapers week after week during the autumn of 1896. Furthermore, although an out-of-state newspaper might or might not choose to report every speech that McKinley delivered, they were likely to report a speech given to a delegation from the newspaper's own community, just as the September 12 Homestead speech received good press in Pittsburgh.

Did McKinley win votes with the Homestead speech? It strains credulity to think that he changed the minds of the Homestead workers. The thousands of steelworkers, who gave up a Saturday to come on the train, wearing McKinley buttons on their lapels, were seemingly going to vote for him no matter what he said. McKinley's opponents were not likely to travel to Canton by the thousands to hear him speak. Not even fence sitters were likely to give up their time to come. Any workers who opposed McKinley were likely to stay home, or to stay quiet, on September 12.

Therefore, the key factor in the Homestead speech, as in the many other speeches that McKinley gave during the campaign, was its newsworthiness. The Republicans could have only two reasons to organize events like this, week after week. One was to provide an occasion for McKinley to speak, an occasion important enough that texts of and excerpts from the speech could appear in the newspapers. A second was to provide for an exciting, colorful demonstration full of cheers, songs, parades, and flags to attract further news coverage.

As McKinley finished his speech and his handshaking, the bands and hearty cheers of the next group, a delegation of workers from the Pennsylvania Railroad, wafted across the steamy streets of Canton's hot September day. It was already time for his next speech on that busy Saturday. Dark, threatening clouds rolled in and a thunderstorm drove McKinley away from his porch to a nearby meeting hall. He thundered various statistics to the railroaders, and so the campaign continued.[58]

McKinley's address adapted both to the Homestead crowd and to the national audience. This shows in the markings on his rough draft, which survives in the Library of Congress.[59] The draft was typed on the back of several pages of McKinley's personal stationery. It contains a number of corrections and minor revisions, which appear to be in McKinley's hand. McKinley often dictated speeches to his secretary and then revised them carefully, often in response to whatever comments and suggestions he could get.[60] The transcript of the speech as printed in the *Canton Repository* was, in accordance with newspaper practice of the time, presumably based on a shorthand record of the speech.

McKinley followed his rough draft loosely at times. The opening line of the newspaper's transcript, "I am very glad to have at my home and give welcome to the workingmen of Homestead," occurs in his rough draft, but a few words changed in the delivery.[61] When he spoke, McKinley changed "workingmen of Pennsylvania" to "workingmen of Homestead."[62] His thought as he delivered the speech was to acknowledge his listeners in a more specific way. McKinley strove to show from the outset of the speech that he thought about and cared about each group that came to see him. He also extemporized various changes in the order in which he presented his sentences. For example, his comment "The Republican party has always believed in 'homesteads'" moved closer to the beginning of the speech when he delivered it. This change put at the forefront the impression that McKinley was thinking particularly of the Homestead workers.

A number of the handwritten corrections and minor revisions from the rough draft appeared in the speech as McKinley delivered it, including his praises of Carlisle's "speech of great power and eloquence." McKinley's comment that Carlisle's words were "of truth and soberness and I commend them to the working men of the country everywhere as well entitled to their most serious and warmest consideration" was added to the typed rough draft in McKinley's own hand. McKinley delivered this comment in the oral presentation of the speech, although polished to "These are the words of truth and soberness and I commend them to the workingmen of Homestead (applause) and to the entire country everywhere as well entitled to their most serious and earnest consideration."[63] This phrasing was smoother than the rough draft and added another personal touch.

McKinley's final comments, including "I thank you more than I can tell for this call from the men who toil" and his promise that "it will be my further pleasure to shake, if possible, each and every one of you by the hand," do not appear in his rough draft. They were apparently spontaneous. Perhaps an unpremeditated phrasing added to the personal touch that marked McKinley's speaking. They expressed his concern for working men without promising any audience-specific policies.

Only a few thousand voters heard this speech in person. Since various newspapers published written accounts of the speech, however, McKinley's words could reach across the nation. For example, the Republican newspapers *Canton Repository* and *Sunday Akron Journal* published complete texts of the speech.[64] The Democratic (but pro-gold) *New York Times* printed a lengthy excerpt.[65] The pro-silver, Democratic *Cleveland Plain Dealer* also published a condensed text of the Homestead speech.[66] Even the pro-silver, out-of-state *St. Louis Post-Dispatch* briefly mentioned the speech. (The *Post-Dispatch* did publish a complete text of another of McKinley's speeches of September 12.)[67]

In his "Cross of Gold" speech only two months earlier, Bryan had distinguished between the laboring masses and the business interests, between easterners and the prairie dwellers of the West, between rich and poor. He implored on that day: "What we need is an Andrew Jackson to stand as Jackson stood against the encroachments of aggrandized wealth."[68]

Unlike Bryan, however, McKinley sought everyone's votes. McKinley showed that he had taken the time to think a little about the Homesteaders. He established a sense of rapport with them. He spoke to them from a chair on an unpretentious front porch in an ordinary midwestern city. Yet he gave the same issue positions as always and pointed them toward working people in general.

A winning presidential candidate must appeal to a broad audience. Understanding this, McKinley walked a tightrope. No one could have forgotten the tragic events of the Homestead lockout. That event, however, had limited appeal for the national voting public and even less for McKinley's supporters in the business community. Andrew Carnegie himself issued a statement against free silver in September.[69] The lockout found no place in McKinley's speech. McKinley instead let the gold standard, the tariff, and the affection of his supporters carry him toward the White House.

A question larger than McKinley's political success is: what happened to the voices of Homestead? One could think that in the course of a full and open exchange of political views, the Homestead lockout deserved at least a casual mention. In this sense, McKinley did not merely ignore the lockout; his rhetoric silenced the issue as far as his campaign was concerned. How many of his supporters were even conscious of McKinley's silence about labor strife and the lockout? Perhaps no one will ever know, but for the most part such concerns did not appear, and for those persons there may have been no negation at all. As a critic, one notices the audience's failure to react to McKinley's silence as a nothingness of its own. Yet McKinley's silence is ultimately ambiguous, its meaning coming only from what the audience expected. These expectations themselves were obviously not uniform.

Nothing required McKinley to take the workers' side about the lockout. All the same a significant message, albeit a message not helpful to the Republican cause in 1896, vanished as if had never existed. The Homestead workers, carefully organized, sporting identical McKinley campaign buttons, waving identical American flags, showed up under the supervision of their employers as if for a company picnic. There is no reason to doubt the sincerity of their enthusiasm for McKinley. There is also no way to know if any of them were lockout veterans. McKinley's silence was neither dishonest nor disrespectful. It was a rhetorical adaptation, a sort of a nontrope. His silence let him generalize to the situation of the factory worker at large.

The alternative interpretation of silence is that power can suppress the rhetoric of the powerless. Did this occur in Canton on September 12? The answer depends on one's point of view, on the negations that one perceives. The workers, given the limits of McKinley's rhetoric, would benefit from renewed prosperity but not from the resurrection of a dramatic, indeed horrific, event of the recent past. In this sense it was not McKinley who was silenced but the ideas.

In a similar way, McKinley carefully avoided sectional or local issues throughout the campaign. When he discussed local hardships in other speeches, always tried to show that sound money and a protective tariff would help to relieve those problems. His gaze focused unwaveringly on the larger picture.

McKinley's silence thus grew out of identification, in Burke's sense. McKinley's rhetoric did not picture the voting public as a coalition of varying people with varying interests. He did not intend to cobble together the votes of various special groups. He repeatedly asserted that Americans' needs and interests were the same throughout the nation. Silence about sectional and divisive issues was the most reasonable strategy open to him. By ignoring local concerns, as he did throughout the campaign, McKinley concentrated on issues that could give his supporters a sense of common cause, of unity, and of shared principles.

CHAPTER 8

Bryan's Railroad Campaign in September, 1896

ONCE HE EXPLODED into the public's view at the 1896 Democratic convention with "A Cross of Gold," anyone could see that Bryan's campaign would feature oratory. In his September campaign speeches, Bryan created a vision in which the gold standard, devised by a conspiracy of evil financiers, caused ordinary working Americans to suffer from economic hardship. His rhetoric was often powerful, vigorous, and divisive. Bryan continued to advocate the unlimited coinage of silver as the solution to the nation's financial, social, and moral problems.

His campaign speeches, however, were nothing like "A Cross of Gold." Bryan's tendency to act like a debater, to give reasoned advocacy for his beliefs, to refute arguments of his opponents, became increasingly pronounced. Contrary to what one might at first think, this quality of his speaking was entirely in line with Bryan's image as a radical. Once again, he was really not a radical on the issues. Many respectable politicians advocated silver coinage. Bryan's speaking, however, epitomized radical rhetoric.

Bryan spent most of September touring the nation on the railroad, speaking several times a day at stops en route. These speeches characteristically expressed *cause and effect reasoning,* and as Richard Weaver points out, such reasoning tends to indicate a pragmatic, nonphilosophical inclination that often leads to exaggeration. All of these qualities marked Bryan's speaking, and his continuing attempts to tie himself to the tradition of the nation's political and economic authorities did little to counter the negative impression that Bryan's opponents tried to create of his character.

Hence Bryan's strategies may have been in large part attempts to defuse the charge that he was a dangerous, ignorant fanatic, yet paradoxically, they are precisely the strategies that one would expect a social reformer to employ. Thus despite his arguments, which were often quite sensible, Bryan sank more and more deeply into a mire largely of his own making.

Bryan brought up issues of cause and effect in "A Cross of Gold," but he subordinated them to the flag issue of free silver. As September progressed, Bryan depicted free silver less and less as a symbol of his advocacy of the common citizen and more as a viable economic program in its own right.

Richard Weaver maintains that the characteristic major premise that a speaker uses in argumentation reveals the speaker's basic moral position. In Weaver's view, a speaker might use one of four principal kinds of major premises. Each leads to a different kind of argument (or topic, as Weaver calls them): (1) the argument from genus or definition, which argues from "the nature of a thing"; (2) the argument from cause and effect, which he also calls the argument from consequences; (3) the argument from analogy; and (4) the argument from circumstance, which refers simply to perceived facts and "is the least philosophical of all the sources of argument." Weaver considers the argument from circumstance to be the argument typical of the liberal, and the argument from genus to be the argument typical of the conservative.[1] Sometimes Weaver treats the argument from circumstance as a variety of the argument from cause and effect.[2] Finally, the argument from authority depends on the other types, according to the authority's pattern of reasoning: every argument from authority is also an argument from genus, circumstance, or what have you.

Considering cause and effect to be a low form of argument because it does not point back to universal categories, Weaver warns that those who employ it "are under a temptation to play too much upon the fears of their audience by stressing the awful nature of some consequence or by exaggerating the power of some cause." He says "those who are characteristically pragmatic in their way of thinking" often prefer cause and effect argument.[3]

Cause and effect argument gives "a forecast of results."[4] Weaver also points out that a frequent feature of cause and effect argument is that "a grave effect implies a grave cause and consequently, a grave cause implies a grave effect."[5]

Bryan's rhetoric bears out all of these characteristics of cause and effect argument. He repeatedly argued that the tight money policy caused an economic depression, and therefore he blamed the gold standard for profound evil. Furthermore, Bryan repeatedly argued that bimetallism would save the nation. His claim that the gold standard was important relied on his argument that tight money caused the depression. Economic hard times were obviously a grave harmful effect. This rhetorical strategy thus implied that bimetallism would revolutionize the economy and provide for the needs of common people. In addition to pragmatic cause and effect arguments on behalf of bimetallism, Bryan made cause and effect arguments about his opponents, attributing their statements to greed rather than to logic or goodwill. Similarly, he attributed the continuation of the gold standard to the covetous efforts of eastern financiers. These strategies inevitably made his rhetoric more divisive.

Bryan gave two different kinds of speeches in September. While traveling, he often stepped out of his train car and spoke briefly to the crowds that waited on the platform. Sometimes he did not even get off the train, and spoke from the car's rear deck. In larger cities Bryan often left the train and went to a large public hall, or more commonly a park, and spoke to crowds of sometimes awesome size. These speeches tended to be long and detailed, frequently approaching tediousness. Nonetheless, the newspapers covered these speeches quite well. Newspaper reporters copied most of them in shorthand and published them in full.

Scholars often mention but seldom study Bryan's railroad campaign. Trent and Friedenberg's important books about political communication point out that the relatively newly developed, highly reliable network of railroads made Bryan's campaign tour possible.[6] One critic, commenting on Bryan's speaking, claims that Bryan used examples and analogies and also notes Bryan's use of "historical precedent."[7] Another notes Bryan's excellence in figurative language, although also recognizing Bryan's use of close argument.[8] A rhetorical historian implies that Bryan's campaign efforts were quite admirable when one takes into account McKinley's much greater resources.[9] Springen's book about Bryan's rhetoric calls Bryan's 1896 railroad campaign "legendary."[10] Coletta said "Bryan had set a new record for campaigning."[11]

As the gold Democrats were forming their splinter party in Indianapolis, Bryan began September by speaking at a mass rally at the state capitol grounds in Columbus, Ohio.[12] The newspapers estimated the crowd at between twenty and thirty thousand, making it Bryan's largest audience yet.[13] Bryan was apparently overwhelmed by the enormous crowd, their numbers defeating his attempts to make himself heard. He frequently asked them to be quiet. As a practical matter, many in the crowd may not have heard the various speakers at all. Bryan walked around to different parts of the stage to face different sections of the audience. He did not review the material that they might have missed while he was speaking in another direction.[14] This event, one could presume, was a remarkable expression of enthusiasm for, or at least curiosity about, the famous orator. However, like many of the mass rallies to follow, it did not provide the ideal forum for the rational discourse that Bryan wished to present.

The spectacle easily equaled McKinley's Front Porch speeches. Bryan spoke from a twenty-foot-high covered platform, bedecked with flags, facing the front of the capitol. He paraded to the platform in a fancy horse-drawn carriage, accompanied by several free silver clubs, who presumably organized to participate in just such an event. Bands played and huge silver dollars were bandied about.[15]

Bryan continued to stress bimetallism. He reviewed the crime of 1873, in which Congress adopted the gold standard. He refuted the compromise plan to coin silver at the ratio of thirty-two to one, saying that it would change "four billion of silver dollars into two billion of silver dollars." This was a simple cause and effect argument. Always alert to prove that he was not an anarchist, he quoted George Washington against the dangers posed by foreign problems, asking: "What anarchist do you suppose wrote that?" He concluded that the nation needed to declare financial independence by adopting free silver ahead of the nations of Europe.[16]

After accusing the advocates of gold of refusing to come "into open battle," Bryan continued the speech by offering a number of cause and effect arguments. He referred Senator John Sherman, a leading advocate of gold, to one effect: that the nation needed to add $40 million a year to the money supply just to keep up with growth. Bryan continued that "a gold standard means a rising dollar. A rising dollar means falling prices, falling prices mean hard times," clearly stating a cause and effect sequence. He advocated that silver be coined at the ratio of sixteen to one by weight with gold because "the gap between gold bullion and silver bullion has been caused by hostile legislation." Bryan opened an assault against the advocates of gold, attributing their beliefs not to personal conviction but rather to greed. He asserted that the Republican platform "was written by men who are interested in making money scarce."[17] Although this was still cause and effect argument, it was directed toward his opponents' motives rather than toward the issues.

Continuing with that theme the next day while traveling through Ohio, Bryan spoke briefly in Kenton to a group of over six thousand. He argued against "the idle holders of idle capital." In a type of incident that became common in the campaign, the railroad platform collapsed under the crowd. Not missing a beat, Bryan retorted that "these platforms may be frail . . . but the [Democratic Party's] Chicago platform is built on a solid rock and can hold all that come," thus turning a near-disaster into an opportunity to assert the benefits that the bimetallist platform would cause.[18] A short time later, in Findlay, Bryan restated his basic cause and effect argument: "How can you make a dollar large? By making few dollars. How can you make a dollar fall in value? By making more dollars."[19] Bryan's voice was once more starting to fail from the stress of speaking, but he did manage to explain the cause of the farmers' troubles. Some complained of the potato bug, the chinch bug, or the army worm, he said, but "the gold bug is destroying more crops than all of them."[20] He once again found the cause of the nation's financial problems in the malice of gold advocates. This was a very pragmatic, straightforward attribution.

Steaming into Toledo by the afternoon, Bryan delivered two speeches to immense audiences that, as he told them, could be "measured by the acre rather than the head." After urging them to be quiet so they could hear, he repeated many of the themes of the Columbus speech.[21] He also protested against the Republican "sound money" clubs, complaining that they should be honest and call themselves gold clubs. He asked: "Why do they attempt to conceal the word 'gold' under the euphonious name of 'sound money?'" He had gotten hold of a membership application for a sound money club and spent some time attacking the language in which it was phrased. Noting the blanks on the form, Bryan mentioned that "the man who issued this considered the employe [sic] a blank (laughter)."[22] An attack against the railroads, it would seem, would have pleased Bryan's populist supporters.

Bryan did not rely completely on rational argument, and his regionalism had not yet passed away. In Elkhart, Indiana, he paused to criticize the pro-gold East in biblical terms: "I am constrained to believe that there is only one passage of the Scripture with which they are familiar, and that is that passage which says that a great many years ago certain wise men came from the East. (Great laughter and applause.) They think that they have been coming from that direction ever since. (Laughter.)"[23]

Bryan continued with cause and effect arguments about his opponents and about the issues. He appeared to be determined to give clear, concise statements of his views and to offer constructive arguments on their behalf. That he often phrased his points with flair, and sometimes with arrogance, does not change the underlying quality of his campaign rhetoric. In this respect, "A Cross of Gold" was an aberration from Bryan's usual oratory. Bryan felt able to criticize the gold forces for their failure to offer the kind of clear cause and effect argument that he routinely presented. When McKinley said "sound money" instead of "gold standard" or used "law and order" as a code phrase to attack the income tax, he was confusing matters and precluding a rational discussion of the issues, Bryan implied.[24] He would bring this grievance to a head in a few more weeks.

Later the same day, Bryan spoke briefly to a huge crowd in South Bend, Indiana. He argued that ordinary people could grasp the money question. Once again faced with a large audience, Bryan urged them to stop "crowding." Displaying his unfailing gift for the apt phrase, he commented that "an honest dollar is a dollar which, when melted, loses none of its value."[25]

These themes recurred many times before the month ended. At National Park in Milwaukee, Bryan denied McKinley's charge that he was appealing to class conflicts and compared the gold standard to a "burglar."[26] Bryan had arrived late for the speech, which although quite long in any case, was shortened by rain. He stated that the extreme gap between the prices of silver and gold "has been produced by hostile legislation," so that "friendly legislation" would result in gold and silver coins of equal value. He attributed the economic troubles to a chain of events in which the "money-owning and money-changing classes have been making dollars dearer and therefore have been making dollars scarcer." Their motive in doing so, he stated, was that "they are interested in having money to go out." He concluded that the ordinary workers were entitled to defend themselves from "a conspiracy to destroy the value of your property. (Applause.)"[27]

Bryan continued that the gold standard had wrecked the nation's economy.[28] In a remarkable if unpolished outburst of his celebrated and well-balanced eloquence, Bryan attacked the gold standard further: "We think that any standard that gives us a rising dollar and falling prices, any standard which makes the money owner great and the man who produces wealth dependent; a policy which makes money the master and all things else the servant, we believe that that policy is bad, and being bad [*sic*] we are opposed to submitting to it any longer."[29]

The reasoning in this speech posited the gold standard as the cause of the nation's economic and moral woes and denounced the nation's wealthy interests as the gold standard's cause. Bryan attributed wondrously evil effects to the gold standard, implying in turn that removing the gold standard would relieve the nation's problems. It should seem extraordinary that Bryan would lay at the feet of the gold bugs such an array of effects. This is, however, typical of what Weaver predicted from cause and effect argument. As if to prove Bryan's point, it was at this point that steel magnate Andrew Carnegie issued his public letter to his workers against free silver.[30]

This was actually one of Bryan's milder attacks against the gold bugs' personal motives. He stated that farmers routinely advocated silver because they thought bimetallism would benefit them. The gold bugs, he said, advocated gold on the grounds that it would be good for others. In response, Bryan contended that greed was the cause of everybody's views on the money question. The farmers, he explained, were at least honest about their motives. Thus Bryan advocated cause and effect positions both on the issues and on the motivations of the advocates. In one instance, at a supposedly nonpolitical speech in Chicago's Sharpshooter Park, Bryan told an amusing story about hogs in Iowa and concluded that "one of the important duties of government is the putting of rings in the noses of hogs." He stated that "we are all hoggish."[31] While Bryan was in Chicago, his friend Charles Dawes called on him and the two young political stars talked for a while. "Bryan," Dawes wrote, "somehow, imagines he has a chance to be elected President."[32]

Early in the month, Bryan decided to make a second campaign trip to the East.[33] This may have been a curious campaign decision, since he ended up campaigning in states that he must have known he could not hope to win. Just at that time, the press quoted Dawes's statement that the real campaign was in the Mississippi Valley states.[34]

Returning to his home in Lincoln, Nebraska, on September 8, Bryan was welcomed by a parade with two bands and two free silver clubs as escorts. He spoke from an outdoor platform near the state capitol, with a huge photograph of himself displayed over his head. Bryan complained about being called an "anarchist." He commented on being very tired.[35] The night before, his staff had awakened him several times to speak to small crowds in Iowa. By September 9, the National Silver Party formally notified Bryan of his nomination.[36] He took note, apparently with pride, of the still-polarized electorate: "I have not found a lukewarm man anywhere. They have been for us or against us and they have been earnestly for us or against us."[37] The radical, divisive rhetoric of "A Cross of Gold"—indeed, of Bryan's entire campaign—was bearing fruit.

Bryan seems to have changed something significant in his campaign a few days later when he issued his Letter of Acceptance for the Democratic nomination. In this well-publicized letter, a formality from an earlier age, Bryan reviewed his thoughts on the issues. He covered the Constitution, public bonds, the Monroe Doctrine, Civil War pensions, injunctions, labor arbitration, railroad regulation, civil service (which he opposed in any strong version), and numerous other questions.[38] What is interesting here is that whereas early in the campaign he had stressed the money question to the exclusion of all else, after issuing his Letter of Acceptance Bryan began to speak about all manner of other issues.

Bryan left Lincoln early on the morning of September 12, accompanied to the station by a parade and brass bands. His plan was to pass through Kansas City, to give some speeches in Missouri, and then to tour through Kentucky, Tennessee, and North Carolina and finally up the eastern seaboard to New England. The schedule for the latter half of the trip was not yet firmed up.[39] Speaking at the time of his departure from Lincoln, Bryan tried to sound conciliatory, mentioning that he had called the East "the enemy's country" but that on touring this region he "found down there just as much enthusiasm as there is in Nebraska."[40]

In a brief speech from the back of his railroad car in Kansas City, he made an analogy to explain how free silver would cause economic prosperity: "Some of our opponents tell us that the thing to do is to open the mills, instead of the mints. That reminds me of the man who said that his horse would go all right if he could just get the wagon started. (Laughter and applause.) It is putting the cart before the horse. . . . There is no more effective way of destroying the markets for what the mills produce than to lower prices upon the products the farmer has raised so that they will not bring him enough to pay him for raising them."[41] Even this analogy, however, expresses an underlying cause and effect argument that farmers were causes of the prosperity of factories, and thus turned back to the money issue to imply why the mills were closed.

Bryan's first major appearances during this tour were in St. Louis, where he planned to speak at the Auditorium, Concordia Park, and Sportsman's Park. All three events were free to the public. Each venue featured a series of speakers during the evening, with Bryan scheduled to appear at each meeting in turn.[42] His train arrived on time at 6:15 P.M., to be met by thousands of admirers.[43] Local reception committees escorted him to his hotel for dinner and then to the speech venues.[44] At the Auditorium he found a crowd of about sixteen thousand, several thousand more people having been turned away.[45] Judging from a newspaper reporter's sketch, the audience consisted entirely of men.[46] Bryan's arrival set off nearly a half hour of cheering. He mentioned that it was in this same hall that the Republicans' national convention a few months earlier had adopted what he characterized as a half-hearted gold plank: "Gold is a coward. It will not meet its enemies in an open fight." Continuing to analyze the political situation in cause and effect terms, Bryan denied that the silver controversy had driven gold out of circulation: "Gold is not scarce because of agitation, but agitation exists because gold was scarce before agitation began. (Loud cheering.)"[47]

Arriving at Concordia Park, a vast outdoor amphitheater in the woods, Bryan spoke to a crowd estimated at twenty-five thousand. The speaker's platform being centrally located, he announced that he would turn to different parts of the throng in turn. He began by stating his pro-silver thesis and was soon heckled by McKinley supporters. Bryan retorted: "We are glad to have our opponents here. We need them here because they need speaking to more than our own people do. (Great applause and cheering.)" Bryan then cited Treasury Department reports to establish the decline in the supply of money.[48]

He followed this by listing the evil effects of the shrinking money supply: "We find the contraction of the currency shown by the reports of the treasury department; we find property falling in value; we find labor out of employment; we find business paralyzed; we find that men do not want to invest in property for fear that they will lose; everybody wants to invest in money, because money is the only thing that is rising."[49]

Bryan then stated that his opponents "propose no plan. Why not? Because the policies of the Republican party are dominated by Wall street, where they do not want money plenty."[50] Thus he explained that the cause of the tight money policy of his opponents was the reprehensible influence of the finance industry. The evening's third speech, also outdoors, was canceled when the speakers' platform collapsed, leaving Bryan dangling from a railing.[51]

Shortly afterward, Bryan passed through Kentucky, escorted on the train by several prominent Democrats.[52] During three speeches to mass crowds in Louisville, he complained about the "syndicates" of "money grabbers."[53] The same day, speaking outdoors in Henderson, Bryan accused the gold bugs of trying "to fasten upon the American people a foreign financial system."[54] His speech in Frankfort, Kentucky, might have been an excellent opportunity—with the railroad tracks right in front of the state capitol building and a large crowd waiting—but was shortened by rain.[55]

Speaking in Asheville, North Carolina, on September 16, Bryan boasted that the silverites had "rescued" the Democratic Party "from the people's despoilers."[56] Bryan tied together his cause and effect arguments, relating the nation's economic difficulties both to the gold standard and to the greedy financiers: "The restoration of bi-metallism is demanded on behalf of those who are the strength of every nation and the gold standard is desired by those who profit most as business is paralyzed and the masses impoverished."[57]

A day later in Salisbury, North Carolina, Bryan paraded to a park escorted by the Hornet's Nest Riflemen and the mounted Knights of Pythias (a fraternal organization) to speak to a crowd estimated in the thousands. Continuing to attribute the depression to the gold standard, Bryan explained that the rising dollar resulted in depressed prices, which in turn hurt working people. He cited a government publication showing that the supply of money was down by $59 million. "These are statements," Bryan assured his listeners, "of one of our opponents, so short a time ago that even they have forgotten that the truths they stated are still alive. (Applause.)"[58]

Even in his brief whistle-stop speeches, which offered little time for detailed argument, Bryan reiterated cause and effect relationships. He spoke for only three minutes in Concord, North Carolina, commenting that one would not know if free silver would provide the right amount of money unless it was tried. By this statement, Bryan uncharacteristically admitted how uncertain cause and effect prediction can be. In Salisbury he asserted that a gold standard "means a lower order of civilization" and that unless the gold standard were abolished, "we will sink down where the few own all the wealth."[59]

Bryan had already warned the laborers not to desert the farmers. In Greensboro, North Carolina, speaking from a much-bedecked stand in town, he switched to the issue of peacetime bonds. He assured the audience that he would enforce the law against the rich investors as well as against the poor.[60] Yet a short time later in Goldsboro, North Carolina, he commented on the union of the disparate free silver groups. He continued that "the money question rises paramount." His attack against the motives of the gold bugs became more vicious: "Money changers have never in the history of the human race listened to anything but force. They have no heart. They cannot feel." He added that "they know nothing but greed and avarice."[61]

Shortly afterward, speaking in an auditorium in Richmond, Virginia, Bryan cited a Treasury Department report showing a reduction in the money supply of $150 million in the last two years. He stated the importance of supply and demand in setting the value of money.[62]

By September 19, Bryan reached the nation's capital and spoke in the baseball stadium. Bad weather thinned the crowd and forced him to cut the speech to thirty minutes. Bryan spoke against life tenure civil service, quoted a letter on the money issue by Secretary of the Treasury Carlisle, and reviewed inconsistencies in the Cleveland Administration's policies. He concluded that the people "can distrust their candor and frankness." He cited George Washington.[63]

George Washington came into Bryan's rhetoric again later that day in Fredericksburg, Virginia. After arriving at the train station in an ordinary day coach, he mentioned in a brief speech that in this very place Washington had thrown a silver dollar across the river. "Would you believe, my friends," Bryan asked, "that a silver dollar which was good enough to be handled by the father of his country is now so mean a thing as to excite the contempt of many so-called financiers?" Hinting about the tariff issue, he continued that "I am not so much worried about our dollars which travel abroad. I want a dollar that won't be ashamed to look a farmer in the face."[64] Whirling through a few other Virginia towns, Bryan spoke briefly in Ashland, but in Milford the train pulled out before he could open his mouth.[65]

On Saturday, September 19, Bryan arrived in Washington and hurried to a series of speeches and public and private meetings. The pro-gold *Washington Evening Star* admitted that the demonstration for Bryan was "such as has not been witnessed here for years." With a late summer storm impending, Bryan was greeted by cheers, a marching demonstration by the Lakeland Democratic Club, and a band. He spoke in favor of admitting several western territories to the Union and again opposed civil service. In very un-McKinley-like fashion, he adapted to his audience by advocating home rule for the residents of the District of Columbia. He quoted Washington against the dangers of foreign alliances, turning this to the undesirability of adopting bimetallism by international agreement. A storm ended his speech after about a half hour.[66]

Bryan got a quiet day on Sunday, September 20, in Washington. This gave him a chance to rest his voice and to meet with several members of Congress. He was scheduled to reach Baltimore that evening and would travel from there to Dover, Delaware, and then to Philadelphia. His dramatic trip east was now under way. Acting against Bryan's wishes, the Delaware Democratic Committee decided that he should leave early for Dover. On the twenty-third the New Jersey Democratic Committee was to meet to set Bryan's schedule for a few days. Thus he had little control over his hectic schedule, which continued to be coordinated state by state.[67]

Bryan started to harp on a recent statement by Otto von Bismarck, former chancellor of Germany, in favor of bimetallism. He turned this against his opponents, sarcastically commenting that "I suppose they will call Bismarck an agitator."[68] When he reached Philadelphia, he spoke at the Academy of Music, which held for Bryan far more than its usual capacity of six thousand. Bryan had to sneak through an alley to get to the hall. He was unable to address a subsequent open-air audience because of noise from the crowd.[69]

Reaching Brooklyn, Bryan was scheduled to speak at the Music Hall, where the King's County Democratic Party was meeting. He arrived late, while Judge William J. Gaynor was defending the party against the charge of being anarchists and communists. Police escorted Bryan into the hall. The audience members held little flags, and flag-draped pictures of Bryan and vice presidential candidate Arthur Sewall adorned the room. Perhaps this was an attempt to meet McKinley's patriotic appeals. In his speech Bryan praised Brooklyn, declared "warfare" against the gold standard, and defended several planks of the Democratic platform. Bryan spoke against federal interference with local rights, in what may have been in part a veiled appeal to the racist vote.[70] He defended the income tax, quoting Lincoln that the Supreme Court was sometimes wrong, and defended himself against the charge of being lawless. He finally turned to the money issue, claiming that financiers used the gold standard to cheat. He attacked the "Rothschild-Morgan syndicate and all the rest of them" as "just like any other criminal." He denied that the money issue was sectional, stating that it started in the West but spread everywhere.[71]

Bryan was soon scheduled to swing back into the nation's capital. The organizers arranged the speech so that, depending on when Bryan would be able to arrive, noted Democrats would both precede and follow him, with the speechmaking beginning about an hour before Bryan's arrival.[72] This procedure ensured that the crowd would not be left listless if the train ran late.

In New Haven, Connecticut, Bryan got too much of a taste of Yale University. About five hundred students, assisted by a brass band from the National Guard, made enough noise to break up his speech. Bryan turned the potentially embarrassing incident to his advantage, stating that "I am not speaking now to the sons who are sent to college on the proceeds of ill gotten gains."[73] He swept through a few Connecticut towns, either not speaking at all or speaking very briefly. He warned a crowd in Bridgeport that "the farmers of the country are the Samsons, and when they fall they will pull down the pillars of the temple with them."[74] This turned his usual cause and effect pattern around somewhat, returning to the argument from "A Cross of Gold" that the nation's prosperity rested on the farmers.

September 25 found Bryan in Boston. He arrived late at the Boston Commons to face an audience that may have exceeded sixty thousand. Bryan immediately announced that he would not try to make himself heard by the entire crowd. Overcoming the regionalism that marred some of his earlier speeches, Bryan stated that "though far from my Nebraska home, I am glad I can greet you as fellow citizens of a common country." He quickly identified an adequate money supply as the cause of prosperity. Lampooning the gold bugs, he continued that "our opponents plant themselves upon the doctrine that the less money the whole people have the more money each individual will have. (Laughter and applause.)" Bryan then once more attributed greatly harmful effects to the gold standard, explaining that the only argument for gold was "the misery which has followed it wherever it has been tried."[75]

Leaving Boston that day on the train, Bryan met a committee of Democrats from Springfield who accompanied him for part of his journey. In Windsor Locks, Massachusetts, Bryan's speech consisted of the single sentence, "I am glad to see you." In Springfield he spoke at the Court Square and cited Jefferson in favor of freedom of speech. He also mentioned a Budapest conference that had endorsed bimetallism. He took time to renew his accusation that his opponents were distorting terms: "A man who does not believe that he is right is the man who has filled the dictionary with ambiguous terms and fills his speech with words of double meaning."[76] He continued that "the man who talks about 'sound money' and refuses to tell you what sound money means can only get a certificate of honesty from himself." Mocking a characteristic phrase of McKinley's, Bryan retorted that "we must not only have money which is good, but we must have money which we can get hold of. (Applause.)"[77]

By September 28 Bryan was on his way to New York City. Disharmony had entered the campaign, as the Populist Party candidate for vice president, Thomas Watson, asked Sewall to resign as vice presidential candidate. The skirmish apparently died down quickly.[78]

At an appearance en route to New York, Bryan got into an argument with an audience member about the merits of free silver. As the reporters transcribed the brief debate, Bryan asked his interlocutor, "Are you in favor of a gold standard?" The man said he was, and Bryan asked why. He said that "every nation will accept a gold dollar for a dollar." Bryan retorted, "Why? I will tell you. Because of its value. The reason why our gold dollar and our bullion are worth the same is because the law says you can convert the bullion into a dollar at the mint." Not only did Bryan seem to enjoy the exchange, but in this extemporaneous debate he also quickly resorted to a cause and effect argument about the valuation of gold.[79]

Bryan frequently depicted himself as the candidate of the people, and McKinley, even today, is often seen as the candidate of the bosses. Despite Bryan's anti-machine protestations, a group from Tammany Hall met him on September 29 at the train station in New York City.[80] Tammany organized huge, enthusiastic crowds to greet Bryan. He reached a steamy, overcrowded Tammany Hall in the rain at 8:00 P.M., accompanied by Sewall. Everyone was equipped with an American flag. The hall was decorated with flags and paintings of Bryan and Sewall. Bryan spoke: "I was in this hall once before. It was on the Fourth of July when I was permitted to take part in one of your celebrations." He continued that it was no surprise that Tammany, "which reads every year the Declaration of American independence gives enthusiastic support to a platform which declares financial independence." Bryan criticized "trusts, stock gamblers and money grabbers." He was then unable to give a scheduled speech outside Tammany Hall because of exhaustion.[81]

In a display of excessive anti-silver zeal, the Democratic but pro-gold *New York Times* took advantage of Bryan's visit to cite medical experts who questioned Bryan's mental stability. The argument, basically, was that no sane person would advocate silver.[82] They also editorialized that Bryan's open affiliation with the "unsavory" Tammany Hall would harm his chances for election.[83] At the end of the month, the *Times* endorsed the ticket of the Gold Democrats, thus denying their support to either McKinley or Bryan.[84] After the election Bryan praised Tammany's contribution to his campaign and asserted that Tammany's support almost enabled him to carry New York City.[85]

Bryan's persuasive attempts were somewhat ambivalent. On the one hand, he repeatedly stressed that the different classes would vote on the silver issue in accordance with their own best interests. On the other hand, he constantly tried to persuade them with detailed cause and effect arguments of the benefits of free silver to the whole nation. If indeed the nation was divided into classes with mutually inconsistent needs, argument along these lines may have been futile from the start. Nevertheless, Bryan was not ambivalent in his evangelism. He preached free silver with the enthusiasm of a religious enthusiast. He spoke as if convinced that if he explained himself clearly enough, and gave enough proof, and answered enough questions, he could get his listeners to agree with his cause.

Yet although his speeches contained abundant biblical references, at this stage of the campaign he stressed cause and effect reasoning. Apparently seeing himself as a responsible social and economic reformer, Bryan presented detailed, cleverly phrased arguments to establish that the gold standard caused the nation's troubles, that an increase in the money supply would alleviate these hardships, and that the farmers were the backbone of the economy. He attributed all manner of evil to the gold standard. This is precisely the kind of exaggerated cause and effect argument that Weaver predicted. Free silver came across in these speeches not as a dogma but as a means to an end, which was to improve the lot of ordinary people by increasing the money supply and devaluing the currency. Bryan's campaign rhetoric was pragmatic. The people knew there was a problem; Bryan visited their cities and towns to explain in detail how free silver would alleviate it.

From a point of view like Weaver's, the argument from genus or definition is the characteristic argument of the conservative or the idealist because definitions and categories are enduring, and the conservative speaks of that which endures. The liberal, on the other hand, characteristically employs the argument from circumstance, Weaver maintains. Trying to predict change, a speaker who uses the closely related argument from cause and effect has a closely related moral stance.[86] If a problem arises, and if the already known solutions do not work, then a speaker requires not the weight of tradition but reasoned predictions to justify a novel solution. Yet no universal principle underlies such argument. Thus, just as Weaver suggests, this is indeed a characteristically liberal manner of thinking.

This was precisely Bryan's approach. A reformer cannot cite prior experience to predict the effect of as yet untried policies. In the abstract, although Bryan often cited tradition in an effort to bolster his credibility, a reformer by definition cannot rely on tradition. Indeed, these two features of Bryan's rhetoric struggled with each another. Bryan challenged the gold advocates to come out into the open and fight the issues point by point. He depicted gold as evil because the gold standard restricted the money supply. He then pictured a variety of evil effects that resulted. Since gold produced evil effects, the eastern financiers who advocated gold must also be evil. Thus the pragmatic, pro-silver argument did not really begin with a moral anti-gold premise; the harmful effects of gold money proved the moral claims. This was exactly the kind of rhetoric that Weaver expects a cause and effect arguer to produce.

Bryan's most famous speeches, particularly "A Cross of Gold," featured striking metaphors, bold images, and figurative analogies. His September campaign speeches, although sometimes entertaining, were not notable for bold figures of speech. Despite the tincture of sarcasm, these speeches stressed cause and effect reasoning. Bryan was the evangelist of a reformist social and economic platform that he proposed and defended by argument. He wished to diagnose a problem and identify a solution that removed that cause, thus producing beneficial effects.

Bimetallism was good, Bryan argued, not because of some basic principle but simply because it would bring prosperity to the ordinary American. Bryan held gold to be evil not because of some inherent quality that a gold-based economy possessed but because the gold supply was as a matter of *circumstance* not sufficient to serve the economy. Just as Weaver cautioned a century later, Bryan exaggerated the importance of the cause and effect processes that he discussed. Thus Bryan built a towering edifice of moral superiority on the uncertain foundation of causal reasoning. He talked like a traditionalist yet used the arguments of a social reformer. As October came, this approach would run aground against McKinley's relaxed, self-confident, and often rather vague rhetoric.

CHAPTER 9

The Closing Weeks of the Front Porch Campaign

McKINLEY CONTINUED his by now well-organized and efficient Front Porch campaign during October 1896. Delegations flocked to hear him speak, sometimes in overwhelming numbers. His campaign reached a frenetic peak during these last few weeks, especially on Saturdays when thousands of visitors poured down Market Street, to the point that McKinley was often hard-pressed even to speak to all the visiting delegations. He stuck to the protective tariff and the dangers of free silver as if those two issues were his personal possessions.

In this chapter I consider McKinley's explicit and implicit use of time, in the sense of *timeliness,* as a line of argument in his rhetoric.

McKinley's rhetoric had taken a ceremonial tone all through the campaign. This does not mean all his speeches were ceremonial but simply that they had many ceremonial qualities. Ceremonial rhetoric, also called epideictic rhetoric, often features display. Such rhetoric is often flowery and general in content and usually brings up policy issues only in an indistinct way. Ceremonial rhetoric often maintains that the audience should learn from the example of the wise people of the past. It frequently helps to set the standards for political decision by establishing and reinforcing values.[1]

Ceremonial rhetoric often takes on a more dignified tone than crisply argumentative rhetoric. Ronald Reagan, for example, the quintessential rhetorical president, sometimes used ceremonial forms of rhetoric to discuss policy issues.[2] McKinley relied on this type of rhetoric throughout October. The next chapter shows how Bryan's increasingly deliberative, argumentative approach to persuasion contrasted ever more sharply with McKinley's more general rhetoric.

The Greek word *kairos* expresses one of the concepts lying behind McKinley's epideictic approach to oratory in this campaign. This word could be translated as "timeliness." The ancient Greek language discriminates between two concepts of time.[3] Greek words commonly translated as "time" include *chronos,* time as it can be measured, and *kairos,* which refers to "fittingness, timing, and the opportune moment of decision."[4] Timeliness or *kairos* may include the sense of the "right time"; a time of tension or conflict, a time of crisis; or "a time when an opportunity for accomplishing some purpose has opened up."[5]

Of these, rhetorical theorists, ancient and modern, often concentrate on the third, the notion that there is a best time for a particular act of rhetoric. Does a speaker speak at the best time? Does a speaker put a particular argument in the right part of a speech? These are important matters, which I examine later.

In his study of the New Testament, Dale Sullivan argues for the existence of a very old conception of timeliness that goes beyond Aristotle's view of the proper moment to do something. This is more akin to the second of Smith's three meanings.[6] The present discussion focuses on this second meaning of timeliness, the idea of a time of crisis that calls for action. In this sense, timeliness becomes a line of argument that a speaker can present to establish a point. That right now is the critical time for patriotic Americans to vote for McKinley is not the kind of thing one proves with argument. It is an almost mystical assertion: incontestable and unprovable. It depends not on reason but on how the audience perceives the speaker's reputation and the quality of the event.

The growing excitement as the campaign reached its conclusion, the ever larger crowds that were by now overwhelming Canton, and the fervency of McKinley's rhetoric all combined to broadcast the inevitable triumph of McKinley's cause. His speeches frequently stressed timeliness. These campaign speeches tended to suggest a series of events that one might paraphrase something like this:

- When it lived by its traditions, the nation was prosperous with a gold standard and a protective tariff.
- However, the Democratic administration adopted a free trade policy, throwing the nation into troubled times.
- Now, Bryan wants to retain free trade and to attack the nation's currency, posing a critical challenge to the nation.
- The nation is thus at a pivotal moment. Only the inevitable Republican victory, bringing a return to the wise policies of the past, can bring the nation back to the prosperity of the past.

McKinley appealed to the cultural values that he shared with his audience. As was typical of his rhetoric, he wove his themes from seemingly unmatched threads. The wisdom of the past would guide the nation to a solution of the crisis that it faced in the present. McKinley often stressed that the nation was at a *critical juncture* in its history, when the people faced a choice between the traditional policies that would bring prosperity and an alternative path consisting of dangerous experiments. McKinley entwined into this implied argument a view of the nation as having overcome the traumas of the Civil War to become a united republic that knew no sectional differences. These perceptions combined to show that the times conspired to bring McKinley and his Republican cause to the presidency and that he fully recognized the pivotal nature of the rhetorical moment. That the rhetorical moment was largely the creation of McKinley's own rhetoric, the growing excitement the simple consequence of McKinley's own pseudo-events, hardly seemed worth mentioning at the time.

Throughout the month, McKinley's Front Porch campaign continued to generate enormous amounts of newspaper coverage. Major Republican papers published good reports of his campaign events, typically printing at least some full-text speeches.[7] The Democratic press, also, gave McKinley good coverage. For example, the Democratic (but fairly conservative) *Kansas City Star* published excellent reports of many of his speeches, often including full texts.[8] Many of these reports appeared to be taken verbatim right off of the wire services, as the reports in the Democratic papers were generally word-for-word (albeit sometimes condensed) versions of the same material that the Republican press offered.

McKinley addressed the question of timeliness on Thursday, October 1. Bad weather drove him indoors to a large auditorium to speak to a group of about a thousand people from nearby Portage County, Ohio. After stating that "we propose in this contest to protect our money from debasement" at the same time as protecting "our industries from foreign competition," McKinley emphasized the critical nature of the times: *"This is the year* to settle *for all time* that our National honor will not and can not be tainted" (emphasis added).[9]

On October 3 McKinley was again forced away from his front porch, not by weather but by the huge crowds. For the arrival of a group of bicycle makers, the Republicans constructed a reviewing stand. This was necessary because the delegations were no longer able to press through the crowd to reach the porch. One crowd encompassed seven distinct delegations. A railroad agent informed the newspapers that more than thirty-eight hundred people arrived on a single railroad on October 3, not counting the delegations that traveled on two other railroads also serving the city.[10] This was enough visitors to overwhelm the small city.

In his speech to the gigantic group of seven delegations, McKinley stressed a return to "normal prosperity." This implied that the times were not normal in 1896. He told the audience that they carried "the same sacred principles in your hearts."[11] In another speech on that bustling day, McKinley stressed the importance of restoring the nation to its time of prosperity. He commented that "we have good money in the United States, and we propose to have that stay with us too." McKinley warned his listeners not "to adopt the Mexican and Chinese system of finance," by which he presumably meant silver coinage.[12] (It is interesting that each candidate attacked the other's financial policies as foreign.)

In every political campaign, there seems to come a moment of unexpected but revealing honesty. In a speech to a group of Union veterans, McKinley began by discussing the sacrifices of war and the value of liberty. He informed his audience of an upcoming delegation of Confederate veterans, "who will bring me testimony of their devotion to the great principles for which, *temporarily,* I stand" (emphasis added).[13] Perhaps McKinley slipped because he was feeling guilty about his turnabout on the silver issue; perhaps the reporter simply transcribed the speech wrongly. But this obscure comment laid bare the real nature of the campaign by both candidates—to advocate any position that seemed likely to yield an election victory. Perhaps McKinley admitted, for a moment, that the timeliness of his campaign was wholly artificial.

The development of the times continued to be a theme that day when McKinley spoke to a group of Pennsylvania farmers. He implied a need to return to the wisdom of the past, the classic approach of the ceremonial speaker. He advised the delegation that "the wisdom of the statesmanship of Hamilton and Blaine was unheeded in 1892." McKinley also warned the group of the danger to the farmer of free trade and inflated currency.[14]

A few days later, driven from his open-air reviewing stand by inclement weather, McKinley spoke indoors to a group from Syracuse, New York. The crowd of several hundred arrived on a special train. They included a marching club. Wheelmen on bicycles rode up and down Market Street behind the marchers.[15] McKinley took some time to give his views about political persuasion. "It is their intelligence," he said of the citizens who supported Democrats, "we seek to reach; it is their sober judgment we invoke; it is their patriotism to which we appeal." McKinley continued that "it is to persuade, not to abuse, which is the object of rightful public discussion." He drove this home by hoping that Americans would "reflect before they add either dishonor to our credit or our currency."[16] This whole discussion may have been an oblique criticism of Bryan's emotionally charged rhetoric. It is ironic, however, considering the lack of detailed argument in McKinley's speeches.

This speech continued McKinley's appeal to the needs and issues of the times. He reviewed the "prosperity" that Syracuse enjoyed "under a protective system," citing some economic statistics to support his point. He then continued: "What her condition has been since 1890 you know better than I, but your beautiful city is, indeed, most fortunate if it has escaped the business depression and wreck of trade." Finally, McKinley advised them to return to the wisdom of the past: "We must return to that policy which gave us such wonderful triumphs in manufacturing." This is an interesting rhetorical technique, for true arguments from tradition usually assert the tradition but do not prove that the traditions are valid. In contrast to Bryan, this is exactly what McKinley did.

McKinley thus continued to display the attitude of a ceremonial speaker. He then apologized for the poor weather and excused himself so that he could address the next delegation.[17]

As the month continued, McKinley still stood on the tariff and sound money. When he did refer to other issues from Bryan's platform or his own, he did so briefly and quickly turned them back to his main themes. For example, he advised a delegation from Goodland, Indiana, that the government should raise funds by taxing imports, not by taxing internal income. Thus he was able to dispense with the income tax in a few words while concentrating on his own pro-tariff ground.[18] He once again pointed out the critical nature of the times: "We are engaged *this year* in a great national contest, the result of which will determine *for years to come* the public policies which shall govern this country" (emphasis added).[19]

Excitement for the McKinley candidacy surged on October 10. Forty special trains brought delegations to Canton, temporarily swelling its population to the breaking point. McKinley and his family reviewed hours of parades, the Canton Troop marching in front.[20] The speechmaking became so tightly scheduled that McKinley had to apologize to one group while he turned to the other side of the reviewing stand to speak to the next group, which was already waiting.[21] The crush of the crowds seems to have contributed to the impression that McKinley's election was inevitable.

McKinley continued to develop his theme that the campaign was a timely struggle against the Democratic-silver-free trade conspiracy. Commenting that one delegation combined traveling salespersons from Ohio and Missouri, McKinley asserted that "there is one thing glorious about our campaign *this* year—it is national in character" (emphasis added). He continued: "This year, as in all the years of the future, I trust we have no North, no South, no East, no West (cries of "Good, good,") but union and union forever." As if this call for unity were not clear enough, McKinley added that "this year patriotism is above party."[22] His views of the times came to the fore again in a brief speech the same day to a delegation from Indiana, who heard the Republican candidate tell them that "I am glad to know that in this vast throng no voice of repudiation is heard and that *this year,* as in 1880, when you voted for the distinguished and illustrious Garfield (Applause), you will vote *this year* for the same party and the same principles, which they represented" (emphasis added).[23]

He told a group of traveling salespeople that "nobody knows sooner than the commercial travelers whether times are good or bad." McKinley cautioned them about the evil of the times, asserting: "Business has been stopped, the wheels of industry are not running, idle men are on the streets." He continued that "you are not doing as well as you were in 1892. (Cries of 'That's right,' and 'No, sir, we are not.')" McKinley assured them that he hoped for "a return to the splendid prosperity of four years ago."[24]

The depression, McKinley's theme ran, was a serious problem, and loyal Americans should look to help their own before helping those overseas. On that same busy October 10, a group of steelworkers from Cleveland listened to McKinley tell them "we should look after our own people (great applause and cries of 'That's the stuff,') before we look after the people of other lands." He related this to the issue of the times, stating that "I hope and fervently pray that we will enter upon an era of prosperity."[25] He tied these themes together further in a short speech to a delegation from Pittsburgh: "This is a year when partyism counts for but little and when patriotism counts for everything." This assertion was a bit odd, following as it did mere seconds upon McKinley's advocacy of "Republican party, Republican principles, sound money and a protective tariff," but all the same it characterized the 1896 election as a time for patriotism.[26]

Similarly, McKinley told the Polish Club of Cleveland that he welcomed them to "this great fight of 1896 for a protective tariff, for a good currency, for peace and law and order, and the triumph of right and justice."[27] He advised another delegation that the protective tariff could be tied back to the 1856 document that founded the Republican Party.[28] The day ended with a lively speech in which McKinley interacted with the cheers of a group of railroad workers, finally telling them that "you are the last to come, for they have been coming since 8 o'clock this morning."[29]

The theme of urgency recurred a few days later as McKinley delivered a speech to a delegation from McDonald, Pennsylvania. The group of several hundred, said the newspaper reports, included oil and coal workers, farmers, and "a number of ladies." They brought with them a band and the "McDonald McKinley and Hobart club, gaily uniformed."[30] McKinley welcomed them "as valuable allies in the great contest in which we are engaged for national honor, for public morals, for good currency, and a protective policy." Laying stress on the inexorable nature of the campaign, McKinley said: "Nothing has long impeded our march."[31]

Indeed, the very existence of the Front Porch campaign had long since become evidence of its timeliness. This implied reasoning ran in a circle, but ceremonial rhetoric does not feature logic. On Saturday, October 17, McKinley's hometown Republican newspaper reported that the candidate "spoke almost without interruption during the day, and he spoke half a dozen times after the glare of electric light was turned upon his lawn." Delegations assembled on all sides of the house. Music from the bands of other delegations interrupted speeches. One group carried a banner that read: "What Bryan wants is a fat office, 16 to 1 he won't get it." The article trumpeted that the crowds were "unparalleled in the Political History of the World."[32] This exaggerated claim suggested public excitement reaching such a peak that McKinley was not merely going to be elected but rather proclaimed.

With the arrival of about five hundred train cars full of energetic supporters, McKinley again gave up his porch and spoke from the reviewing stand.[33] It is impossible to give more than a flavor of the content of McKinley's speaking on that busy day. His speeches began to sound a bit frayed at the edges, as if the candidate had too little time to prepare them. He told a group from Ohio that "Good honest dollars hurt nobody."[34] During one speech, he assured his listeners that "there is no conflict—natural conflict between the men who work and the men who employ them." He wearily advised them that "I have already addressed eighteen to twenty delegations to-day."[35] In a very brief speech, he told another group that "I have spoken many times today and if I read your banners right it is very evident to me you do not need any further argument."[36] He mistakenly stated that a group from Cuyahoga County, Ohio, was from nearby Summit County.[37]

Nonetheless, several speeches from that Saturday developed the campaign's themes with clarity and force. Furthermore, McKinley continually stressed the significance of the times, presenting his candidacy as the solution to the situation that the times presented to the nation. This became a theme of his speech to the Garfield Club of Louisville, Kentucky. Early in the speech, McKinley cited those famous Kentuckians Clay and Tilden on the subject of the tariff. Although this was in part a device to appeal to the delegation, it also placed McKinley's views into the traditions of the nation. He continued to weave themes of timeliness into his rhetoric: "We have put the past behind us," McKinley told the Kentuckians, the nation now had "no North, no South, no East, no West, but a perpetual Union of indestructible States." Making a subtle attack against Bryan's regionalism, McKinley continued "that there are no longer any sectional lines to divide us (great applause), and that we have but one flag—the glorious old stars and stripes (great cheering), the same our grand sires bore upon many a field." He warned his listeners that he did "not know, my fellow citizens, when it will be possible to bring back the prices of 1892." This speech also further emphasized the crisis of the times: "This is the hour and the era for the exhibition of the highest patriotism. (Applause.)"[38] This dramatic language, stressing timeliness so precisely, seems more appropriate for a national crisis such as imminent war than for the discussion of the gold standard or foreign trade policy.

Connected with this whole way of thinking was McKinley's persistent claim to go back to what he described as the wise policies of the past. This again is a fundamentally ceremonial appeal. McKinley told one of the October 17 delegations: "There is no danger of a workingman ever becoming a slave if he has American wages (three tremendous cheers), the wages he had from 1860 to 1890, under the glorious policy of a protective tariff."[39] In this statement, McKinley presumed his candidacy as a restoration of old times. In a much briefer speech on the same day, he told a delegation from West Virginia: "People . . . believed that involved in a republican [sic] triumph is public confidence and the restoration of better times."[40]

McKinley also placed himself in a historical context in a speech to a delegation from Grand Rapids, Michigan. He began by recalling a George Washington birthday celebration that he had attended in Grand Rapids. In a veiled allusion to a ritual of his

Methodist Episcopal faith, he termed that celebration a "great Republican love feast." Stressing that the Republican Party meant unity, McKinley assured his audience that "the Republican party ... can celebrate the anniversaries of all the great American statesmen, no matter to what party they may have belonged, who stood for the country and its honor." He even mentioned the names "of Jefferson, Jackson and Benton."[41]

This highly ceremonial praise led McKinley to move from the past into the present. He continued: "This year, it seems to me, Republicanism more than ever before, proud as has been its record in the past, [is] synonymous with patriotism and represents all that is best in the past records and teachings of all American parties and statesmen."[42] In this way McKinley pointed out the critical nature of the gathering crisis, while establishing a sense that his party could not fail to triumph.

Even at this late, highly emotional point in the campaign, McKinley continued to steer away from all divisions. In one interesting exchange on October 17, he said: "We want every mine in the country to be busy." A voice from the crowd called out, "Not the silver mines," to the laughter of the crowd. McKinley quickly retorted, "My friend says 'not silver mines.' (Renewed laughter.) We are willing that our silver mines shall be busy," and he continued for a few more sentences about the importance of the mines.[43] This appeal for unity, for universal prosperity, made for an interesting contrast to Bryan's typically competitive interactions with his audiences. McKinley, as usual, preferred to achieve identification with everyone.

In one of the month's last speeches, McKinley stressed the history-setting importance of the election as he told a visiting delegation that "the Republican Party occupies this year a post of most distinguished honor and responsibility." He continued: "It has been given to few parties in the history of the American Republic to take the position thus occupied by our grand old party to-day, standing, as it does, for country, sound currency, public honor, the supremacy of the law, and the great Federal courts."[44] In this way, with the election only a few days away, McKinley advised his auditors (as well as the newspaper readership) of the crucial nature of the times and assured them that this election fell at a critical moment.

The Republicans declared October 31, 1896, to be Flag Day. This was a time to honor the flag, to honor the country, to honor the veterans, to honor McKinley, to honor trade restrictions. It somehow all made perfect sense. McKinley's campaign had long since adopted the American flag as its symbol, and Marcus Hanna himself had initiated the drive to declare a special celebration in honor of the flag.[45] It certainly did not hurt the McKinley campaign to hold Flag Day a few days before the election. This timing neatly placed the Democrats and Populists in a double bind. They could not speak against Flag Day, which would be unpatriotic. Yet Flag Day was an obvious Republican contrivance. The Republicans had co-opted the times, at least for the day.

The Front Porch campaign reached a peak of excitement during its last few weeks. The growing tumult that filled Canton, the seemingly endless series of trains delivering fervent Republicans, the constant cheers, and the vast throngs that trampled the small city all conveyed an overwhelming feeling that the election result was preordained. As fully as did McKinley's words, the setting conveyed the theme that McKinley himself was rising to the crisis of the times.

In an obvious way, the stress on timeliness was an effort by McKinley to puff up the importance of his campaign. The nation was at peace and, despite the depression, was not in particularly bad shape, at least not for the long run. Bryan and McKinley both seemed to feel some need to inflame the passions of the voters: Bryan by stressing that free silver was an issue of the ordinary American, and McKinley by focusing on the dangers that Bryan's radical experiments meant for the nation. McKinley, by emphasizing to the voters that the need for their votes was urgent, that later would be too late, conveyed a perhaps contrived but nonetheless interesting sense of time.

The ancient concept of timeliness points out the need to put universal values to work in actual circumstances as a guide to practical action.[46] McKinley was not madly stumping the country for votes. Instead, he stayed at home while dozens upon dozens of delegations descended on Canton to endorse and cheer for their candidate. Furthermore, McKinley's rhetoric during this campaign was founded on a concept of time or timeliness that is difficult to express, much less to clarify, in the English language. It was not a matter of measurable time, *chronos,* but instead a concept of time that took on moral implications.

In his rhetoric, McKinley repeatedly advised his audiences that Election Day, 1896, was a critical moment in history. Logically this was a circular argument, for McKinley claimed the election to be critical precisely because it afforded the voters an opportunity to vote for him. Nonetheless, the entire atmosphere of the campaign, and the content of its rhetoric, contributed to an air of pending coronation, the notion that the time had come for McKinley's installation as president. The election was not to be a time of decision but a moment of predestined triumph. Combined with this implication was McKinley's promise to restore the nation to a time of past prosperity. He assured the voters that he was ready to accept the responsibilities that the times imposed upon him and that it was necessary for them to do their patriotic duty by voting for him in the upcoming election.

Can speeches like these, which offer minimal rational argument, yet be reasonable? To answer this, one must for a moment step aside to look at how people think reasonably. Raymie McKerrow distinguishes between *rational* thought, which reaches conclusions by analysis and calculation, and *reasonable* thought, which includes social means of making decisions. For example, one might adopt a practice because "this is the custom," in which case one's reasons are cultural. In contrast, one might adopt a practice in the belief that there are good reasons for it, in which case one engages in rational analysis.[47]

Cultural reasons, however, tend to be opaque. The reasons behind many traditions are long forgotten.[48] People may act as tradition dictates without understanding how the tradition evolved. Thus to say that a speaker cannot give rational arguments for a tradition does not prove that it is wrong.

Epideictic rhetoric embodies fundamental cultural values.[49] Rosenfield explains: "Far from forcing his ideas on an audience with cold logic, the orator charms his listeners; he enchants them so that they, *like him,* are 'attracted' to a mode of thinking."[50]

This is what McKinley was doing in his campaign speeches. He did not argue for values; he assumed them. His policies, and indeed his entire candidacy, became the application of those values. Ceremonial rhetoric often shows off or makes noticeable "what might otherwise remain unnoticed or invisible."[51] McKinley was not *arguing* that his candidacy was the timely solution to the nation's crisis; he *assumed* it; his speeches merely illuminated what the audience might have to take as obvious.

One might object that ceremonial rhetoric deals with the present, whereas politicians speak to the future. However, all speech intends to lead to action, and action "can only concern the future."[52] From that point of view, one might expect ceremonial forms to creep into political rhetoric.

McKinley's approach depended to the highest degree upon his prestige, his credibility as a speaker. Only a speaker who claimed a strong reputation could rely so exclusively on ceremonial themes. That McKinley could succeed with such a strategy suggests that his credibility prevailed over Bryan's. Bryan's argumentative strategy itself even began to seem weak—McKinley could assume and assert, while Bryan was desperately involved in logical refutation of McKinley's position. Thus McKinley's strategy put his candidacy in the forefront, with Bryan on the defensive. In modern terms McKinley was more presidential, an orator who could speak on his own authority.

Charles Larson distinguishes between the *pragmatic* style of language and the *unifying* style of language. *"Pragmatic persuaders,"* he explains, try to offer convincing persuasion to those who may not agree with them. *"Unifying persuaders,"* however, reinforce the beliefs of people who already believe what the speaker plans to say. Unifying persuaders do not find it necessary to rely so heavily on argumentative language. Among other tactics, a unifying persuader can appeal to the glorious times when things were better than they are now.[53]

This, of course, is what McKinley was up to. It was this quality of McKinley's rhetoric that enabled him to rely on ceremonial forms.

The nature of McKinley's audience made this approach possible, or at least made it more effective. McKinley's audiences generally went to a great deal of trouble to visit him. His own staff was able to exercise some control over the speaking situation in front of the candidate's house. Hecklers like the obnoxious Yale students who troubled Bryan were not likely to come and were likely to encounter a hostile environment if they did. The American population as a whole held diverse opinions about the campaign's candidates and issues, but McKinley's auditors tended to support him.

Thus when McKinley spoke to his visitors, he could assume that they agreed with him. Their very presence proved that they did. No close argument was needed to persuade them; at the most, they merely required support and encouragement for the beliefs that they already preferred.

This was entirely a strategy of identification. Near the end of the campaign, McKinley told a Canton audience that "I do not teach the doctrine of hate. I prefer the doctrine of hope. Never give up as long as you have the ballot."[54]

CHAPTER 10

The End of Bryan's First Battle

WHILE MCKINLEY'S SUPPORTERS were swarming into Canton to ratify their hero, an increasingly frustrated Bryan was trying to overcome his rival's appeals to time-honored policies and engage him in exactly the sort of point-by-point dialogue that McKinley had so studiously avoided. Not all political debating occurs in a setting in which both candidates stand on the same stage at the same time, pointing fingers at each other and reacting instantly to each other's arguments in exciting repartee. The ongoing exchanges during an election campaign can also constitute something like an extended debate. In his campaign speeches of October, 1896, Bryan employed such basic debating strategies as point-by-point refutation, argument by analogy, cause and effect reasoning, and appeal to the testimony of authorities. Even though the candidates never met face to face, Bryan treated the campaign like a debate. However, McKinley's refusal to respond in kind frustrated Bryan. All the same, Bryan's increasing reliance on refutation and insistence on close argument may have been inherently weak both as debating strategy and as political persuasion.

Bryan's speeches in this campaign thus reveal a much different speaker than the dogmatic, intellectual lightweight of *Inherit the Wind*. Bryan repeatedly acted more like a debater than like the blowhard political candidate that his critics so often pictured him to be. He relied on argumentative discourse to persuade the voters. Although it was nothing new for Bryan, the Democratic candidate's one-sided attempt to engage McKinley in a sort of ongoing debate became particularly noticeable during the last few weeks of the campaign. McKinley's campaign strategy was given more to ringing endorsements and bald appeals to patriotism than to open debate. One could equally question, however, whether Bryan's campaign, full of hurried whistle-stop speeches and bizarre demonstrations, was capable of stimulating systematic debate.

Bryan's reputation would not lead one to suspect that he preferred to debate. Early in the campaign the *Chicago Evening Post* called Bryan "the boy orator of the platitudes" rather than the more common "boy orator of the Platte."[1] Scholarly opinion about Bryan's intellectual stature in this campaign, and indeed his entire career, is mixed. Some who have written about him repeat the charge that Bryan was uninformed or that he presented few facts in his speechmaking, although it is occasionally noted that his congressional speeches were closely reasoned.[2] One authority notes that Bryan knew something about economics.[3] Thus Bryan's reputation gives little reason to suspect that the famous orator would turn out to be a debater at heart. Bryan's congressional speeches, one of which is briefly discussed in chapter 2, were strongly emotional, although they did indeed include facts, figures, and expert quotations.

"The fact the critic of argumentation must take into account," writes Edwin Black, is that one always finds "a protagonist and antagonist in the argumentative situation."[4] Surely this could be said of the 1896 campaign, but the matter is not as simple as that, because the two opponents did not follow the same rules.

Douglas Ehninger and Wayne Brockriede codify several assumptions about debate in their textbook *Decision by Debate*. Ehninger suggests that certain premises underlie the use of debate to settle controversies by critical thinking.[5] The idea behind the ancient Greek method of dialogue was that the careful testing of ideas, following prescribed conventions, was the best way to ensure their truth. Plato's dialogues are often presumed to be models of this process. These dialogues often begin with a question, followed by one character's answer to that question, followed by a discussion finding fault in that answer.

Theories about argumentation and dialogue usually endorse conclusions that survive testing in critical competition.[6] The idea behind debate contests, court trials, and other organized disputes seems to be that full, fair, and free discussion of the issues will lead an audience, or an impartial judge, or even the disputants themselves to reach the correct conclusions.

To such an end, Ehninger and Brockriede propose that (1) the two sides should "enter contrasting beliefs into full and fair competition, so their relative worth may be assessed" and (2) the debate should occur in two steps. In the first, the debaters make a constructive case for their own position, and in the second, they see if they can defend it against knowledgeable criticism. The debaters also tacitly agree not to reach an outcome until both sides have had a chance to lay out and defend their positions; and they agree on certain conditions by which a "judging agency" will consider the arguments and determine the victory.[7] Ehninger stresses that in debate both contestants have "an equal opportunity" to develop their ideas, that each debater asks "the other to set forth for public examination the facts and reasoning upon which that view is based.[8] Their assumptions are, one suspects, typical of those made by many debaters. In any case, Bryan appears to have had such notions in the back of his mind during the campaign, and particularly during this critical last month.

There is no question about McKinley and Bryan's joint acceptance of the democratic process, which placed the voters in the position of a judging agency. There was a considerable gap, however, in how McKinley and Bryan treated the dialectic of the campaign as expressed in Ehninger and Brockriede's first two premises. Bryan sought to state and prove his case while refuting the errors that he perceived in the views of his opponent and critics. But as the last chapter shows, McKinley seldom seemed to take a similar approach. In August, the Democratic Party attempted to interest McKinley in a joint debate appearance with Bryan, but the Republicans never took the offer seriously. One Republican newspaper explained McKinley's reluctance to debate as due to the Ohioan's desire to "preserve a dignified course during the campaign."[9] By this point it should be obvious that dignity was never the principal feature of the Front Porch campaign. Also, McKinley rarely made much effort in his usually brief Front Porch speeches to prove the validity of his policies, at least not in any depth.

McKinley refuted Bryan's arguments, if at all, only in elusive terms. A typical example occurred near the middle of October when he glibly advised a Polish-American audience that they were part of "this great fight of 1896 for a protective tariff, for a good currency, for peace and law and order, and the triumph of right and justice."[10] The reference to law and order implied, at most, a subtle attack against Bryan's advocacy of silver money and the income tax. (Since the Supreme Court had ruled against the income tax, its advocacy was presented as lawlessness.) Indeed, McKinley never mentioned Bryan's name in any campaign speech. Any cut-and-thrust debating in which McKinley engaged thus tended to be very elliptical.

Bryan, on the other hand, was eager for a scrap. Speaking on October 2 in Huntington, West Virginia, Bryan offered a series of fresh arguments on behalf of the free coinage of silver. Criticizing the Republican practice of using the vague term *sound money* rather than the more precise term *gold standard,* Bryan explained that "money may be good, splendid, but there may be none of it. (Applause.)" Bryan then offered an interesting analogy: "It is of money as it is of food. You have got to combine quality and quantity. Suppose that a person tried to feed himself on bread of the very best quality and yet not enough of it to sustain life. (Applause.)" Making the application, Bryan asserted that "the gold standard is of no advantage unless you can find enough gold to furnish the standard money." He continued that the gold bugs could not supply enough gold to back the currency, that "all over the world today the nations are scrambling to get all the gold there is."

A voice from the crowd cried out, apparently in agreement with Bryan: "There's only fourteen billion dollars." Bryan quickly retorted, "Fourteen billions? Only four billions, my friends, if the statistics furnished by the treasury department are correct." Carrying the point further, Bryan claimed that actually only about half of the nominal U.S. gold supply of $600 million could be accounted for.[11] Thus Bryan had at the tip of his tongue a quantity of statistical and economic information and used it to support his platform.[12] He was ready to engage in quick, point-by-point dialogue.

Bryan himself felt that his own rhetoric was the driving force behind his campaign. For example, en route to St. Louis the next day, he told a 7:00 A.M. crowd that he was "commencing today's work pretty early" because he felt that "we have to make up in public speaking and in hard work what we lack in daily newspapers and campaign funds for the circulation of litera-ture."[13] Bryan continued to insist that the "money issue," as he called it, was paramount over McKinley's tariff issue. Alluding to the Republican's insistence that bimetallism be adopted only by international agreement, Bryan stated that "until they put a prohibitory tariff on foreign financial policies they cannot talk tariff to me."[14] This implied that bimetallism should not wait for an international agreement, as was called for in the Republican platform.

Later that day Bryan's train made a brief stop in his birthplace, Salem, Illinois, where he told the waiting crowd that "if you heard any rumors of my failing health . . . they are from the enemy." Reaching St. Louis on October 3, Bryan spoke in an auditorium that had been packed to capacity for more than an hour before he arrived. After fifteen minutes of cheering from the crowd, Bryan praised Thomas Jefferson, whom the Democratic clubs organiz-ing the mass meeting had adopted as a symbol. He stressed that his policies were traditional: "We today can advance no new principles; we are seeking no new truths."[15]

In East St. Louis the same day, Bryan once again went head-to-head against his opponent in point-by-point refutation. He asserted that "we propose something; our opponents propose nothing." Responding directly to a claim of McKinley's, Bryan said: "Our opponents say, 'Open up the mills instead of the mints.'[16] Yes, my friends, you can open the mills as much as you want to, but if the people can't buy what the mills produce you will simply close the mills again."[17] This simple cause and effect argument directly attacked one of McKinley's assertions.

Bryan often complained that the advocates of gold not only failed to argue but even used language to obfuscate their policies. The "full and fair competition" of debate called for by Ehninger and Brockriede, one assumes, would feature a forthright statement of one's position.[18] Wenzel finds "candidness" to be the purpose of the dialectical perspective on argument.[19] McKinley's lack of candidness seemed to disturb Bryan.

Swinging down into Tennessee, Bryan's train arrived in Mem-phis, where he initially put forward some more cause and effect reasoning: "The gold standard gives us a rising dollar and a rising dollar means bondage, distress, and misery." He then took issue with the candidness of McKinley's terminology: "They call the gold dollar an honest dollar. They know it is not an honest dollar and those who love that dollar most love it because it is the most dishonest dollar the world has ever seen." Bryan asserted that "an honest dollar would be a dollar of which the purchasing power would be stable; a dollar which rises in purchasing power is as dishonest as one which falls in purchasing power." He reiterated that "quantity in money is as essential as quality."[20] In this way, Bryan was not refuting the gold advocates' position but was instead complaining about their failure to observe conventions of proper debating.

This would not be the last time that Bryan expressed distress at his opponents' unwillingness to state their position precisely. On October 6 he gave five speeches in Indianapolis. Speaking at the Indiana Statehouse, after attacking the pro-gold Democrats, Bryan asserted: "The gold standard never fought an open fight. It carries the knife of the assassin and does its work behind the mask of a burglar." He complained that the gold standard "is not an open enemy, never was and never will be."[21]

Bryan's hopes notwithstanding, this may not have been an ideal forum for rational discourse and subtle argument. A wire service reporter estimated that "less than one-fourth of the audience heard his speech, but those who were able to get within the sound of his voice were enthusiastic to a degree."[22] The same day, on a train through Indiana, Bryan stopped in Seymour and told the waiting throng that "the people of the west have been paying an exorbitant interest to the east until they are impoverished."[23]

A few days later Bryan took time to attack McKinley personally for hypocrisy. This may have been argument *ad hominem,* but argument it was. At an early morning whistle-stop speech in Burlington, Iowa, a local committee met Bryan at the station and organized a parade to the local Coliseum, complete with mounted police, a band, a carriage for the candidate, women on horseback, more bands, and uniformed silver clubs who had organized to serve at such occasions. After several minutes of cheering, and some heckling from local Republicans, Bryan restated the principles of the bimetallist platform. A voice from the crowd called out, "Hurrah for McKinley." Bryan's supporters hissed, to which Bryan retorted, "My friends, I beg you to refrain from any manifestations of displeasure."

He said he was happy to hear from McKinley's supporter, and asked: "Which McKinley he is for, the McKinley of 1890 or the McKinley of 1896?" Bryan then quoted from McKinley's 1890 speech in favor of bimetallism and McKinley's 1891 speech in favor of an increased money supply. In this manner, Bryan turned a potentially ugly, emotional scene into an opportunity for refutation. After this sharp bit of on-the-spot debating, Bryan commented, "My friends, they tell you they want sound money. If they were honest instead of using ambiguous phrases they would tell you what kind of money they thought was good, but they do not say that."[24]

On October 8 Bryan delivered several short speeches while railroading through Iowa. In Sioux Falls he appealed once again to tradition, discussing the "ancient place" of silver money. He again criticized McKinley's use of terms like *honest money*, pointing out that any witness in court who uses "ambiguous phrases" or "words of double meaning" is open to fair criticism. He expressed disapproval of his opponents who said "sound money" instead of "gold." Criticizing "that deceptive phrase, 'sound money,'" Bryan reiterated that "no dollar is honest which rises in value."[25] In this way, Bryan countered his opponents' shifty nonargument with a line of reasoning about what is honest.

Whirling into Fargo, North Dakota, on October 10, Bryan turned the tables on the Republican Party, whose platform advocated bimetallism by international agreement, stating that they wished to "get rid of the gold standard and to substitute the double standard just as soon as other nations will let us." If bimetallism is good, Bryan explained, the nation should have it now and permanently.[26]

A Sunday of rest and church going for Bryan followed.[27] This provided an occasion for Catholic Archbishop John Ireland to speak against silver money: "I stand by the platform and the presidential candidate of the Republican convention."[28] Bryan was not the sort to turn the religious advantage over to the gold bugs. He got back to campaigning on October 12. At the Exposition Hall in Minneapolis, Bryan quoted the Bible in favor of helping the poor.[29] Needless to say, Bryan implied that bimetallism would benefit the poor. In Duluth a day later, he advised his audience to elect a pro-silver Congress and reasserted: "The money question is paramount in this campaign." He again complained of the Republicans' failure to state their position forthrightly: "My friends, we have been compelled to wage warfare against deception. Our opponents have not come out in the open field." He promised that if his opponents had openly advocated the gold standard, they "would have been answered by the protest" of the population.[30]

Earlier on October 13, Bryan had flurried through several Minnesota towns on the incongruously named railroad car "Idler." During his brief appearance in St. Cloud a few hecklers called out. Bryan expressed happiness to see them, as soon the advocates of the Republican platform would "be so few, that he will draw a high price when they come around and want him for a museum."[31] In Little Falls, speaking from a platform near the tracks, Bryan returned to a slightly less personal form of rhetoric and proclaimed: "Truth is truth and right is right even if they don't have bankers and railroad presidents on their side."[32]

In Minneapolis Bryan appeared before an audience of women and asserted: "I believe this is the first political meeting where a candidate has addressed his remarks to ladies entirely in the discussion of an economic question. . . . I deem it a great honor." He spoke to them rather eloquently about hard times: "Go into the house where the mortgage has been foreclosed; go into the homes where the husband and wife started out with that laudable ambition to own a home, where they paid down with what they had saved and expected to pay the balance." He lamented that the gold standard and the depression had taken their homes from them. Bryan told his audience that the financial magnates had gained what the families had sacrificed. He continued at length upon the importance and virtue of "the common people."[33] Thus Bryan presented thoughtful arguments on behalf of his policy. This attitude made an interesting contrast with McKinley's earlier rhetoric to a women's group, in which the Republican candidate, avoiding all discussion of campaign issues, had averred that: "It is in the quiet and peaceful walks of life where her [woman's] power is greatest and most beneficial."[34]

Bryan's tendency to employ debating tactics sometimes led him to take a defensive posture. He stressed his ideology when he told an audience in Watersmeet, Michigan, that "this is not a matter of personality, my friends. Candidates stand for ideas."[35] He defended himself against the charge that he was an agitator: "Agitation is the result of a condition, and when you remedy that condition you will stop agitation, and not before."[36] Cause and effect statements of this kind may have been cogent and helpful responses to the slanders that the Republicans and pro-gold Democrats had repeatedly heaped upon the young Nebraskan orator but were nonetheless so defensive in quality that they may have called more attention to the calumnies.

The "honest dollar" controversy came up again during a short speech at Petroskey, Michigan, on October 15 at 5:30 A.M. The newspaper reported that many of the early risers in the audience wore yellow badges, presumably symbolizing gold, inscribed with the legend "An Honest Dollar." Bryan asked the seemingly unreceptive members of the crowd to explain whether the term "honest dollar" meant a silver dollar or a gold dollar. A friendly voice called out "sixteen to one," and Bryan, apparently feeling that his point was made, moved to another topic.[37]

In the Traverse City speech, Bryan continued to argue the issues. He explained that "the gold standard means that money shall be dearer, and money cannot be dearer unless property is cheaper." He continued that the gold standard would thus lead to hard times and that no candidate would advocate hard times. He supported this cause and effect argument by quoting yet again from McKinley's 1890 pro-silver speech.[38]

Although relentless in his arguments, Bryan presented his rhetoric in an often irrational context. A newspaper sketch published at about this time showed a scene from a Bryan whistle-stop speech. The sketch shows Bryan standing on the rear platform of a train car. Gathered on the tracks and around the train stand a crowd of men in hats, some with their arms raised as if to cheer. Three other men are crowded onto the platform with Bryan. He is wearing a suit with a vest and is gesturing with one hand.[39] It is difficult to imagine that much close reasoning could be communicated in such a setting. This scene cannot have been entirely typical, however, for newspaper reports repeatedly describe Bryan as speaking from a temporary platform or nearby public park.

Furthermore, odd, highly nonargumentative irrelevancies continually crept into the campaign. As Bryan came into Ohio, a Cleveland department store advertised the "First Great Bargain Bulletin of the Campaign," offering for sale various items of clothing.[40] The Democratic, pro-silver *Cleveland Plain Dealer* complained about Republican National Committee Chairman Marcus Hanna's declaration of Flag Day on McKinley's behalf, terming it a "desecration."[41]

In the midst of this commotion Bryan continued his efforts to bring arguments to the voters' attention. Traveling through Lima, Ohio, he spoke from a park bandstand: "We not only believe in sound money, but we tell you what we mean by sound money." He urged his supporters to participate in Flag Day right along with McKinley's supporters.[42]

Steaming into Dayton, Bryan asserted his superiority in argument and criticized his opponents for personal attacks. He claimed victory in the campaign's debate: "We have forced the battle on the money question and after we have made an answer to every argument that can be advanced in favor of the present financial system; after we have driven the advocates of a foreign policy from the field, they then turn and try to abandon the money fight and appeal to the people to save the country from Anarchists." Bryan defiantly continued: "Those who stand upon the [Democratic] Chicago platform are not Anarchists." Continuing on that theme, Bryan asserted that he stood "for those policies which are democratic in the broadest sense of that term. (Applause.)" To support this claim that his ideas were traditional, Bryan again cited Thomas Jefferson and Andrew Jackson.[43] Then in Rochester, Pennsylvania, Bryan digressed to discuss the income tax plank from the Democratic platform.[44]

Bryan may well have been right that he had offered refutations of the pro-gold arguments. Nonetheless, McKinley's refusal to respond with precise cut-and-thrust refutation of his own rendered Bryan's victory hollow: Bryan won the debate about the money issue not by superior argument but by default, because McKinley refused to debate at all.

As Bryan approached Akron, Ohio, the Democratic committee busied itself decorating the city for him, supposedly with bipartisan support from the local merchants.[45] Arriving in Akron on October 20, Bryan encountered such huge crowds that he had to give up on his planned appearances at lecture halls and instead gave four speeches at downtown's Grace Park. A parade honored the candidate.[46] When Bryan headed east to Ravenna, Ohio, several local Democratic dignitaries joined him on the train.

In Youngstown, Bryan reasserted his appeal to tradition: "We stand for the money of the constitution."[47] In Fort Wayne, Indiana, on October 21, Bryan told an audience at the Princess skating rink that the only real issue in the campaign was gold versus silver, that his opponents "propose nothing; they present no plan, they offer no relief." This was essentially a complaint that McKinley and his supporters were not engaging the issue. In another speech in Fort Wayne on the now familiar theme, Bryan advised his audience to consider why his opponents said "sound money" instead of "gold standard."[48]

By the next day, it turned out that the Indiana Democratic Committee, which controlled the candidate's itinerary in that state, had scheduled Bryan for nineteen speeches in a twenty-four-hour period. The scheduling pressure seemed to energize his speaking. In Peru, Indiana, Bryan quoted in depth from the writings on monetary policy of J. Laurence Laughlin, identified as a professor "of the Chicago university" (presumably another reference to Laughlin's book opposing bimetallism). In Delphi, Bryan again quoted at length from McKinley's 1890 pro-silver speech. In Lafayette, speaking alternately from three sides of the courthouse, Bryan criticized a pro-gold speech by Benjamin Harrison, who had been elected on a bimetallist platform, Bryan said.[49] A day later, speaking at the Tabernacle in Peoria, Illinois, Bryan criticized an anti-gold disturbance at a pro-gold speech given by Secretary of the Treasury John Carlisle.[50]

Bryan then turned again to economic arguments. He cited a recent increase in European interest rates as due to the insufficient stock of gold. He warned that overseas governments and banks had a "string to that gold" and could affect the business of the United States "whenever they want to by jerking out the foundations from under our system." Then, without offering proof, he accused the New York banks of "receiving their instructions from their London correspondents."[51]

Speaking at the Armory in Chicago on October 27, Bryan found himself once more arguing on the defensive, denying that he was an anti-Semite or a demagogue.[52] The next day he gave a series of speeches in Chicago. At St. Stanislaus hall he spoke to an audience of several thousand, the majority of whom were reported to be women. He spoke about the good judgment of women on vital issues and stated that if he could convince the women, nothing could deny him the votes of "the husbands and the brothers and the sons."[53]

The same day, back at the Armory on the Chicago lakefront, Bryan offered additional close reasoning for his position. He told a shoulder-to-shoulder crowd of businessmen: "Wealth must be created before it can be distributed. . . . You could not live if the producers of wealth go out of business." He presented interesting arguments, well adapted to the audience. For example, he complained again about the "deception" of those advocating the gold standard and made an analogy to the audience's line of endeavor: "Do you have to resort to deception when you are selling something which has merit? Not at all." He also criticized the practice of taking foreign bonds, arguing that "if we need money from abroad, it is conclusive proof that we have not enough money in this country." He denied the common allegation that bimetallism would mean the repudiation of debts. He spoke for the rights of debtors.[54]

Bryan continued to refute his opposition. At one campaign stop, he spoke coldly of those who worried about the safety of their bonds: "You say that that is repudiation. I deny it. They bought our bonds only a short time ago and they made a difference between coin bonds and gold bonds, charging for the risk they took, and now let them have the risk they were paid for."[55] This argument may have been economically sound, but it could not have endeared him to securities investors.

Canvassing Illinois towns by train on October 29, Bryan defended himself against various criticisms.[56] In Elgin, he mentioned a book of the 1850s by an economist named Chevalier and concluded that "you will find the identical arguments used against silver now were used against gold then."[57] At Rockford,

Bryan mentioned that England had been bimetallist before 1816. This may have established that the English were hypocritical to advocate the gold standard, or perhaps that the gold standard had an honorable history. He then quoted from a speech that "Hon. William Lathrop of this city made in the house of representatives on Feb. 14, 1879" in favor of silver. Bryan mockingly asked, "Was this the speech of a demagogue? Was this the speech of an Anarchist?"[58] Like many of Bryan's arguments, this point met at least some standard of argumentative proof, but the implied conclusion, once again, may have been defensive rather than constructive. Bryan seems to have been saying that reputable politicians had advocated silver, proving that Bryan was himself a reputable politician. In Freeport, rain drove Bryan indoors to speak, where he told his audience that "Washington, in his farewell address, warned the people of this country against the evil effects of foreign influences."[59] This attacked the position in the Republican platform that the nation should adopt bimetallism only by international agreement.

Bryan returned to St. Stanislaus to speak that evening. To invite his audience to serve as rational judges of the free silver dispute, he told the group of Polish Americans there: "You have heard arguments, you have studied the question and as if events themselves were coming to our aid in this great currency struggle, you have read only in the evening's papers how scarce money is in New York, where they tell us there is enough and to spare." He mentioned the sharp rise in interest rates. Bryan reiterated that "there is not money enough in this country to do the business of the country."[60]

On October 30, with the campaign nearing its end (October 31 was Sunday, and the election was Tuesday), Bryan swept through the doubtful state of Wisconsin, giving almost all of his speeches from the back of his train car. On Monday he delivered a large number of speeches during his return to Nebraska, although he noted that "the meetings were so short that no extended argument was possible."[61]

Most particularly, Bryan repeatedly attempted to engage his opponents in a rational discussion of the issues. He stated his views in succinct, precise terms. He sometimes quoted academic and political authorities to support his views. He brought up data about interest rates, although less frequently and less specifically than he had done earlier in the campaign. Over and over, he railed against the ambiguity of "honest money." He complained that the advocates of gold should do as he did—state forthrightly what program they advocated and give the reasons for it. He advised his audiences to weigh the pros and cons of the arguments on both sides. Yet speaking forums that featured hurried comments made from the rear of a train with a schedule to keep, mass outdoor crowds so huge that many people could not hear, and a general atmosphere of bustle and conflict may not have been well adapted to the kind of dialectic Bryan had in mind.

Although the Republicans distributed extensive popular literature about the money issue, McKinley himself had largely devoted his speeches to warm, friendly comments about his audience combined with vague discussions of the issues.[62] This obviously frustrated Bryan, who must have felt that he was debating against an opponent who refused to fight but who was winning just the same.

The typical objective of political rhetoric is to gain election to public office, and this was most certainly Bryan's goal. At the same time, Bryan gave every impression of wishing to win not only votes but minds. He seemed to feel that he could defeat the advocates of the gold standard in point-by-point argumentation. McKinley refused to play by Bryan's rules and yet ultimately won the election. McKinley rarely tried to prove his points by research or close argument and seldom gave specific attention to Bryan's arguments. Thus the testing of argument that Ehninger and Brockriede consider essential to debating never fully developed during this campaign. Bryan felt that an exchange of ideas would lead to the triumph of his views. The Republican Party issued a considerable amount of "educational" campaign literature. Nevertheless, with McKinley unwilling to debate, either face to face or otherwise, and given the realities of how the campaign was being conducted, it is doubtful whether a dialectical exchange really took place.

Many of Bryan's arguments continued to be defensive rather than constructive. He attacked his opponents for their hypocrisy and flip-flopping, often with more energy than he used to advocate his own positions. He directed his proofs less to a claim such as "silver money is good" than to a claim like "I, William J. Bryan, am neither a revolutionary nor an anarchist." Thus, these refutations did not prove Bryan's case. They aimed at character questions, so important in a presidential campaign but irrelevant to the dialectic that Bryan wished to conduct. The slanders stung Bryan, who commented after the election that "as the campaign drew to a close the canards increased in number and variety." Bryan complained about the appeals to religious prejudice and pointed out contradictions among the charges raised against him. In Madison, Wisconsin, during the closing days of the campaign, he took out time to speak against the charge that he belonged to an anti-Catholic organization.[63] Nonetheless, Bryan soon after commented that "I look back with much satisfaction to the fact that the four political contests through which I have passed, two successfully and two unsuccessfully, have been free from personalities."[64]

The custom in debating is that the advocate of change must prove a constructive case in favor of that change. From the standpoint of the theory of debating, this can be traced at least back to the eighteenth-century British author Richard Whately, who suggests that "there is a Presumption in favour of every existing institution." This does not imply that existing institutions are good, Whately makes clear—merely that as a matter of order and common sense the burden of proof lies with the advocate of change.[65] An advocate of change, particularly a change as radical as bimetallism was perceived to be, needs to offer to the adjudicators of the matter, the voters, a convincing argument. Bryan's personal attacks and personal defenses could not accomplish such a purpose.

Given Bryan's implicit attempt to engage McKinley and the gold bugs in debate, a certain portion of his rhetoric certainly should consist of the refutation of his opponents' views. Nonetheless, in advocating ideas that much of the public perceived to be a major change in economic policy, Bryan needed to overcome the presumption in favor of the monetary policy then in effect. To do so required making positive arguments in favor of the proposed change. Furthermore, it was not entirely issue-oriented defense. The feeling that the Republicans were on the attack put Bryan in a weak position, even if (as is surely true) the Republicans' attacks against Bryan's character were insupportable.

Similarly, Bryan's appeals to tradition seemed just a little out of the ordinary. Genuine arguments from tradition start by assuming the tradition. Tradition implies an almost unthinking transmission of ideas from generation to generation. The wisdom of the past comes down to us in the present. If a speaker needs to prove that X, Y, and Z are actually traditions, then they probably are not. People normally have no need to argue about whether something is a tradition. If circumstances have changed, of course, traditions become outdated and irrelevant. Bryan repeatedly offered proof that his positions were traditional. As fate had it, a majority of the voters did not accept that line of reasoning.

Just as McKinley tended to rely on what Larson might call a unifying style, so Bryan was forced into a pragmatic style. Typical methods of the pragmatic style include the use of language that is "concrete," a reliance on "facts instead of images." Pragmatic persuaders, explains Larson, focus on "immediate problems familiar to the audience." Curiously, Larson comments that "their language is concrete and prosaic."[66] Although Bryan's speech was concrete, few would call him prosaic.

His reputation as an eloquent, firebrand orator notwithstanding, Bryan's speaking in this campaign, especially near the last days, was much more notable for argument and reasoning than for fiery language. Although he retained his extraordinary ability to strike to the heart of an issue with a single well-chosen phrase, his October speeches contained relatively little of the high mode of rhetorical expression. At the Democratic convention, he had been speaking to true believers and could rely on the unifying style. Touring the country, however, Bryan faced diverse and often hostile audiences. He did not enjoy McKinley's luxury of being able to speak exclusively to friendly visitors. This may explain, at least in part, Bryan's habitual reliance on debating strategies as well as his frustration when McKinley refused to join the contest as Bryan had defined it. In contrast to McKinley's more or less ceremonial style, Bryan saw the campaign as an opportunity to prove his points and refute McKinley's points.

For these reasons, Bryan the debater could well have triumphed argument by argument and yet failed to make a compelling case for his election to the presidency. Bryan was not, however, the sort of person to lie down and give up. Shortly after the election, he published *The First Battle,* to show that the fight for silver had just begun.

Conclusion

Identification and Timeliness Revisited

CKINLEY WON a convincing victory in the November 3 election. The Democratic *Kansas City Star* grudgingly admitted that "the victory of yesterday was distinctly non-partisan," pointing out that McKinley won the votes "of states which have not been anything but Democratic for more than a quarter of a century."[1] McKinley's tactics of identification and unity seem to have been antidotes to Bryan's rhetoric of hostility and division.

As discussed in chapter 9, McKinley used timeliness as a line of argument. The ancient Greeks, in contrast, thought timeliness was a critical element of rhetoric: to speak at the right time, to say the right things at the right part of a speech.[2] It was in this kind of timeliness, the older conception of the idea, that McKinley bested Bryan. This rhetorical quality became apparent with the candidates' efforts to identify with or separate themselves from the voters.

Many persons falsely assume that the Greek philosophers favored moderation; that is, to do everything a little but not a great deal. Nothing could be farther from the truth. To an ancient Greek, the correct amount of food to eat would indeed be moderate, neither too much nor too little. The correct amount of exercise is moderate, neither so much as to cause injury nor so little as to cause feebleness. However, the right amount of adultery is none. The right amount of theft is none. The right amount of happiness is a great deal. Along these lines, the right time is not the time in the middle but rather the time that is best.

The timing of the rhetoric in relation to election day became critical. Both candidates in this election had something to say; however, neither was running for office solely to make an ideological point. Both men wanted to be elected. McKinley, an experienced and confident politician, understood almost instinctively the importance of appealing to a large coalition of voters. Skillfully wrapping himself in the flag, repeatedly explaining that the whole nation would benefit from his rather vague policies, McKinley said as few things as possible that might offend any voters. He attempted to establish identification between himself and almost everything good: the flag, the country, patriotism, prosperity, labor, capital. With ever-increasing crowds of ardent supporters traveling to Canton, McKinley's campaign reached its fervent peak shortly before voting day. His speeches in October were not quite as good as those he gave in September, but the vigor of the campaign hit its highest point just before the election.

McKinley's campaign also used time in another way. In a sense, his campaign speeches gave the impression of timelessness. That is, the key themes of his campaign never changed. Within a few days after Bryan's nomination, McKinley settled on the sound money and the protective tariff. He rarely allowed any other issues to interject themselves into his rhetoric. He relied on the same characteristic turns of phrase—something like, "not only do they want to deny work to American labor, but they also want to reduce the value of the worker's wages"—which he repeated, over and over, with just enough variation to keep people interested. Thus McKinley's Front Porch campaign gave the impression of a crescendo, with the campaign gradually reaching its peak focused on the same two issues with which it had begun. The cumulative effect of his rhetoric was thus more powerful than any individual speech.

McKinley's Front Porch campaign capitalized on Bryan's divisive approach. For example, as noted earlier, McKinley had stated in a campaign speech: "The attempt to inflame the passions of the west and south against the east is, therefore, but a mischievous and unpatriotic effort to arouse prejudice and hatred against men of their own calling."[3]

Bryan, on the other hand, acted as if he wanted not only to win but also to convert the entire nation to his way of thinking. Nonetheless, Bryan was quick—too quick—to dismiss as "enemies" anyone who disagreed with him. It became too difficult for him to gain the support of fence sitters, for his radical-sounding rhetoric seems to have scared too many people right off the fence. Thus in this election, identification proved to be a more powerful strategy than was division. Remarking about the extent of the "conservative victory," the *Kansas City Star* also urged against Bryan's divisive tactics: "There should be an end of the always foolish and mischievous talk about the West and the East and the enemy's country. The result has been brought about by the vote of the great Center."[4] That a Democratic, western paper would go to the extent of mimicking McKinley's characteristic phrasing clearly shows how persuasive the Republican candidate's rhetoric had been—not only about the correct positions on the issues but, more important, in stealing Bryan's thunder and building the framework about what the issues really were.[5]

The *Review of Reviews,* a magazine that gave thoughtful and relatively unbiased political commentary, remarked near the end of the 1896 campaign that "Mr. William Jennings Bryan has immeasurably surpassed everything in the history of oratorical political canvasses by his stumping of the United States." Its editors estimated that he had averaged about five speeches a day, although some of them were brief. They speculated that in West Virginia, perhaps half of the voters had heard Bryan speak. Yet they noted, quite correctly, that as the campaign continued Bryan became "more bitter."[6] They also noted that without the printing press, "the orator's words could reach but a limited number."[7] This was certainly true, but Bryan's habit of repeating characteristic phrases and arguments reduced the appeal of his campaign to newspaper editors, who naturally wished to have news every day. McKinley also repeated characteristic phrases, but he managed to put just enough variety into his presentations to avoid boring the news reporters.

As the campaign ended, the *Review of Reviews* noted—perhaps a little too sanguinely—that "all of these speeches have been reported and published in the newspapers."[8] Even Republican and pro-gold Democratic newspapers published abbreviated accounts, and sometimes texts, of Bryan's campaign oratory.[9]

Bryan's loss of the Solid South, the traditional loyalty of former slave states to the Democratic Party, is not consistent with a claim that his campaign met with remarkable success. In October a Republican newspaper attributed the swing toward McKinley in Maryland and other doubtful states to the defection of pro-gold Democrats.[10] Bryan became the first Democratic candidate since the end of Reconstruction to lose the former slave-holding states of Kentucky, West Virginia, Maryland, and Delaware.[11] McKinley carried Kentucky because of a strong showing in Louisville, while the rural areas of the state went to Bryan. In general, McKinley did well in urban areas of the South.[12]

To the Greeks, mastery of timeliness meant that the speaker presented materials, information, or ideas at the right time: not too early, not too late, but at the time that was best. Here also McKinley seemed to best Bryan during the campaign. Wishing to conduct an enthusiastic campaign from start to finish, Bryan toured the country vigorously, giving hundreds of speeches throughout large portions of the Northeast, Midwest, and West and portions of the South. He discussed the many themes and ideas of his campaign in considerable depth and often with zest. Although he said the money issue was paramount, he devoted thousands of words to various other issues. By early October he had said most of what he had to say. The newspapers continued to report his campaign but not with the same enthusiasm as in September. Bryan was repeating himself too much, and the physical strain of the campaign had taken its toll on the quality of his speaking.

By that point in the campaign, even the pro-silver newspapers were beginning to lose interest. Whereas a month earlier the pro-silver press routinely published complete texts of even his lengthiest speeches, by now they were often publishing only excerpts. Reporters dismissed some of his shorter speeches with such remarks as "He went over the same ground already covered by him," so that at this critical late stage of the campaign, Bryan's arguments were at times dropping slightly below the horizon.[13] Bryan reinforced this attitude at Traverse City, Michigan, admitting that "sometimes when I am weary and my voice shows signs of wear, it is encouraging to meet an audience like this and to be informed by so many people that I am all right." He promised nonetheless to campaign vigorously right to the end and that he would work even harder "on the last day of the campaign." His explanation was that he needed to do this because of lack of support from newspapers.[14] October produced fewer memorable speeches than any other portion of Bryan's campaign.

As the election neared, Bryan's campaign seemed to have passed its peak. In a letter to Senator James Jones, the powerful Democratic leader William J. Stone had urged that Bryan not begin his speaking tour until September.[15] Disregarding that advice, Bryan went out, starting in August, on one frantic railroad canvass of the nation after another.[16] By late October, Bryan's speeches seemed frazzled and disorganized. Thus just as McKinley's carefully orchestrated Front Porch campaign reached its peak, Bryan's campaign was sputtering out. Only occasionally in October did Bryan rise to the heights of eloquence, and even more rarely did he present long discourses of the kind that marked the earlier stages of the campaign. Trent and Friedenberg estimate that Bryan appeared to audiences totaling over five million persons during this campaign.[17] His railroad tours of the nation were indeed remarkable rhetorical events, but they reached their zenith too soon.

Bryan's rhetoric fell short of timeliness in another way. He started the campaign as a one-issue advocate of free silver. By October, Bryan was often addressing issues such as the income tax, civil service reform, and so forth. Thus as the election neared, Bryan's campaign had to some extent lost its focus. By peaking early and then digressing, Bryan's rhetoric may have lost some of its impact.

McKinley's campaign, however, reached its high point during the last few weeks. This was in part the consequence of the structure of the campaign itself. As the voters' excitement increased in October, thousands of visitors descended upon Canton to pay homage to their hero and to hear him speak. McKinley responded with an appropriate speech to each delegation. As the great historian Lewis Gould points out, McKinley did a superb job of staying "on message."[18]

This is not to deny that McKinley's rhetoric sometimes seemed as frayed at the edges as Bryan's. By October, McKinley sometimes found himself too rushed or exhausted to present a speech to every unannounced delegation; he asked them to read his speeches in the newspaper.[19] He also occasionally cut short speeches given to unannounced delegations or to delegations that were arriving on too tight a schedule. Overall, however, the campaign appeared to reach a high level of precision and energy in October. Certainly, each Saturday in October brought with it a larger number of delegations with a larger number of members. Furthermore, the simple fact that McKinley gave more of his speeches on Saturday than any other day was serendipitous. Delegations were more likely to come to Canton on Saturday because they could get off work. Speeches delivered on Saturday would in turn be reported in the Sunday newspapers, which were often larger and may have had larger circulations than weekday editions. Thus, the timing of McKinley's speeches was arranged for maximum effect.

In certain respects Bryan was obviously a superior speaker to McKinley. Bryan's gift for effective, concise language and clear expression was obvious in every speech, including those that were void of fiery eloquence. Although at times the enormous crowds defeated even Bryan's remarkable vocal talents, the campaign tour enhanced Bryan's reputation as a public speaker. Nonetheless, there are respects in which McKinley's speaking was noticeably superior. McKinley never failed to make personal, often charming comments that were specifically adapted to his individual audience. At the same time, unlike Bryan, McKinley never, even once, lost sight of the national audience long enough to say something that was likely to give offense to any voters. He even corrected hecklers who said anything against anyone. In an editorial, the Republican newspaper *Washington Evening Star* commented that McKinley consistently "spoke to the whole country daily, and always in words of soberness and truth."[20] McKinley's approach made such a partisan observation credible.

Indeed, McKinley often demonstrated his talent for being correct and sociable. Early in October he presented a speech to a group of pastors belonging to the African-American Episcopal Church. Befitting the nonpolitical nature of the delegation, McKinley offered a brief speech in which he praised the group, offered encouragement to the African-American race, and glorified freedom and the United States Constitution. McKinley presented them with some statistics about the growth of their religious denomination. He shook each minister's hand. This very gracious speech perhaps did as much to advance his campaign as any overtly political speech could have done. At the same time, the very fact that the group came to greet him symbolized something about McKinley's support among African-American voters.[21]

McKinley's campaign speeches depended on media technology for their effect. Newspapers and wire services served the function that was later served by television. Texts and accounts of the speeches appeared, in whole or in part, in newspapers across the country. It is impossible to escape the feeling that McKinley always had his eye on the representatives of the press, who carefully took down every word that he uttered. A perusal of the newspapers of the time shows that they covered McKinley's homey Front Porch campaign just as thoroughly as Bryan's frenzied whistle-stop tours. Bryan was aware of the press, as he repeatedly mentioned in his book *The First Battle,* but his instincts were, often enough, to interact intimately with his immediate audience in ways that might be unappealing to other groups of voters.

The Front Porch campaign contributed to a sense of inevitability. Thousands and thousands of people, almost all of whom were McKinley's supporters, came to Canton. They came in such numbers as to overwhelm the city's capacity. Together with the accompanying marching bands, drill teams, and riders on horseback, their arrival gave a seemingly clear impression that the nation was rising up to endorse McKinley's candidacy.

To be sure, Bryan also spoke to huge, enthusiastic crowds accompanied by marching bands and drill teams. His crowds, however, were mixed. Many in his audiences openly supported gold. Bryan often dealt with heckling and dissension from his audiences. Thus one never got the same impression of an overwhelming tide of support rising up to a peak by election day.

Both McKinley and Bryan used the appeal to tradition. They did so, however, in different ways. McKinley stressed that the policies of the past, particularly the protective tariff, were wise. A return to those policies, he contended, would bring renewed prosperity. This was the approach of the ceremonial speaker, who ties ideas to tradition with only minimal argument. Bryan rarely took the view that silver money was wise because it was traditional. More often, he took the defensive approach that he was not an anarchist or a fanatic because silver money had once been fundamental to the nation's currency.

McKinley's concern with prosperity, incidentally, continued during the few years that remained to him; Ivie points out that one of the reasons that McKinley offered for invading Cuba in 1898 was the failure of Spanish rule to offer prosperity to the people of Cuba.[22]

The results of this campaign may also, in part, reflect the inherent nature of a two-party political system. Bryan was in theory the nominee of the Democratic, Populist, and National Silver parties. As a result, the pro-gold press called Bryan and his supporters "Popocrats." In real life, however, after Bryan's nomination, the so-called "fusion" of these parties resulted in the Populist and National Silver parties being practically subsumed into the Democratic Party, at least at the national level, for Bryan hardly ever mentioned them in his speeches.

It may well be in the nature of the two-party system that radical views, or even views that are perceived as being radical, are unlikely to result in election victory. In rhetorical terms, the rhetoric of division is unlikely to prevail in a two-party election. Bryan received an enormous number of votes, but this may have been not so much because he was popular as because the entire electorate became energized during the extraordinarily vigorous 1896 presidential campaign. Contrary to some of Bryan's remonstrations, the election, although well contested, was not all that close. It is also possible that the high voter turnout in large part resulted simply from population growth: more voters, more votes.

In addition, as a matter of political communication, Bryan may have been unwise in choosing which states to canvass. He had no need to campaign in the Deep South, which was obviously going to vote for him regardless of what he said during the campaign. In this post-Reconstruction period, a Republican candidate, and Union veteran to boot, was unlikely to receive any significant number of votes in Georgia or Alabama. Indeed, even Bryan's trip through North Carolina may have been a waste of time and money. One might also question Bryan's decision to campaign extensively in the extreme northeast portion of the country. Although his reception in that part of the country was occasionally polite, he could not possibly have expected to win many votes there. He certainly was not going to win votes by visiting people to call them his enemies. One speculates that Bryan's main interest was to proselytize the region, not to win their votes.

The results of the election, much as Dawes had predicted, were decided in the states of the Ohio and upper Mississippi valleys. It could be said in Bryan's defense that his travels throughout the country may have helped him overcome the impression that he was a regional candidate; however, he might have accomplished the same goal simply by refraining from comments about "the enemy's country."

In contrast, McKinley did not have to worry too much about where his supporters traveled from. He spoke to whatever delegations appeared. Nonetheless, most of McKinley's visitors came from such states as Pennsylvania, Ohio, Indiana, Michigan, Illinois, and Kentucky, all of which were pivotal states in the election. The central location of Canton to those regions was opportune. Some delegations came from the Northeast or the West. In addition, McKinley received just enough delegations from Virginia to give the impression that he was getting national support.

Bryan's speech at the Chicago convention may have made his defeat inevitable. The election in November came almost four months after "A Cross of Gold" and was obviously influenced by factors other than that one dramatic speech. Most obviously, Bryan's other campaign speeches and McKinley's skillfully conducted campaign surely influenced the outcome.[23] Nonetheless, Bryan's radical tactics of polarization and division, his reliance on flag individuals and flag issues, started a trend that seems to have led to a polarized voting public in November. One Democratic (but anti-silver) newspaper noted this clearly: "The contention over the sound money question has created a new line of demarkation in American politics. On the one side," they explained, "are the discontented and those who are dissatisfied with the existing order." These, of course, were Bryan's supporters. "On the other side," the editorial continued, "are those who believe in our institutions and appreciate their beneficence."[24]

The election returns from November 3 showed a pattern that is consistent with a still-polarized public. Bryan received excellent support from voters in the West, but this support was not as complete as the silverites might have anticipated from the campaign's rhetoric. For example, Bryan lost Minnesota and California. Oregon went for McKinley, possibly because of opposition from the press.[25]

Bryan received significantly better support from rural areas than from urban regions.[26] Although he received excellent support from farming communities, his most natural constituency, the pattern of that support was rather curious. He received the votes of many tenant farmers but got fewer votes from small land-owning farmers.[27] This is surprising because the free silver issue would seem to have its greatest appeal to debtors.

This result suggests that Bryan's reputation as the Great Commoner, the supporter of the poor, had more influence on the election results than did the economics of free silver. Once one realizes, however, that the silver question was a flag issue in "A Cross of Gold," and on its face continued to serve as a *flag issue* in Bryan's subsequent rhetoric, it should be no surprise that the poorest farmers would support Bryan the most. Free silver was the vehicle by which Bryan symbolized his advocacy of the needs of the poor, working-class American over the rich and powerful forces of business. The voting public apparently sensed this and responded accordingly.

The silver issue may have gained Bryan some votes of wage laborers, most of whom were poor but suffered no crushing debts. Nonetheless, despite the endorsement of political machines and labor unions, Bryan was not able to carry the voters in eastern industrial states, most of whom sided with McKinley.[28] Thus Bryan's rhetoric was inflammatory, noteworthy, and eloquent, but the existing evidence is not consistent with a view that it achieved the results he wanted. McKinley perceived more clearly, almost instinctively, the virtue of "we must welcome everybody in," and he thus had an easier time appealing to a sufficient coalition of voters.

A century later, to many of us, the 1896 campaign seems like a remote relic of the past. In his hometown of Canton, Ohio, McKinley is remembered in the name of a local high school and its renowned football team. The house in which McKinley lived and from which he campaigned has long since given way to urban development. On the outskirts of the city, joggers run up the long outdoor staircase leading to McKinley's massive memorial, enjoying it as a convenient way to exercise and oblivious to the four coffins, two large and two small, that lie within.

Bryan is today best remembered for his feeble performance in the 1925 Scopes trial. His grave in Arlington National Cemetery carries the legend, "He Kept the Faith."[29] Bryan began the revolution of the Democratic Party that Franklin Roosevelt completed: he made his party the representative of the poor and downtrodden. McKinley set forth the themes and rhetorical style, with its emphasis on ceremonial forms of speech, that Republican presidents have followed ever since and that Ronald Reagan brought to perfection. The influence of the surprisingly modern 1896 campaign remains with the United States today.

Notes

Introduction

1. "Bryan Receives a Great Ovation," *Cleveland Plain Dealer,* 1 September 1896, 3.

2. William J. Bryan, *The First Battle: A Story of the Campaign of 1896, Together with a Collection of His Speeches and a Biographical Sketch by His Wife* (Chicago: W. B. Conkey Company, 1896), 11.

3. "No Man, Woman or Child," Editorial, *Canton Repository,* 4 October 1896, 4.

4. Note, for example, the dismissive account of McKinley's campaign in Paolo E. Coletta, *William Jennings Bryan,* vol. 1: *Political Evangelist, 1860–1908* (Lincoln: University of Nebraska Press, 1964), 167.

5. Jerome Lawrence and Robert E. Lee, *Inherit the Wind* (New York: Random House, 1955).

6. Michael J. Hostetler, "William Jennings Bryan as Demosthenes: The Scopes Trial and the Undelivered Oration, *On Evolution,*" *Western Journal of Communication* 62 (1998): 166-67; 176-78.

7. Judith S. Trent and Robert V. Friedenberg, *Political Campaign Communication: Principles and Practices,* 5th ed. (Lanham, Md.: Rowman & Littlefield Publishers, 2004), 96, give a brief but accurate review of McKinley's 1896 campaign.

8. There has been little study of Bryan's "Cross of Gold" speech from the 1896 Democratic Convention and virtually no study of the speeches that he gave while touring the nation four times during the campaign. Most studies of Bryan's rhetoric cover his entire speaking career, giving only brief mention to the 1896 campaign; see Myron G. Phillips, "William Jennings Bryan," in *A History and Criticism of American Public Address,* vol. 2, ed. William Norwood Brigance (New York: McGraw, 1943), 891–918; compare Margaret Wood, "William Jennings Bryan, Crusader for the Common Man," in *American Public Address: Studies in Honor of Albert Craig Baird,* ed. Loren Reid (Columbia: University of Missouri Press, 1961), 151–69. Wood's paper includes a few scattered paragraphs about the "Cross of Gold" but does not mention other 1896 campaign speeches. See also David B. Valley, *A History and Analysis of Democratic Presidential Nomination Acceptance Speeches to 1968* (New York: University Press of America, 1988), 34–37, for a brief discussion of Bryan's speaking.

9. Aristotle, *On Rhetoric: A Theory of Civic Discourse,* trans. George A. Kennedy (New York: Oxford University Press, 1991), p. 36, n. 34.

10. The importance of publications was noted at the time; see "Bryan's Unprecedented Canvass," *Review of Reviews* 14 (1896): 519.

11. Stanley L. Jones, *The Presidential Election of 1896* (Madison: University of Wisconsin Press, 1964); Paul W. Glad, *McKinley, Bryan, and the People* (Chicago: Dee-Elephant, 1991); Margaret Leech, *In the Days of McKinley* (New York: Harper and Row, 1959).

12. See, e.g., Edwin Black, *Rhetorical Criticism: A Study in Method* (Madison: University of Wisconsin Press, 1978), 75–82; Wayne C. Minnick, "A Case Study in Persuasive Effect: Lyman Beecher on Duelling," *Speech Monographs* 38 (1971): 262–76.

13. LeRoy Ashby, *William Jennings Bryan: Champion of Democracy* (Boston: Twayne, 1987), 67.

14. Phillips, "William Jennings Bryan," 906.

15. Daniel J. Boorstin, *The Image: A Guide to Pseudo-Events in America* (New York: Harper, 1964), 11–12.

16. Robert L. Ivie published an interesting study of a speech that McKinley gave during the Spanish-American War, "William McKinley: Advocate of Imperialism," *Western Speech* 36 (1972): 15–23. Ivie also devoted a section of his doctoral dissertation to McKinley's "War Address" to Congress: see Robert Lynn Ivie, "Vocabularies of Motive in Selected Presidential Justifications for War," Ph.D. diss. (photocopy), Washington State University, Department of Speech, 1972, University Microfilms #73-58, 37–42. See also Robert L. Ivie, "Presidential Motives for War," *Quarterly Journal of Speech* 60 (1974): 337–45, esp. 343; and Robert L. Ivie, "Issues of Savagery in American Justifications for War," *Communication Monographs* 47 (1980): 279–94, esp. 287.

17. Martin J. Medhurst, "The Academic Study of Public Address: A Tradition in Transition," in *Landmark Essays on American Public Address,* ed. Martin J. Medhurst (Davis, Calif.: Hermagoras Press), xxv.

18. Stephen E. Lucas, "The Renaissance of American Public Address: Text and Context in Rhetorical Criticism," *Quarterly Journal of Speech* 74 (1988): 247.

19. Kenneth Burke, *A Rhetoric of Motives* (New York: Prentice-Hall, 1950), 19–27.

20. Donald T. Campbell, *Methodology and Epistemology for Social Science: Selected Papers,* ed. E. Samuel Overman (Chicago: University of Chicago Press, 1988), 479.

21. "Governor M'Kinley's Response," *Canton Repository,* 2 July 1896, 1.

22. See various typescripts in the Western Reserve Historical Society, McKinley Papers, #4674, container 3, folder 13.

23. See W. S. Lloyd, "William Jennings Bryan's Tour," *Cleveland Plain Dealer,* 11 August 1896, 1; "His Journey's End," *Cleveland Plain Dealer,* 12 August 1896, 1.

24. "Kissed the Major," *Cleveland Plain Dealer,* 28 September 1896, 1.

1. E.g., Donald H. Ecroyd, "The Agrarian Protest," in *America in Controversy: History of American Public Address,* ed. DeWitte Holland (Dubuque, Iowa: Wm. C. Brown Company Publishers, 1973), 171–84; Wood, "William Jennings Bryan, Crusader"; Phillips, "William Jennings Bryan."

2. Bryan, *First Battle.*

3. Robert T. Oliver, *History of Public Speaking in America* (Boston: Allyn and Bacon, 1964), 485–86; Glad, *McKinley, Bryan,* ch. 8; Coletta, *William Jennings Bryan,* 1:200; Bryan, *First Battle,* pp. 616–20.

4. "Late News by Wire," *Washington Evening Star,* 6 November 1896, 2.

5. Bryan, *First Battle,* 617–18.

6. Coletta, *William Jennings Bryan,* 1:199.

7. Ibid., 1:200.

8. Donald K. Springen, *William Jennings Bryan: Orator of Small-Town America,* Great American Orators 11, ed. Halford Ryan (New York: Greenwood Press, 1991), 19.

9. Glad, *McKinley, Bryan,* 170; see also Oliver, *History,* 485.

10. Phillips, "William Jennings Bryan," 904.

11. W. S. Lloyd, "Hanna's Wad," *Cleveland Plain Dealer,* 26 September 1896, 1.

12. Charles G. Dawes, *A Journal of the McKinley Years,* ed. Bascom N. Timmons (Chicago: Lakeside–R. R. Donnelley, 1950), 106; Leech, *Days of McKinley,* 86–87.

13. Oliver, *History,* 485.

14. Coletta, *William Jennings Bryan,* 1:189.

15. "Eleven of 'Em" *Cleveland Plain Dealer,* 27 September 1896, 1.

16. "Bryan at Home," *Cleveland Plain Dealer,* 9 September 1896, 8.

17. "Truth or Lies," *Cleveland Plain Dealer,* 26 September 1896, 1.

18. LeRoy Ashby, *William Jennings Bryan: Champion of Democracy* (Boston: Twayne, 1987), 67–68.

19. Wm. M. Osborne, to William McKinley, 11 August 1896, and Wm. M. Osborne to William McKinley, 1 September 1896, both in Library of Congress McKinley Papers, microfilm, series 1, reel 1; Jones, *Presidential Election,* 279–83.

20. "Bryan and Hill Meet," *Washington Post,* 26 August 1896, 1, 3.

21. "Up in Michigan," *Cleveland Plain Dealer,* 15 October 1896, 1.

22. "Great Crowds," *Canton Repository,* 18 October 1896, 1.

23. "A Day of Rest," *Cleveland Plain Dealer,* 21 September 1896, 1.

24. "On the Offensive," *Cleveland Plain Dealer,* 23 October 1896, 6.

25. "In Old Virginia," *Cleveland Plain Dealer,* 20 September 1896, 7.

26. See, e.g., "Bryan at Home," *Cleveland Plain Dealer,* 9 September 1896, 8.

27. "Mr. Bryan Has No Doubts," *Kansas City Star,* 3 October 1896, 1.

28. See, e.g., "Labor for Bryan," *Cleveland Plain Dealer,* 9 September 1896, 2.

29. On Powderly, see "Sound Truths," *Akron Sunday Journal*, 13 September 1896, 4.

30. "Labor for Bryan," *Cleveland Plain Dealer*, 24 September 1896, 8.

31. Coletta, *William Jennings Bryan*, 1:93; Selig Perlman, *A History of Trade Unionism in the United States* (New York: Macmillan, 1923), 139–41; John R. Commons, David J. Saposs, Helen L. Sumner, E. B. Mittelman, H. E. Hoagland, John B. Andrews, and Selig Perlman, *History of Labour in the United States* (New York: Macmillan, 1926), 2:514; Philip Taft, *The A. F. of L. in the Time of Gompers* (New York: Harper and Row, 1957), 130.

32. Coletta, *William Jennings Bryan*, 1:169.

33. Philip S. Foner, *History of the Labor Movement in the United States*, vol. 2: *From the Founding of the American Federation of Labor to the Emergence of American Imperialism*, 2nd ed. (New York: International Publishers, 1975), 2:336.

34. "Bryan at Brooklyn," *Washington Evening Star*, 24 September 1896, 1.

35. Foner, *History of the Labor Movement*, 2:336.

36. "Up at Daybreak," *Cleveland Plain Dealer*, 16 October 1896, 2.

37. "Methods and Tactics of the Campaign," *Review of Reviews* 14 (1896): 558.

38. Bryan, *First Battle*, 612–20.

39. Bryan, *First Battle*, 612–20; "The Associated Press Reports," *New York Evening Post*, 12 September 1896, 7.

40. E.g, "Bryan Talks at Chicago," *St. Louis Post-Dispatch*, 8 September 1896, 6; "Bryan Back in Nebraska," *St. Louis Post-Dispatch*, 8 September 1896, 2; "Bryan Defends the Platform," *St. Louis Post-Dispatch*, 17 July 1896, 2.

41. E.g., "Mr. Bryan at Canton," *Washington Post*, 11 August 1896, 1, 4; "Bryan in West Virginia," *Kansas City Star*, 2 October 1896, 10.

42. "It Started in Nebraska," *New York Times*, 23 September 1896, pt. 1, p. 6.

43. Coletta, *William Jennings Bryan*, 1:148.

44. "Hanna's Brazen Boodle Campaign," *St. Louis Post-Dispatch*, 7 September 1896, 1.

45. Bryan, *First Battle*, 616–18.

46. Springen, *William Jennings Bryan*, 19.

47. Glad, *McKinley, Bryan*, 169.

48. Paul Kleppner, *Who Voted? The Dynamics of Electoral Turnout, 1970–1980* (New York: Praeger, 1982), 58–59.

49. Jefferson Myers, Salem, Oregon, to W[illia]m. J. Bryan, Lincoln, Nebraska, 4 October 1896, William Jennings Bryan Papers, Manuscript Division, Library of Congress, Washington, D.C., box 4.

50. Coletta, *William Jennings Bryan*, 1:252; "Tammany at the Front," *New York Times*, 29 September 1896, pt. 1, p. 4; "Tammany to Endorse Bryan," *New York Evening Post*, 20 July 1896, 1; Gustavus Myers, *The History of Tammany Hall* (New York: Boni, 1971), 281; E. Vale Blake, *History of the Tammany Society of Colombian Order from Its Organization to the Present*

Time (New York: Souvenir, 1901), 162–64; William L. Riordon, *Plunkitt of Tammany Hall: A Series of Very Plain Talks on Very Practical Politics* (Boston: Bedford–St. Martin's, 1994), 21; Myers, *History of Tammany Hall,* xiii–ix.

51. Jones, *Presidential Election,* 345.

52. "Hits at Carlisle," *Cleveland Plain Dealer,* 17 September 1896, 8.

53. Paul Lewinson, *Race, Class, and Party: A History of Negro Suffrage and White Politics in the South* (New York: Russell, 1963), 79–81; Robert M. Goldman, *A Free Ballot and a Fair Count: The Department of Justice and the Enforcement of Voting Rights in the South, 1877–1893* (Garland: New York, 1990), 254.

54. Kleppner, *Who Voted?* 66.

55. Steven F. Lawson, *Black Ballots: Voting Rights in the South, 1944–1969* (New York: Columbia University Press, 1976), 8–11.

56. William Diamond, "Urban and Rural Voting in 1896," *American Historical Review* 46 (1941): 281–305, see 293.

57. Ronald W. Walters, *Black Presidential Politics in America: A Strategic Approach* (Albany: State University of New York Press, 1988), 10.

58. Dawes, *Journal,* 61.

59. Jones, *Presidential Election,* 170.

60. E.g., "A Delegation of Colored Callers" and "Colored Callers from Stark County," in *McKinley as a Candidate: His Speeches Since His Nomination, June 18 to August 1, 1896,* comp. Joseph P. Smith (Canton, Ohio: Repository Press, 1896), 11, 39–40; "The Colored Rifles of Cleveland," in *McKinley's Speeches in August,* comp. Joseph P. Smith (Canton, Ohio: Repository Press, 1896), 85–87; "Afro-Americans" *Canton Repository,* August 20, 1896, 5; "Every Agency for the Public Good" *Canton Repository,* October 11, 1896, 6. These sources report speeches given to sizable delegations of African-American voters who visited McKinley during his Front Porch Campaign in 1896.

Russell H. Davis, *Black Americans in Ohio's City of Cleveland: George Peake, the First Black Settler to Carl Stokes, the First Black Mayor* (Washington: Associated Publishers, 1972), 130–41.

61. "Colored Rifles."

62. Lewinson, *Race, Class, and Party,* 77–78; Lawson, *Black Ballots,* 9–10; Jones, *Presidential Election,* 344.

63. Bryan, *First Battle,* 616–17.

64. E.g., "Mark Hanna, the New Boss," *St. Louis Post-Dispatch,* 14 June 1896, 9; "The New Boss and the Push," *St. Louis Post-Dispatch,* 15 June 1896, 3.

65. Jones, *Presidential Election,* 139–57; T. Bentley Mott, *Myron T. Herrick, Friend of France: An Autobiographical Biography* (Garden City: Doubleday, 1929), 48; Charles Dawes to William McKinley, 13 March 1896, Library of Congress McKinley Papers, microfilm, series 1, reel 1.

66. Dawes, *Journal,* 66.

67. Ibid., 3, 29, 74 (quotation), 89.

68. "Bryan's Unprecedented Canvass," *Review of Reviews* 14 (1896): 519

69. "Shouts for Silver," *Pittsburg Press,* 9 August 1896, 1.

70. "The Burden of Bryan," Editorial, *New York Times,* 11 August 1896, pt. 1, p. 4.

71. "Bryan Greeted by Thousands," *St. Louis Post-Dispatch,* 9 August 1896, 2; "Arrival at Chicago," *St. Louis Post-Dispatch,* 9 August 1896, 2.

72. "Wm. J. Bryan en Route East," *St. Louis Post-Dispatch,* 8 August 1896, 1.

73. "Methods and Tactics."

74. "Bryan, Free Silver, and Repudiation," *New York Times,* 11 July 1896, pt. 1, p. 1.

75. Dawes, *Journal,* 66.

76. Ibid., 6.

77. Ibid., 97.

Chapter 2

1. E.g., Ecroyd, "Agrarian Protest," 173; Jones, *Presidential Election,* 3–35.

2. J. Laurence Laughlin, *The History of Bimetallism in the United States,* 4th ed. (1896; repr., New York: Greenwood Press, 1968), 4.

3. Peter B. Kenen, *The International Economy* (Englewood Cliffs, N.J.: Prentice-Hall, 1985), 9.

4. L. Rangarajan, "The Politics of International Trade," in *Paths to International Political Economy,* ed. Susan Strange (London: George Allen and Unwin, 1984), 141–42; Robert M. Dunn Jr. and John H. Mutti, *International Economics* (London: Routledge, 2000), 156.

5. Irwin Unger, *Greenback Era: A Social and Political History of American Finance, 1865–1897* (Princeton: Princeton University Press, 1964), 203.

6. John A. Garraty, *The New Commonwealth, 1877–1890* (New York: Harper and Row, 1968), 44–46; Lawrence Goodwyn, *The Populist Moment: A Short History of the Agrarian Revolt in America* (Oxford: Oxford University Press, 1978), 20–27.

7. John H. Sloan, "American Imperialism," in *America in Controversy: History of American Public Address,* ed. DeWitte Holland (Dubuque: Brown, 1973), 123–34; Glad, *McKinley, Bryan,* ch. 4.

8. Milton Friedman, *Money Mischief: Episodes in Monetary History* (New York: Harcourt Brace Jovanovich, 1992), 75–76.

9. Gretchen Ritter, *Goldbugs and Greenbacks: The Antimonopoly Tradition and the Politics of Finance in America* (Cambridge: Cambridge University Press, 1997), 74–76.

10. "Dun's Trade Review," *Akron Evening Journal,* 12 September 1896, 2.

11. "Free Turnpikes by Force," *Akron Evening Journal,* 12 September 1896, 2.

12. "Panicky in New Orleans," *New York Times,* 12 September 1896, pt. 1, p. 1.

13. See, e.g., Paul Krause, *The Battle for Homestead, 1880–1892: Politics, Culture, and Steel* (Pittsburgh: University of Pittsburgh Press, 1992), 12–43; Leon Wolff, *Lockout, the Story of the Homestead Strike of 1892: A Study of Violence, Unionism, and the Carnegie Steel Empire* (New York: Harper, 1965), 100–26.

14. Jones, *Presidential Election*, 15.

15. Goodwyn, 239–63.

16. Jones, *Presidential Election*, ch. 2, esp. 12, 27.

17. Ibid., 3–18; Sloan, "American Imperialism," 126; Glad, *McKinley, Bryan*, ch. 4; [William H. Harvey], *Coin's Financial School*, Coin's Financial Series, vol. 1, no. 3 (Chicago: Coin Publishing Company, June 1894).

18. See the chart in Steven P. Reti, *Silver and Gold: The Political Economy of International Monetary Conferences, 1867–1892*, Contributions in Economics and Economic History 194 (Westport: Greenwood Press, 1998), 185–86.

19. Ted Wilson, *Battles for the Standard: Bimetallism and the Spread of the Gold Standard in the Nineteenth Century* (Aldershot: Shagate, 2000), 182.

20. Ritter, *Goldbugs*, 76.

21. Coletta, *William Jennings Bryan*, 1:206.

22. Ritter, *Goldbugs*, 75.

23. "Wakes 'Em," *Cleveland Plain Dealer*, 20 October 1896, 2.

24. Angela Redish, *Bimetallism: An Economic and Historical Analysis* (Cambridge: Cambridge University Press, 2000), 222–24.

25. Ibid., 234–36.

26. Ibid., 11.

27. Ibid., 237.

28. Jones, *Presidential Election*, 19.

29. Friedman, *Money Mischief*, 75–78.

30. Richard M. Weaver, *The Ethics of Rhetoric* (Chicago: Regnery, 1953), ch. 9.

31. Jones, *Presidential Election*, 3–19; Sloan, "American Imperialism," 126; Glad, *McKinley, Bryan*, ch. 4; Harvey, *Coin's Financial School*.

32. E.g., William McKinley, "The Silver Bill: Speech in the House of Representatives, Fifty-First Congress, June 25, 1890," in *Speeches and Addresses of William McKinley from His Election to Congress to the Present Time* (New York: D. Appleton and Company, 1893), 454–55.

33. William J. Bryan, "Remarks," *Congressional Record*, 53rd Congress, 1st session, 1893, 400–11.

34. "Seems to Lack Vitality," *New York Times*, 5 May 1895, 1.

35. As Bryan himself later noted; William J. Bryan and Mary Baird Bryan, *The Memoirs of William Jennings Bryan* (Philadelphia: United Publishers, 1925), 110.

36. William McKinley, "Letter of Acceptance," in *McKinley's Speeches in August*, comp. Joseph P. Smith (Canton: Repository Press, 1896), 115–27; Jones, *Presidential Election*, 166.

37. "The Republican Platform," *New York Times*, 19 June 1896, pt. 1, p. 1.

38. Samuel W. McCall, "Remarks," *Congressional Record*, 53rd Congress, 1st session, 1893, 395–97.

39. McKinley, "Silver Bill," 454–55.

40. "M'Kinley Gets to Work," *New York Times*, 23 August 1891, 5.

41. "Call to Patriotic Men," *Canton Repository*, 3 September 1896, 1.

42. "Favors Independence," *Canton Repository*, 8 October 1896, 2.

43. "To a Call from the Sixfooters," *Canton Repository*, 11 October 1896, 2.

44. "The Money Plank," *Washington Evening Star*, 11 June 1896, 1.

45. "McKinley Wanted More Silver," Cartoon, *St. Louis Post-Dispatch*, 7 August 1896, 1; "Alas the Major!" *Cleveland Plain Dealer*, 30 September 1896, 1; "His Own Mouth," *Cleveland Plain Dealer*, 9 September 1896, 1; "Tariff Changes Blamed," *Kansas City Star*, 3 October 1896, 9; "Bryan Quotes McKinley," *New York Times*, 2 October 1896, 3.

46. Mark Hanna, *His Book* (Boston: Chapple Publishing Company, 1904), 62.

47. Henry Clay, "In Defence of the American System," in *The Life and Speeches of the Hon. Henry Clay*, ed. Daniel Mallory (New York: Robert P. Bixby, 1843), 2:6–55.

48. "M'Kinley and Bryan," Editorial, *Kansas City Star*, 2 October 1896, 4.

49. Fletcher W. Hewes and William McKinley Jr., *What Are the Facts? Protection and Reciprocity Illustrated: Questions of To-Day Answered in One-Hundred Graphic Studies Embracing a Century of American Politics, Industries and Finance* (New York: Henry F. Clark, 1892).

50. William McKinley, "The Tariff of 1883. Speech in the House of Representatives, Forty-Seventh Congress, January 27, 1883," in *Speeches and Addresses*, 106, 122.

51. William McKinley, "The Morrison Tariff Bill: Speech in the House of Representatives, Forty-Eighth Congress, April 30, 1884," in *Speeches and Addresses*, 159.

52. William McKinley, "The Tariff of 1890. Speech in the House of Representatives, Fifty-First Congress, May 7, 1890," in *Speeches and Addresses*, 425.

53. McKinley, "Tariff of 1890," 430.

54. "M'Kinley Gets to Work."

55. Joseph P. Smith, ed., *History of the Republican Party in Ohio and Memoirs of Its Representative Supporters* (Chicago: Lewis Publishing Company, 1898), 2:692.

Chapter 3

1. "Mr. Bryan's Trip to Chicago," *St. Louis Post-Dispatch*, 9 August 1896, 5.

2. Cartoon, *St. Louis Post-Dispatch*, 5 September 1896, 2.

3. "In Self–Defense," *Cleveland Plain Dealer*, 4 September 1896, 10.

4. Note, for example, the dismissive account of McKinley's campaign in Coletta, *William Jennings Bryan*, 1:167.

5. Edited texts from Front Porch campaign speeches are found in Republican campaign literature such as William McKinley, *McKinley as a Candidate,* ed. Joseph P. Smith (Canton: Repository Press, 1896); McKinley's *Speeches in August,* ed. Joseph P. Smith (Canton: Repository Press, 1896); and *McKinley's Speeches in September,* ed. Joseph P. Smith (Canton: Repository Press, 1896). The *Canton Repository* published less edited versions of almost all of the speeches. Numerous speech texts appeared in various other newspapers, some of which were not published in the sources cited. Many of the newspaper accounts appear to be based on shorthand records of the speeches. Most of these transcripts appear to be complete, while others contain selections from the speeches.

6. "No Man, Woman, or Child," Editorial, *Canton Repository,* 4 October 1896, 4.

7. Burke, *Rhetoric of Motives,* 20–22, introduces the concept of identification.

8. Boorstin, *Image,* 11–12; Dan Nimmo, *The Political Persuaders: The Techniques of Modern Election Campaigns* (Englewood Cliffs, N.J.: Prentice, 1970), 26–27.

9. Burke, *Rhetoric of Motives,* 19–29.

10. E.g., in "Bryan's Great Speech," *Cleveland Plain Dealer,* 10 July 1896, 2.

11. Boorstin, *Image,* 12.

12. Trent and Friedenberg, *Political Campaign Communication,* 62.

13. William R. Brown, "Television and the Democratic National Convention of 1968," *Quarterly Journal of Speech* 55 (1969): 241.

14. Wm. M. Osborne, New York, to William McKinley, Canton, 11 August 1896, Library of Congress McKinley Papers, microfilm, series 1, reel 1.

15. Bryan, *First Battle,* 168.

16. "People's Choice," *Canton Repository* 13 August 1896, 2.

17. G. H. W., "Chat with M'Kinley," *Washington Evening Star,* 2 July 1896, 12.

18. "Hobart Here," *Canton Repository,* 2 July 1896, 3.

19. "M'Kinley on the Stump," *Washington Evening Star,* 13 August 1896, 1.

20. "Maj. and Mrs. McKinley," *St. Louis Post-Dispatch,* 16 August 1896, 6.

21. William McKinley, "Major McKinley at Alliance," "Speech on the Campus," and "To Alliance Workingmen," in Smith, *McKinley as a Candidate,* 52–54, 55, 55–56.

22. "McKinley in the Campaign," *Akron Beacon and Republican,* 10 August 1896, 1; Mott, *Myron T. Herrick,* 64.

23. Allan Peskin, *Garfield: A Biography* (Kent, Ohio: Kent State University Press, 1978), 482–83, 498–500; Margaret Leech and Harry J. Brown, *The Garfield Orbit* (New York: Harper and Row, 1978), 212–14.

24. Julia B. Foraker, *I Would Live It Again* (New York: Harper and Row, 1932; reprint, New York: Arno Press, 1975), 133.

25. Mott, *Myron T. Herrick,* 64.

26. G. H. W., "Chat".

27. Edward Thornton Heald, *The William McKinley Story*. (Canton, Ohio: Stark County Historical Society, 1964), 75–77; Jones, *Presidential Election*, 278; Leech, *Days of McKinley*, 89–90.

28. "Neighbors Congratulate Him," *New York Times*, 20 June 1896, pt. 1, p. 5.

29. "McKinley's Response," *Canton Repository*, 21 June 1896, 7.

30. A. R. Manning to William McKinley, Canton, 23 October 1896, Library of Congress McKinley Papers, microfilm, series 1, reel 1. This reel also contains manuscripts of speeches of greeting that were presumably submitted for review, and the Western Reserve Historical Society McKinley Papers, #4674, container 3, folder 13, contains one such draft, full of misspellings and grammatical errors.

31. "Served with M'Kinley," *Washington Post*, 13 August 1896, 3.

32. William McKinley, "Greetings from the Empire State," in Smith, *McKinley as a Candidate*, 10.

33. "From McKinley's Birthplace," *New York Times*, 21 June 1896, pt. 1, p. 2.

34. "Loyal Niles," *Canton Repository*, 21 June 1896, 1.

35. "Rush on Canton Wires," *New York Times*, 20 June 1896, pt. 1, pp. 1, 5.

36. "More to Come," *Canton Repository*, 25 June 1896, 5.

37. "The Campaign at Canton," *Review of Reviews* 14 (1896): 519.

38. William McKinley, "Zanesville Sends a Large Delegation: Major McKinley's Response," in Smith, *McKinley as a Candidate*, 16–17.

39. "From Wheeling," *Canton Repository*, 21 June 1896, 1–2.

40. "A Tinplate Demonstration," *New York Times*, 21 June 1896, pt. 1, p. 2.

41. "From Wheeling."

42. "Rush on Canton Wires."

43. William McKinley, "The Canton Ratification and Parade: Major McKinley's Response," in Smith, *McKinley as a Candidate*, 22.

44. See Dawes, *Journal*, 86–87.

45. John Thurston, "Senator Thurston's Notification Address," in Smith, *McKinley as a Candidate*, 23–24.

46. "Governor M'Kinley's Response," *Canton Repository*, 2 July 1896, 1.

47. Dawes, *Journal*, 87.

48. "Big Gathering," *Canton Repository*, 28 June 1896, 1.

49. "Foraker Club," *Canton Repository*, 12 July 1896, 1

50. "Bryan," *Cleveland Plain Dealer*, 11 July 1896, 1.

51. "What He Says of It," *Canton Repository*, 12 July 1896, 1.

52. Ibid.

53. Ibid.

54. "Many Women," *Canton Repository*, 16 July 1896, 1.

55. Ibid.

56. William McKinley, "Comrades from Cleveland: Major McKinley's Response," in Smith, *McKinley as a Candidate*, 45–49, see 48.

57. "Comrades from Cleveland: Major McKinley's Response," 48.

58. "Through Ohio," *Akron Beacon and Republican,* 10 August 1896, 1.

59. "M'Kinley Talks," *Akron Beacon and Republican,* 12 August 1896, 2.

60. Ibid.

61. "Glass Workers," *Canton Repository,* 26 July 1896, 1.

62. "Speaks to Colored Men," *Canton Repository,* 20 August 1896, 6.

63. "Afro-Americans," *Canton Repository,* 20 August 1896, 5. The L'Ouverture Rifles were founded in 1895 and eventually became part of the Ohio National Guard (National Rites of Passage Institute, "Cleveland and the Black Serviceman," accessed 21 June 2002, http://www.ritesofpassage.org/m-cleveland.htm).

64. "Speaks to Colored Men."

65. William McKinley, "Business and Politics: Major McKinley's Response," in Smith, *McKinley's Speeches in August,* 93.

66. William McKinley, "Letter of Acceptance," in Smith, *McKinley's Speeches in August,* 115–27.

67. Wm. M. Osborne, New York, to William McKinley, Canton, 1 September 1896, Library of Congress McKinley Papers, microfilm, series 1, reel 1.

68. McKinley, "Letter of Acceptance."

69. Dawes, *Journal,* 95

70. Wm. M. Osborne, New York, to William McKinley, Canton, 11 August 1896, Library of Congress McKinley Papers, microfilm, series 1, reel 1.

71. "Gives Warm Welcome for All," *Canton Repository,* 27 September 1896, 6.

72. "Answers Pennsylvania," *Canton Repository,* 23 August 1896, 6.

73. "His Old Comrades," *Canton Repository,* 19 July 1896, 6.

74. "What He Says of It."

75. Boorstin, *Image,* 11–12.

76. Ibid.

77. Ibid., 12.

78. See W. D. Caldwell and Company, Advertisement, *Canton Repository,* 19 July 1896, 5.

79. E.g., "A Bryan Day," *Cleveland Plain Dealer,* 13 August 1896, 1.

Chapter 4

1. Coletta, *William Jennings Bryan,* 1:141; "Bryan's Great Speech," *Cleveland Plain Dealer,* 10 July 1896, 2. This article contains a complete text with running commentary of Bryan's "Cross of Gold" speech, apparently based on a shorthand record. This is preferred to the later published versions, many of which contain changes introduced after the delivery of the speech. Most anthologized versions of this speech appear to rely, directly or indirectly, on the version in William J. Bryan, *The First Battle: A Story of the Campaign of 1896* (Chicago: W. B. Conkey, 1896), 199–206. The version in *The First Battle,* however, appears to have been polished somewhat

and therefore probably less accurately reflects what Bryan said at the convention. In addition, during the campaign the public read the newspaper versions, not the version in a book published after the campaign.

2. Ronald F. Reid, *Three Centuries of American Rhetorical Discourse: An Anthology and Review* (Prospect Heights, Ill.: Waveland Press, 1988), 600.

3. Springen, *William Jennings Bryan: Orator*, 18.

4. James Andrews and David Zarefsky, *American Voices: Significant Speeches in American History, 1640–1945* (New York: Longman, 1989), 389.

5. Oliver, *History*, 478; Valley, *Nomination Acceptance Speeches*, 34–35.

6. Coletta, *William Jennings Bryan*, 1:148

7. Leech, *Days of McKinley*, 85.

8. Wood, "William Jennings Bryan, Crusader," 165.

9. Burke, *Rhetoric of Motives*, 45.

10. For example, Jack Mills, in "The Speaking of William Jennings Bryan in Florida, 1915–1925," *Southern Speech Journal* 14 (1949): 137–69, discusses the speaking of the last ten years of Bryan's life; John H. Sloan, in "'I Have Kept the Faith': William Jennings Bryan and the Democratic National Convention of 1904" *Southern Speech Journal* 31 (1965): 114–23, and "Bryan versus 'Bosses' at Baltimore," *Southern Speech Journal* 32 (1967): 260–72, covers Bryan's public speaking in the 1904 and 1912 conventions, whereas Donald K. Springen, in "The Democrats: Techniques in Destruction, Bryan vs. Underwood," *Southern Speech Journal* 36 (1970): 152–63, studies Bryan's speaking against Oscar Underwood from 1911 to 1924. Hostetler, in "William Jennings Bryan as Demosthenes," examines Bryan's rhetoric in the Scopes trial.

11. Phillips, "William Jennings Bryan," 902–903, 912; Wood, "William Jennings Bryan, Crusader"; Springen, *William Jennings Bryan: Orator*, 15–18; Edgar DeWitt Jones, *Lords of Speech: Portraits of Fifteen American Orators* (Freeport, N.Y.: Books for Libraries, 1937), 217–19; Valley, *Nomination Acceptance Speeches*, 34–35.

12. E.g., Coletta, *William Jennings Bryan*, 1:137–43; Robert W. Cherny, *A Righteous Cause: The Life of William Jennings Bryan*, ed. Oscar Handling (Boston: Little, Brown and Company, 1985), 56–60; Charles Morrow Wilson, *The Commoner William Jennings Bryan* (Garden City: Doubleday, 1970), 213–17.

13. For example, "A Cross of Gold" is one of only two events listed in the *World Almanac's* historical chronology for the year 1896; "United States History," in *The World Almanac and Book of Facts 2000* (Mahah, N.J.: World Almanac Books, 1999), 525.

14. "The Silver Fanatics Are Invincible," *New York Times*, 7 July 1896, pt. 1, p. 1; "'Twill Be Bland and McLean," *St. Louis Post-Dispatch*, 8 July 1896, 1.

15. "Paving the Way for a Silver Ticket," *New York Times*, 9 July 1896, pt. 1, pp. 1–2; "Just a Bit Shy," *Cleveland Plain Dealer*, 8 July 1896, 1–2.

16. "Silver Will Get a Frost," *St. Louis Post-Dispatch*, 11 June 1896, 1; "Ingalls on the Situation," *St. Louis Post-Dispatch*, 14 June 1896, 9.

17. "Hanna Fighting Hard against Morton," *New York Times,* 17 June 1896, pt. 1, p. 1.

18. See, e.g., the analysis in Jonathan I. Lange, "Refusal to Compromise: The Case of Earth First!" *Western Journal of Speech Communication* 54 (1990): 489.

19. James Darsey, *The Prophetic Tradition and Radical Rhetoric in America* (New York: New York University Press, 1997), 57–58.

20. See, e.g., the analysis in Arthur L. Smith [Molefi K. Asante], "Topics of Revolutionary Rhetoric," in *Language, Communication, and Rhetoric in Black America,* ed. Arthur L. Smith (New York: Harper & Row, 1972), 220–21.

21. John W. Bowers, Donavan J. Ochs, and Richard J. Jensen, *The Rhetoric of Agitation and Control,* 2nd ed. (Prospect Heights, Ill.: Waveland, 1993), 34–36.

22. Ernest G. Bormann, *Forerunners of Black Power: The Rhetoric of Abolition* (Englewood Cliffs, N.J.: Prentice-Hall, 1971), 20–22.

23. Bowers et al., *Rhetoric of Agitation,* 34–35.

24. Ibid., 34–36.

25. Saul D. Alinsky, *Rules for Radicals: A Practical Primer for Realistic Radicals* (New York: Random House, 1971), 131–33.

26. Alinsky, *Rules for Radicals,* 15.

27. Lange, "Refusal to Compromise," 475.

28. "The Silver Fanatics Are Invincible," *New York Times,* 7 July 1896, pt. 1, p. 1.

29. "Silver Fanatics"; "The Standard Bearer Not Yet Named," *New York Times,* 10 July 1896, pt. 1, p. 1; "A Wet Blanket for Bland," *Cleveland Plain Dealer,* 9 July 1896, 1; "Wet Blanket"; Coletta, *William Jennings Bryan,* 1:121.

30. "Before Assembling," *Washington Evening Star,* 9 July 1896, 2.

31. Coletta, *William Jennings Bryan,* ch. 7, esp. 1:124.

32. Bryan and Bryan, *Memoirs,* 102–104.

33. "The Chicago Convention," *Wall Street Journal,* 9 July 1896, 1.

34. Dawes, *Journal,* 89.

35. Bryan and Bryan, *Memoirs,* 112.

36. "The Coliseum Where the Convention Will Meet Tomorrow," *Atlanta Journal,* 6 July 1896, 1.

37. "Platform of the Chicago Convention," *New York Times,* 10 July 1896, pt. 1, p. 6.

38. "Silver Fanatics."

39. Coletta, *William Jennings Bryan,* 1:132.

40. "Resolutions Discussed," *Washington Evening Star,* 9 July 1896, 1–2; Louis W. Koenig, *Bryan: A Political Biography of William Jennings Bryan* (New York: Putnam, 1971), 178.

41. "Ablaze!" *Cleveland Plain Dealer,* 10 July 1896, 1; A. E. Heiss, "Made Haste Slowly," *Cleveland Plain Dealer,* 9 July 1896, 3; "Still Nothing But Talk," *Akron Beacon and Republican,* 9 July 1896, 1; "Silverites Worry," *Pittsburg Press,* 8 July 1896, 1.

42. "Bryan's Great Speech."

43. Springen, *William Jennings Bryan: Orator,* 17–18

44. "Bryan's Great Speech."

45. "Ablaze!"

46. "Bryan's Great Speech."

47. "Bryan's Great Speech."

48. Ibid.

49. Bryan and Bryan, *Memoirs,* 104–105,

50. Wood, "William Jennings Bryan, Crusader," 159.

51. "Bryan's Great Speech."

52. Bowers et al., *Rhetoric of Agitation* (1993), 19–20; cf. John W. Bowers and Donovan J. Ochs, *The Rhetoric of Agitation and Control* (Reading: Addison-Wesley, 1971), 18. The author really owes this insight to a long-ago conversation with Richard L. Johannesen.

53. "Bryan's Great Speech."

54. Ibid.

55. Bryan, *First Battle,* 608.

56. Ibid., 606.

57. "Bryan's Great Speech."

58. Ibid.

59. "Bryan the Candidate," *Akron Beacon and Republican,* 10 July 1896, 1; A. E. Heiss, "Bland Losing," *Cleveland Plain Dealer,* 9 July 1896, 3.

60. "The Chicago Convention," *Wall Street Journal,* 10 July 1896, 1.

61. Reid, *Three Centuries,* 600; Andrews and Zarefsky, *American Voices,* 389; Valley, *Nomination Acceptance Speeches,* 34–35; Coletta, *William Jennings Bryan,* 1:148; Leech, *Days of McKinley,* 85.

62. "Bryan," *Cleveland Plain Dealer,* 11 July 1896, 1.

63. "Bryan's Great Speech."

64. "Bryan for President," *St. Louis Post-Dispatch,* 11 July 1896, 4.

65. "A Silver Candidate Named," *Charleston News and Courier,* 11 July 1896, p. 1.

66. "Repudiation Has Won," *New York Times,* 10 July 1896, pt. 1, p. 1.

67. "Bryan, Free Silver, and Repudiation," *New York Times,* 11 July 1896, pt. 1, pp. 1–2.

68. "A Welcome Visitor," *Akron Beacon and Republican,* 10 July 1896, 2.

69. "Bryan's Gospel," Editorial, *Pittsburg Press,* 11 July 1896, 4.

70. "West Gone Loony," *Pittsburg Press,* 8 July 1896, 3.

71. "Call It a Teller Plot," *Chicago Tribune,* 10 July 1896, 5.

72. "Effect of Free Coinage," *Wall Street Journal,* 10 July 1896, 1.

73. Editorial, *Akron Beacon and Republican,* 11 July 1896, 2.

74. Mott, *Myron T. Herrick,* 69.

75. "Daily Public Call," *St. Louis Post-Dispatch,* 10 July 1896, 3rd extra, 1.

76. "Radical of Radicals," *New York Times,* 11 July 1896, pt. 1, p. 3.

77. "The Corner Turned," *Wall Street Journal,* 13 July 1896, 2.

78. "Hill's Speech in Full," *Cleveland Plain Dealer,* 10 July 1896, 2; "Repudiation Has Won."

79. "The Chicago Convention," *Wall Street Journal,* 11 July 1896, 1.

80. "Bryan," *Cleveland Plain Dealer,* 11 July 1896, 1.

81. "The Triumph of Populism," *Washington Evening Star,* 14 July 1896, 6.

82. "Better Than His Platform," Editorial, *Charleston News and Courier,* 11 July 1896, 4.

83. "M'Kinley May Make a Western Tour," *Chicago Tribune,* 11 July 1896, 1.

84. "A Populist Triumph," *Washington Evening Star,* 14 July 1896, 1.

85. "Repudiation Has Won."

86. Editorial, *St. Louis Post-Dispatch,* 11 July 1896, 4.

87. "Bryan En Route," *Akron Beacon and Republican,* 8 August 1896, 1. A campaign document edition of "A Cross of Gold" indeed places the phrases about the "crown of thorns" and "cross of gold" in quotation marks (without attribution) at the top of the first page as a sort of flying heading; William J. Bryan, *Speech Delivered by Hon. William J. Bryan, of Nebraska, before the Democratic National Convention, July 9, 1896, in Concluding the Debate on the Adoption of the Platform* (n.p., ca. 1896). However, many anthologized versions of the speech do not place these passages in quotation marks.

88. Samuel Walker McCall, Remarks, *Congressional Record,* 53rd Congress, 2nd session, 26 January 1894, 1500.

89. Bryan, *First Battle,* 206.

90. "Still Nothing but Talk," *Akron Beacon and Republican,* 9 July 1896, 1.

Chapter 5

1. Aristotle, *On Rhetoric,* 1378a.

2. Ibid., 1356a.

3. Kennedy, in Aristotle, *On Rhetoric,* p. 37, n. 40.

4. Kennedy, commentary, in Aristotle, *On Rhetoric,* p. 91.

5. Sharon Crowley and Debra Hawhee, *Ancient Rhetorics for Contemporary Students,* 2nd ed. (Boston: Allyn and Bacon, 1999), 108.

6. Helen Constantinides, "The Duality of Scientific Ethos: Deep and Surface Structures," *Quarterly Journal of Speech* 87 (2001): 62.

7. Lange, "Refusal to Compromise," 475.

8. Herbert W. Simons and Elizabeth W. Mechling, "The Rhetoric of Political Movements," in *Handbook of Political Communication,* ed. Dan J. Nimmo and Keith R. Sanders (Beverly Hills: Sage Publications, 1981), 428.

9. Herbert W. Simons, "Requirements, Problems, and Strategies: A Theory of Persuasion for Social Movements," *Quarterly Journal of Speech* 56 (1970): 2, 4.

10. Darsey, *Prophetic Tradition,* 203.

11. Valley, *Nomination Acceptance Speeches,* 36.

12. Springen, *William Jennings Bryan: Orator,* 16–19.

13. Wood, "William Jennings Bryan, Crusader," 161.

14. Phillips, "William Jennings Bryan."

15. Jones, *Presidential Election,* 304–305.

16. Kurt W. Ritter and James R. Andrews, *The American Ideology: Reflections of the Revolution in American Rhetoric,* Bicentennial Monographs (Falls Church, Va.: Speech Communication Association, 1978), 77.

17. "Hill's Speech in Full," *Cleveland Plain Dealer,* 10 July 1896, 2; "Repudiation Has Won," *New York Times,* 10 July 1896, pt. 1, p. 1; "Bryan," *Cleveland Plain Dealer,* 11 July 1896, 1.

18. "Bryan in Ohio," *Cleveland Plain Dealer,* 11 August 1896, 1; "Bryan en Route," *Akron Beacon and Republican,* 8 August 1896, 1.

19. "Through Ohio," *Akron Beacon and Republican,* 10 August 1896, 1; "The Silverites Come to Town," *New York Times,* 12 August 1896, pt. 1, p. 3.

20. "Bryan Starts Invasion," *St. Louis Post-Dispatch,* 10 August 1896, 1.

21. "Bryan Moves On," *Pittsburg Press,* 8 August 1896, 1.

22. "Wm. J. Bryan en Route East," *St. Louis Post-Dispatch,* 8 August 1896, 1.

23. "Wm. J. Bryan en Route."

24. Bryan, *First Battle,* 300.

25. "Bryan Greeted by Thousands," *St. Louis Post-Dispatch,* 9 August 1896, 2.

26. "Weary and Worn," *Cleveland Plain Dealer,* 10 August 1896, 1.

27. "Through Ohio."

28. "Through Ohio."

29. W. S. Lloyd, "William Jennings Bryan's Tour," *Cleveland Plain Dealer,* 11 August 1896, 1.

30. Untitled note, *Canton Repository,* 13 August 1896, 4.

31. "A Blast of Death," *Akron Beacon and Republican,* 10 August 1896, 1; "Heavy Storms," *Canton Repository,* 13 August 1896, 6; "Local Notes," *Canton Repository,* 13 August 1896, 8.

32. "Through Ohio"; "Bryan Talks at Canton," *New York Times,* 11 August 1896, pt. 1 p. 3.

33. "Bryan Moves On."

34. "Bryan in Town," *Cleveland Plain Dealer,* 11 August 1896, 8.

35. "Bryan Talks All Day," *New York Times,* 11 August 1986, pt. 1, p. 1; cf. "Bryan's Great Speech," *Cleveland Plain Dealer,* 10 July 1896, 2.

36. "His Journey's End," *Cleveland Plain Dealer,* 12 August 1896, 1.

37. "Guards His Voice," *Akron Beacon and Republican,* 11 August 1896, 1; "Could Not Make Speeches," *New York Times,* 12 August 1896, pt. 1, p. 3; "His Journey's End," *Cleveland Plain Dealer,* 12 August 1896, 1. This author has heard a few brief recordings of Bryan speaking; his voice seemed powerful but also somewhat raspy and nasal. Such vocal technique is an obvious cause of vocal strain. It is, of course, also possible that he had the bad luck to catch a cold.

38. "Bryan's Unprecedented Canvass," *Review of Reviews,* 14 (1896): 519; see, e.g., "Bryan Speaks Twice," *Washington Post,* 18 August 1896, 1, 4.

39. Lloyd; also, "His Journey's End," *Cleveland Plain Dealer,* 12 August 1896, 1.

40. "Through Ohio."

41. "The Burden of Bryan," Editorial, *New York Times*, 11 August 1896, pt. 1, p. 4.

42. "Through the Keystone State," *St. Louis Post-Dispatch*, 11 August 1896, 1.

43. "May Not Speak," *Akron Beacon and Republican*, 12 August 1896, 1.

44. "All Politics in New York," *St. Louis Post-Dispatch*, 9 August 1896, 9.

45. "Mr. Bryan's Trip to Chicago," *St. Louis Post-Dispatch*, 9 August 1896, 5.

46. "Bryan's Bugle Call," *Cleveland Plain Dealer*, 13 August 1896, 1.

47. "A Bryan Day," *Cleveland Plain Dealer*, 13 August 1896, 1.

48. "For To-Night's Meeting," *New York Times*, 12 August 1896, pt. 1, p. 3.

49. "Arrangements for the Bryan Notification," *St. Louis Post-Dispatch*, 9 August 1896, 9.

50. "Bryan Spoke and His Auditors Fled," *New York Times*, 13 August 1896, pt. 1, p. 1; "Miscellaneous," *Wall Street Journal*, 13 August 1896, last ed., n.p.; "Notification Plans," *St. Louis Post-Dispatch*, 8 August 1896, 2.

51. "Mr. Bryan in This City," *New York Times*, 12 August 1896, pt. 1, p. 1.

52. "The Candidates at New York," *St. Louis Post-Dispatch*, 12 August 1896; see also Bryan, *First Battle*, 299.

53. "Dead by Scores," *Cleveland Plain Dealer*, 11 August 1896, 2.

54. "Bryan Spoke."

55. "Bryan's Bugle Call."

56. "Bryan Day."

57. "Bryan Day"; see also "Bryan's Bugle Call."

58. "Bryan's Great Speech."

59. "Speech of Candidate Bryan," *New York Times*, 13 August 1896, pt. 1, p. 2. "Speech of Candidate" contains a complete text, presumably taken from a shorthand record or (more likely) a draft distributed at the occasion of Bryan's Acceptance Speech at Madison Square Garden of August 12, 1896. This text is preferred to the later published versions, many of which contain minor changes introduced after delivery of the speech. The typescript from which Bryan apparently spoke is preserved in the William Jennings Bryan Papers, Manuscript Division, Library of Congress, Washington, D.C., box 4.

60. "Speech of Candidate," 2.

61. Presumably Laughlin, *History of Bimetallism*.

62. "Speech of Candidate," 2–3.

63. "Platform."

64. "Speech of Candidate," 2.

65. Darsey, *Prophetic Tradition*, 204.

66. Ibid., 87–88.

67. "Bryan's Great Speech."

68. "Speech of Candidate," 2.

69. "Bryan Spoke."

70. "Speech of Candidate," 3.

71. Ibid., 2.

72. Ibid.

73. Ibid.

74. Ibid.

75. See, e.g., "He Must Howl," *New York Times,* 10 August 1896, pt. 1, p. 4.

76. E.g., "Bryan Was Notified," *Pittsburg Press,* 13 August 1896, 7.

77. Bryan, *First Battle,* 299.

78. Springen, *William Jennings Bryan: Orator,* 18.

79. "Bryan Spoke."

80. "Arrangements."

81. "The Notification of Bryan," *Charleston News and Courier,* 13 August 1896, p. 1.

82. "Second Speech."

83. "Candidates at New York."

84. "Bryan Day."

85. "Bryan's Plans," *Akron Beacon and Republican,* 14 August 1896, 1.

86. "Candidates Notified," *Washington Post,* 13 August 1896, 1.

87. "Specimens of Bryan," *Pittsburg Press,* 13 August 1896, 4.

88. "Mr. Bryan in New York," *Review of Reviews* 14 (1896): 261–61.

89. "To Bryan Is Given the Banner," *St. Louis Post-Dispatch,* 13 August 1896, 1.

90. "Demand for Bryan's Speeches," *Cleveland Plain Dealer,* 14 August 1896, 1.

91. E.g., "Specimens of Bryan," *Pittsburg Press,* 13 August 1896, 4; "A Bryan Day," *Cleveland Plain Dealer,* 13 August 1896, 1; "Notification of Bryan"; "Points from Bryan's Speech," *Wall Street Journal,* 13 August 1896, 1; "Mr. Bryan's Address," *St. Louis Post-Dispatch,* 13 August 1896, 2; "Mr. Bryan's Speech," *Washington Post,* 13 August 1896, 1, 2, 4.

92. "Talk about Bryan's Speech," *Charleston News and Courier,* 14 August 1896, p. 1.

93. Ibid.

94. "He's Satisfied," *Akron Beacon and Republican,* 13 August 1896, 1.

95. Ibid.

96. "Bryan Spoke."

97. "Specimens of Bryan."

98. "Mr. Bryan's Great Speech," Editorial, *Charleston News and Courier,* 14 August 1896, 4.

99. "To Bryan Is Given."

100. "Bryan's New York Address," Editorial, *Chicago Journal,* 13 August 1896, 4.

101. "Billy Want 'A Cracker?' Nit," *Washington Post,* 23 August 1896, 1.

102. Joseph Benson Foraker, *Notes of a Busy Life* (Cincinnati: Stewart and Kidd, 1917), 1:494.

103. "Some Comment," *Washington Evening Star,* 13 August 1896, 1.

104. Ibid.

105. See, e.g., "Tammany to Endorse Bryan," *New York Evening Post,* 20 July 1896, 1.

106. Darsey, *Prophetic Tradition,* 435.

Chapter 6

1. E.g. "To Canton and Return," Advertisement, *Cleveland Plain Dealer,* 17 September 1896, 10; "Awful Cheap Rates to Canton via Cleveland, Canton & Southern RY., Friday, Sept. 18th, '96," Advertisement, *Cleveland Plain Dealer,* 17 September 1896, 10.

2. "Another Canton Trip," *Cleveland Plain Dealer,* 24 September 1896, 10.

3. Burke, *Rhetoric of Motives,* 20–22; Bernard Brock, "Political Speaking: A Burkeian Approach," in *Critical Responses to Kenneth Burke: 1924–1966,* ed. William H. Rueckert (Minneapolis: University of Minnesota Press, 1969), 444–45.

4. Burke, *Rhetoric of Motives,* 20–22; cf. Barry Brummett, "Presidential Substance: The Address of August 15, 1973," *Western Speech Communication* 39 (1975): 249–59.

5. E.g., Burke, *Rhetoric of Motives,* 23–24, 27–28.

6. E.g., Dennis G. Day, "Persuasion and the Concept of Identification," *Quarterly Journal of Speech* 40 (1960): 271.

7. Burke, *Rhetoric of Motives,* 55.

8. Mark H. Wright, "Burkeian and Freudian Theories of Identification," *Communication Quarterly* 42 (1994): 301–303.

9. Colleen E. Kelley, "The 1984 Campaign Rhetoric of Representative George Hansen: A Pentadic Analysis," *Western Journal of Speech Communication* 51 (1987): 204–17.

10. "The Campaign at Canton," *Review of Reviews* 14 (1896): 519.

11. "Kissed the Major," *Cleveland Plain Dealer,* 28 September 1896, 1.

12. Jones, *Presidential Election,* 311–12.

13. William McKinley, "West Virginia Editors," in *McKinley's Speeches in September,* comp. Joseph P. Smith (Canton: Repository Press, 1896), 156–61.

14. "Call to Patriotic Men," *Canton Repository,* 3 September 1896, 1.

15. Ibid.

16. Wm. M. Osborne, New York, to William McKinley, Canton, 7 September 1896, Library of Congress McKinley Papers, microfilm, series 1, reel 1.

17. "Bryan at Milwaukee," *Chicago Inter-Ocean,* 6 September 1896, 3.

18. William McKinley, "The Home of Senator Quay," in *McKinley's Speeches in September,* 161–64.

19. McKinley, "A Labor Day Visit," *McKinley's Speeches in September,* 164–68; "Workingmen," *Cleveland Plain Dealer,* 6 September 1896, 3.

20. "A Labor Day Visit," *Canton Repository,* 6 September 1896, 1.

21. Ibid.

22. Ibid., 4.

23. William McKinley, "Newspaper Men of Ohio," in *McKinley's Speeches in September,* 168.

24. Jones, *Presidential Election,* 264–75.

25. "Major M'Kinley to the Editors," *Canton Repository*, 10 September 1896, 1.

26. W. S. Lloyd, "A Band of Editors," *Cleveland Plain Dealer*, 9 September 1896, 2.

27. William McKinley, "The Green Mountain State," in *McKinley's Speeches in September*, 176; "Voted for McKinley," *Chicago Evening Post*, 11 September 1896, 1.

28. McKinley, "Green Mountain," 176–78; see also "Voted for McKinley."

29. "Chicago to Canton," *Chicago Evening Post*, 12 September 1896, 1.

30. "One Thousand," *Akron Evening Journal*, 12 September 1896, 1.

31. "Not to Take the Stump," *St. Louis Post-Dispatch*, 12 September 1896, 2.

32. "Crush at Canton," *Cleveland Plain Dealer*, 12 September 1896, 1.

33. William McKinley, "Workingmen from McKeesport," in *McKinley's Speeches in September*, 197; "Got a Wetting," *Canton Repository*, 13 September 1896, 3.

34. "Wool Growers," *Canton Repository*, 17 September 1896, 3.

35. William McKinley, "The Wool Growers of Harrison County," in *McKinley's Speeches in September*, 199, 203.

36. "Fine Addresses," *Akron Sunday Journal*, 13 September 1896, 1.

37. William McKinley, "Stark County Soldiers," in *McKinley's Speeches in September*, 203.

38. W. S. Lloyd, "A Very Tired Man," *Cleveland Plain Dealer*, 17 September 1896, 1.

39. "In Self-Defense," *Cleveland Plain Dealer*, 4 September 1896, 10.

40. "Crush at Canton," *Cleveland Plain Dealer*, 12 September 1896, 1.

41. William McKinley, "Stark County Campaign Opening," in *McKinley's Speeches in September*, 214–15.

42. Joseph Black to William McKinley, 16 September 1896, Library of Congress McKinley Papers, microfilm, series 1, reel 1.

43. "To Call on M'Kinley," *Cleveland Plain Dealer*, 20 September 1896, 5.

44. William McKinley, "Hungarian-Americans from Cleveland," in *McKinley's Speeches in September*, 235.

45. See Burke, *Rhetoric of Motives*, 21.

46. "Canton's Big Day," *Cleveland Plain Dealer*, 18 September 1896, 1.

47. W. S. Lloyd, "On the Jump," *Cleveland Plain Dealer*, 20 September 1896, 1.

48. "Pittsburgh Travelers," *Canton Repository*, 17 September 1896, 1.

49. "Greatest Prosperity," *Canton Repository*, 17 September 1896, 1.

50. "William J. Bryan in Two States," *St. Louis Post-Dispatch*, 4 September 1896, 3.

51. "Voters on the March," *Chicago Sunday Inter-Ocean*, 20 September 1896, 9.

52. "Signals of Danger," *Canton Repository*, 20 September 1896, 1.

53. "To the Steel Workers," *Canton Repository*, 20 September 1896, 6.

54. Ibid.

55. "America Stands First," *Canton Repository,* 24 September 1896, 1.

56. "It's an Honest Nation," *Canton Repository,* 24 September 1896, 5.

57. William McKinley, "Chautauqua and Cattaraugus Counties," in *McKinley's Speeches in September,* 240.

58. "It's an Honest Nation."

59. Ibid.

60. Ibid.

61. "Not a Dollar to be Had," *Canton Repository,* 24 September 1896, 6.

62. "Flowers for McKinley," *New York Times,* 25 September 1896, pt. 1, p. 6.

63. W. S. Lloyd, "Came from Three States," *Cleveland Plain Dealer,* 26 September 1896, 1.

64. William McKinley, "Meadville and Crawford County," in *McKinley's Speeches in September,* 266.

65. William McKinley, "A Great Day in Canton," in *McKinley's Speeches in September,* 271; "A Big Day in Canton," *Cleveland Plain Dealer,* 26 September 1896, 1.

66. "Kissed the Major."

67. William McKinley, "Peoria Commercial Men," in *McKinley's Speeches in September,* 273–74.

68. "Cleveland Women," *Canton Repository,* 27 September 1896, 1.

69. "No Inequality Known," *Canton Repository,* 27 September 1896, 1.

70. "Eleven of 'Em," *Cleveland Plain Dealer,* 27 September 1896, 1.

71. "Twin Delusions and Evils," *Canton Repository,* 27 September 1896, 3.

72. "Making Politics a Business," *Canton Repository,* 27 September 1896, 3.

73. J. N. Bishop to William McKinley, 22 September 1896, Library of Congress McKinley Papers, microfilm, series 1, reel 1.

74. E.g., W. S. Lloyd, "A Band of Editors," *Cleveland Plain Dealer,* 9 September 1896, 2; "A Day Off," *Cleveland Plain Dealer,* 2 September 1896, 5; "M'Kinley to Ohio Editors," *Cleveland Plain Dealer,* 9 September 1896, 2; "Ten Speeches in a Day;" *Cleveland Plain Dealer,* 20 September 1896, 1; "More Pilgrims Hear M'Kinley," *St. Louis Post-Dispatch,* 13 September 1896, 7.

75. Marie Hochmuth, "Kenneth Burke and the 'New Rhetoric,'" *Quarterly Journal of Speech* 38 (1952): 133.

76. Coletta, *William Jennings Bryan,* 1:191; Diamond, "Urban and Rural Voting," 291–92; Glad, *McKinley, Bryan,* 203–204.

77. In August, McKinley wrote to his friend Myron Herrick that "as to Texas, of course I must frankly say I would be astonished if we carry that State." Wm McKinley to Myron T. Herrick, 10 August 1896, TS, Herrick Papers, MS 2925, Western Reserve Historical Society, container 1, folder 4 (microfilm).

78. "Bryan Greeted by Thousands," *St. Louis Post-Dispatch,* 9 August 1896, 2; "Yale Yells," *Cleveland Plain Dealer,* 25 September 1896, 1.

79. Burke, *Rhetoric of Motives,* 45.

80. Burke, *Rhetoric of Motives,* 25–29.

81. Richard E. Crable, "Ike: Identification, Argument, and Paradoxical Appeal," *Quarterly Journal of Speech* 63 (1977): 189, n. 10.

1. The *Cleveland Plain Dealer* reported the Cleveland weather at 91 degrees; 13 September 1896, pt. 1, p. 1.

2. "Bryan's Coming Tour," *Cleveland Plain Dealer,* 10 September 1896, 6; "Bryan Speeding toward St. Louis," *St. Louis Post-Dispatch,* 12 September 1896, 1.

3. For accounts of the 1892 lockout, see Krause, *Battle for Homestead,* 12–43, and Wolff, *Lockout,* 100–26.

4. Vanessa B. Beasley, "Making Diversity Safe for Democracy: American Pluralism and the Presidential Local Address, 1885–1992," *Quarterly Journal of Speech* 87 (2001): 25.

5. "A Busy Day," *Akron Beacon and Republican,* 12 September 1896, 3.

6. "The First Voters," *Akron Evening Journal,* 11 September 1896, 5; "Two Big Crowds," *Cleveland Plain Dealer,* 13 September 1896, 2.

7. Robert L. Scott, "Between Silence and Certainty: A Codicil to 'Dialectical Tensions of Speaking and Silence,'" *Quarterly Journal of Speech* 86 (2000): 11, 110.

8. Barry Brummett, "Towards a Theory of Silence as a Political Strategy," *Quarterly Journal of Speech* 66 (1980): 289.

9. Edwin Black, "Gettysburg and Silence," *Quarterly Journal of Speech* 80 (1994): 29.

10. Martin J. Medhurst, "Truman's Rhetorical Reticence, 1945–1947: An Interpretive Essay," *Quarterly Journal of Speech* 74 (1988): 55, 67.

11. Peter Ehrenhaus, "Silence and Symbolic Expression," *Communication Monographs* 55 (1988): 48, 55.

12. See Ronald Reagan, "Remarks at the U.S. Ranger Monument, Pointe du Hoc, France, June 6, 1984," in Ronald Reagan, *Speaking My Mind: Selected Speeches* (New York: Simon and Schuster, 1989), 217–22.

13. Black, "Gettysburg and Silence," 29.

14. Hazel E. Barnes, "Key to Special Terminology," in Jean-Paul Sartre, *Being and Nothingness: An Essay on Phenomenological Ontology,* trans. Hazel E. Barnes (New York: Philosophical Library, 1956), 629.

15. Hazel Barnes, "Sartre's Ontology: The Revealing and Making of Being," in *The Cambridge Companion to Sartre,* ed. Christina Howells (Cambridge: Cambridge University Press, 1992), 24.

16. Sartre, *Being and Nothingness,* 7.

17. Ibid., 9–11; Peter Caws, *Sartre, The Arguments of the Philosophers,* ed. Ted Honderich (London: Routledge and Kegan Paul, 1979), 67-68.

18. Sartre, *Being and Nothingness,* 10.

19. P. L. Heath, "Nothing," q. v., *Encyclopedia of Philosophy,* ed. Paul Edwards (New York: Macmillan, 1967).

20. Lester C. Olsen, "On the Margins of Rhetoric: Audre Lorde Transforming Silence into Language and Action," *Quarterly Journal of Speech* 83 (1997): 49, 53, 65.

21. Scott, "Between Silence and Certainty," 10.

22. Wm. M. Osborne to Hon. William McKinley, 11 August 1896, Library of Congress McKinley Papers, microfilm, series 1, reel 1.

23. Chaim Perelman and Lucie Olbrechts-Tyteca, *The New Rhetoric: A Treatise on Argumentation,* trans. John Wilkinson and Purcell Weaver (Notre Dame: University of Notre Dame Press, 1969), 19; see also Chaim Perelman, "The New Rhetoric," trans. E. Griffin-Collart, in *The Prospect of Rhetoric: Report of the National Developmental Project,* ed. Lloyd F. Bitzer and Edwin Black (Englewood Cliffs, N.J.: Prentice-Hall, 1971), 115–22; and Chaim Perelman and Lucie Olbrechts-Tyteca, "Act and Person in Argument," in *Philosophy, Rhetoric and Argumentation,* ed. Maurice Natanson and Henry W. Johnstone Jr. (University Park: Pennsylvania State University Press, 1965), 102–25.

24. "Gone to See McKinley," *Pittsburg Press,* September 12, 1896, 4.

25. "Democratic Day," *Akron Beacon and Republican,* 12 September 1986, 1.

26. "50,000 Pilgrims," *Akron Beacon and Republican,* 14 September 1896, 3.

27. "Gone to See McKinley," *Pittsburg Press,* September 12, 1896, 4.

28. "50,000 Pilgrims," 3; "One Thousand," *Akron Evening Journal,* 12 September 1896, 1.

29. "Two Big Crowds."

30. "A Good Time," *Canton Repository,* 13 September 1896, 1.

31. "One Thousand."

32. For example, see "Fine Addresses," *Akron Sunday Journal,* 13 September 1896, 1; "One Thousand"; "Democrats Visit M'Kinley," *New York Times,* 13 September 1896, pt. 1, p. 3; "Two Big Crowds"; "Gone to See McKinley," *Pittsburg Press,* September 12, 1896, 4; also, "McKinley to Steel Workers," *New York Times,* 13 September 1896, pt. 1, p. 3.

33. "One Thousand," 1; "Two Big Crowds," pt. 1, p. 2. Molanthy was a middle-level manager. The press also spelled this name "Molamphy" and "Molamphey."

34. Martha Scott Kessler makes a similar point about the related practice of using surrogate speakers in a late twentieth century campaign, "The Role of Surrogate Speakers in the 1980 Presidential Campaign," *Quarterly Journal of Speech* 67 (1981): 146–56, esp. 148.

35. "Fine Addresses," *Akron Sunday Journal,* 13 September 1896, 1. This article includes excerpts from J. Molanthy's speech of 12 September 1896.

36. "Two Big Crowds."

37. "50,000 Pilgrims," 3.

38. "More Work, More Wages," *Canton Repository,* 13 September 1896, 1. Text of McKinley's speech to a group from Homestead, Pennsylvania, on 12 September 1896. By the *Repository's* usual practice, this text was probably based on a copy taken down by a shorthand reporter. This text probably does accurately reflect what McKinley actually said to the Homestead group, but the text may contain transcribing errors or alterations to correct errors and infelicities of style. A number of other newspapers published lengthy excerpts from this speech. Versions published in McKinley campaign

documents are less desirable because they have been subjected to further editing; judging by the handwriting this editing was presumably undertaken by McKinley's private secretary, Joseph Smith. Smith's edited typescript of the Homestead speech is found in the Western Reserve Historical Society in Cleveland, Ohio, #3201, container 1, folder 1. All of these texts are, of course, subject to the vicissitudes of shorthand reporting.

39. "Bryan's Great Speech," *Cleveland Plain Dealer,* 10 July 1896, 2.

40. "More Work, More Wages."

41. Ibid.

42. "Bryan's Great Speech," 2.

43. Robert Lynn Ivie also notes McKinley's stress on unity in one of his addresses as president; see "William McKinley: Advocate of Imperialism," *Western Speech* 36 (1972): 15–23.

44. "More Work, More Wages."

45. In one interesting incident, labor leader Terence V. Powderly wrote that same day: "Go carefully over Mr. Bryan's speeches and you do not find a single labor measure championed"; "Sound Truths," *Akron Sunday Journal,* 13 September 1896, 4.

46. "More Work, More Wages."

47. Ibid.

48. Ibid.

49. "Bryan Talks at St. Louis," *New York Times,* 13 September 1896, pt. 1, p. 2.

50. "More Work, More Wages."

51. Ibid.

52. Ibid.

53. "Two Big Crowds."

54. "Homestead Men for Bryan," *Cleveland Plain Dealer,* 12 September 1896, 1.

55. "Gives Warm Welcome for All," *Canton Repository,* 27 September 1896, 6.

56. "Favors Independence," *Canton Repository,* 8 October 1896, 2.

57. "All Aspire to Get Better Things, *Canton Repository,* 11 October 1896, 3.

58. "50,000 Pilgrims," 1; "Fine Addresses." The latter article includes passages from McKinley's speeches of 12 September 1896.

59. William McKinley, Speech to delegation from Homestead, Pennsylvania, TS, presumably a rough draft of McKinley's speech of September 12, 1896, Library of Congress McKinley Papers, microfilm, series 4, reel 81. The Library of Congress does not allow scholars to see the actual documents from presidential archives. The microfilm reproduction is clear enough to show through McKinley's letterhead on the reverse.

60. Shorthand notes for several McKinley speeches are found in the Library of Congress McKinley Papers, series 4, reel 81.

61. McKinley, Speech to delegation from Homestead.

62. "More Work, More Wages."

63. McKinley, Speech to delegation from Homestead; "More Work, More Wages," 1.

64. "Fine Addresses"; "More Work, More Wages."

65. "McKinley to Steel Workers," *New York Times,* 13 September 1896, 3.

66. "Two Big Crowds."

67. "More Pilgrims Hear M'Kinley," *St. Louis Post-Dispatch,* 13 September 1896, 7.

68. "Bryan's Great Speech."

69. "Carnegie on Silver," *Akron Evening Journal,* 4 September 1896, 5.

Chapter 8

1. Weaver, *Ethics of Rhetoric,* 57; Richard M. Weaver, "Language Is Sermonic," in *Contemporary Theories of Rhetoric: Selected Readings,* ed. Richard L. Johannesen (New York: Harper, 1971), 172; Richard M. Weaver, "A Responsible Rhetoric," ed. Thomas D. Clark and Richard L. Johannesen, *Intercollegiate Review* 12 (1976–77): 83–84; Richard M. Weaver, *Rhetoric and Composition: A Course in Writing and Reading,* 2nd ed., revised with the assistance of Richard S. Beal (New York: Holt, 1967), 137–41.

2. E.g., Weaver, "Language Is Sermonic," 172.

3. Ibid.

4. Weaver, *Ethics of Rhetoric,* 57.

5. Weaver, "Responsible Rhetoric," 84; see Weaver, *Rhetoric,* 140.

6. Trent and Friedenberg, *Political Campaign Communication,* 74.

7. Wood, "William Jennings Bryan, Crusader," 159.

8. Phillips, "William Jennings Bryan," 913–17.

9. Oliver, *History,* 485.

10. Springen, *William Jennings Bryan: Orator,* 19.

11. Coletta, *William Jennings Bryan,* 1:196.

12. "Two Big B's," *Cleveland Plain Dealer,* 2 September 1896, 1.

13. "Bryan's Triumph!" *Cleveland Plain Dealer,* 2 September 1896, 1; "Thirty Thousand Heard Bryan," *St. Louis Post-Dispatch,* 2 September 1896, 6. Newspaper estimates of audience sizes are obviously rough approximations that must be taken with a grain of salt. Different newspapers often gave varying estimates.

14. "Bryan's Triumph!" 1.

15. Ibid.

16. "Thirty Thousand."

17. "Bryan's Triumph!" 12.

18. "Indefatigable," *Cleveland Plain Dealer,* 3 September 1896, 8.

19. Ibid.

20. "A Scorcher," *Cleveland Plain Dealer,* 3 September 1896, 2.

21. "Fifty Thousand," *Cleveland Plain Dealer,* 3 September 1896, 1.

22. "William J. Bryan in Two States," *St. Louis Post-Dispatch,* 4 September 1896, 3.

23. Ibid.

24. E.g., "Signals of Danger," *Canton Repository,* 20 September 1896, 1.

25. "William J. Bryan in Two States"; "In Hoosierdom," *Cleveland Plain Dealer,* 4 September 1896, 1.

26. "Rainy Weather," *Cleveland Plain Dealer,* 6 September 1896, 6.

27. "Bryan at Milwaukee," *Chicago Inter-Ocean,* 6 September 1896, 3.

28. "Two Speeches by Mr. Bryan," *St. Louis Post-Dispatch,* 6 September 1896, 3.

29. Ibid.

30. "Carnegie on Silver," *Akron Evening Journal,* 4 September 1896, 5.

31. "No Politics in It," *Cleveland Plain Dealer,* 8 September 1896, 1.

32. Dawes, *Journal,* 96.

33. "Pleased with the Prospect," *St. Louis Post-Dispatch,* 6 September 1896, 1; "William J. Bryan at Milwaukee," *St. Louis Post-Dispatch,* 5 September 1896, 2; "Well Satisfied," *Cleveland Plain Dealer,* 5 September 1896, 8.

34. W. S. Lloyd, "Quay's Brains," *Cleveland Plain Dealer,* 4 September 1896, 7.

35. W. S. Lloyd, "His Own Mouth," *Cleveland Plain Dealer,* 9 September 1896, 1.

36. "Routed from Bed," *Cleveland Plain Dealer,* 9 September 1896, 8.

37. "Bryan at Home," *Cleveland Plain Dealer,* 9 September 1896, 8.

38. "Yes, Sir!" *Cleveland Plain Dealer,* 10 September 1896, 5.

39. "Bryan's Coming Tour," *Cleveland Plain Dealer,* 10 September 1896, 6; "Bryan Speeding toward St. Louis," *St. Louis Post-Dispatch,* 12 September 1896, 1.

40. "Bryan Speeding."

41. Ibid.

42. "Great Crowds to Hear Bryan," *St. Louis Post-Dispatch,* 12 September 1896, 1–2.

43. "How Mrs. Bryan Was Received," *St. Louis Post-Dispatch.* 13 September 1896, 1.

44. "Great Crowds," 1.

45. "Bryan at the Auditorium," *St. Louis Post-Dispatch,* 13 September 1896, 1.

46. "William J. Bryan Addressing the Audience at the Auditorium," sketch, *St. Louis Post-Dispatch,* 13 September 1896, 1.

47. "Bryan at the Auditorium," 1–2.

48. "Mr. Bryan at Concordia Park," *St. Louis Post-Dispatch,* 13 September 1896, 5.

49. "Bryan in St. Louis," *Cleveland Plain Dealer,* 13 September 1896, 5.

50. Ibid.

51. "Platform Gave Way," *St. Louis Post-Dispatch,* 13 September 1896, 9.

52. "Rainy," *Akron Beacon.*

53. "In Old Kentucky," *Cleveland Plain Dealer,* 15 September 1896, 2.

54. "Great Welcome in Kentucky," *Cleveland Plain Dealer,* 15 September 1896, 2.

55. "Rainy," *Akron Beacon.*

56. "Hits at Carlisle," *Cleveland Plain Dealer,* 17 September 1896, 8.

57. Ibid.

58. "Bryan's Tour," *Cleveland Plain Dealer,* 18 September 1896, 1.

59. Ibid., 2.

60. Ibid.

61. "A Common Cause," *Cleveland Plain Dealer,* 19 September 1896, 1.

62. "Bryan on Bolters," *Cleveland Plain Dealer,* 19 September 1896, 5.

63. "In Spite of Rain," *Cleveland Plain Dealer,* 20 September 1896, 1–2.

64. "In Old Virginia," *Cleveland Plain Dealer,* 20 September 1896, 7.

65. "In Old Virginia"; "Rain Stops Bryan," *Chicago Sunday Inter-Ocean,* 20 September 1896, 9.

66. "Mr. Bryan's Speech," *Washington Evening Star,* 21 September 1896, 10.

67. "A Day of Rest," *Cleveland Plain Dealer,* 21 September 1896, 1.

68. "Bismarck's Tip," *Cleveland Plain Dealer,* 22 September 1896, 1.

69. "An Awful Crush," *Cleveland Plain Dealer,* 23 September 1896, 1.

70. However, see also "Law as to Riots," *Cleveland Plain Dealer,* 12 September 1896, 6.

71. "Lincoln's Words," *Cleveland Plain Dealer,* 24 September 1896, 1–2; "It Started in Nebraska," *New York Times,* 23 September 1896, pt. 1, p. 6; "Mr. Bryan in Brooklyn," *New York Times,* 24 September 1896, pt. 1, pp. 1–2.

72. "To Help Bryan," *Cleveland Plain Dealer,* 24 September 1896, 7.

73. "Yale Would Not Listen," *New York Times,* 25 September 1896, pt. 1, p. 5; "Yale Yells," *Cleveland Plain Dealer,* 25 September 1896, 1.

74. "Bryan in Connecticut," *Cleveland Plain Dealer,* 25 September 1896, 1.

75. "Bryan in Boston," *Cleveland Plain Dealer,* 26 September 1896, 1.

76. "A Rising Dollar," *Cleveland Plain Dealer,* 26 September 1896, 3.

77. Ibid.

78. "Watson Flares Up," *Cleveland Plain Dealer,* 29 September 1896, 5.

79. "Back in New York," *Cleveland Plain Dealer,* 29 September 1896, 1.

80. Ibid.

81. "A Conqueror," *Cleveland Plain Dealer,* 30 September 1896, 2; "Bryan Tammany's Guest," *New York Times,* 30 September 1896, pt. 1, p. 1; "Wigwam Crowded," *New York Times,* 30 September 1896, pt. 1, p. 2; "Mr. Bryan's Address," *New York Times,* 30 September 1896, pt. 1, p. 2.

82. "Is Mr. Bryan a Mattoid," *New York Times,* 29 September 1896, pt. 1, p. 3.

83. "Tammany at the Front," *New York Times,* 29 September 1896, pt. 1, p. 4.

84. "The Choice," *New York Times,* 30 September 1896, pt. 1, p. 4.

85. Bryan, *First Battle,* 509.

86. Weaver, *Ethics of Rhetoric,* 56–58.

1. Floyd D. Anderson and Lawrence J. Prelli, "Pentadic Cartography: Mapping the Universe of Discourse," *Quarterly Journal of Speech* 87 (2001): 76.

2. Kurt Ritter and David Henry, *Ronald Reagan: The Great Communicator,* Great American Orators 13 (New York: Greenwood Press, 1992), 63.

3. Noted by John E. Smith, "Time, Times, and the 'Right Time': *Chronos* and *Kairos*," *Monist* 53 (1969): 1.

4. Dale L. Sullivan, "*Kairos* and the Rhetoric of Belief," *Quarterly Journal of Speech* 78 (1992): 317; Crowley and Hawhee, *Ancient Rhetorics,* 31, 40.

5. Smith, "Time, Times," 1, 6; John E. Smith, "Time and Qualitative Time," *Review of Metaphysics* 40 (1986): 4.

6. Sullivan, *Kairos,* 321, 332.

7. See, for example, "A Short Money Talk," *Washington Evening Star,* 7 October 1896, 1.

8. E.g., "McKinley on Confidence," *Kansas City Star,* 2 October 1896, 9; "Tariff Changes Blamed," *Kansas City Star,* 3 October 1896, 9. b

9. "Places Protection First," *New York Times,* 2 October 1896, 3.

10. "Hard Road to Travel," *Canton Repository,* 4 October 1896, 1; "Sixteen to One," *Canton Repository,* 4 October 1896, 1, 4.

11. "Patriotism Foremost," *Canton Repository,* 4 October 1896, 5.

12. "Want Good Times to Come Again," *Canton Repository,* 4 October 1896, 6.

13. "Greeting to His Old Comrades," *Canton Repository,* 4 October 1896, 6.

14. "Farmers Not Misled," *Canton Repository,* 4 October 1896, 6.

15. "Syracuse, N.Y.," *Canton Repository,* 8 October 1896, 1.

16. "Favors Independence," *Canton Repository,* 8 October 1896, 2.

17. Ibid.

18. "Cannot Create Money," *Canton Repository,* 8 October 1896, 1.

19. Ibid.

20. "All Crafts," *Canton Repository,* 11 October 1896, 1; "All Records Outdone," *Canton Repository,* 11 October 1896, 4.

21. "Speech to Pennsylvania Miners," *Canton Repository,* 11 October 1896, 6.

22. "Unsullied and Spotless," *Canton Repository,* 11 October 1896, 5.

23. "Greeting to Indiana Callers," *Canton Repository,* 11 October 1896, 6.

24. "Register Waves of Business," *Canton Repository,* 11 October 1896, 2.

25. "Business Threads Interwoven," *Canton Repository,* 11 October 1896, 2.

26. "To a Call from the Sixfooters," *Canton Repository,* 11 October 1896, 2.

27. "To the Polish Club of Cleveland," *Canton Repository,* 11 October 1896, 2.

28. "Keystone, Hawkeye and Sucker Men," *Canton Repository,* 11 October 1896, 3.

29. "Speech to Many Railroad Men," *Canton Repository,* 11 October 1896, 2.

30. "Pennsy Again," *Canton Repository,* 15 October 1896, 1.

31. "Panic and Depression," *Canton Repository,* 15 October 1896, 1.

32. "Great Crowds," *Canton Repository,* 18 October 1896, 1.

33. "Wonders Never Cease in Canton," *Canton Repository,* 18 October 1896, 4.

34. "Markets Versus Maxims," *Canton Repository,* 18 October 1896, 1.

35. "There Is No Conflict," *Canton Repository,* 18 October 1896, 2.

36. "People All Are Patriots," *Canton Repository,* 18 October 1896, 2.

37. "Address to Cuyahoga Callers," *Canton Repository,* 18 October 1896, 2.

38. "Hour and Era for Patriotism," *Canton Repository,* 18 October 1896, 6.

39. "It Never Makes a Slave," *Canton Repository,* 18 October 1896, 3.

40. "People and Nation Have Suffered," *Canton Repository,* 18 October 1896, 6.

41. "It Means Patriotism," *Canton Repository,* 18 October 1896, 6.

42. Ibid.

43. William McKinley, "To Columbus Ohio Railway Club, Oct. 17, 1896," TS, presumably from a collection of McKinley's speeches edited for publication, Western Reserve Historical Society McKinley Papers, #4674, container 3, folder 13, pp. 109–10.

44. "They Are Only Waiting," *Canton Repository,* 29 October 1896, 1.

45. Dawes, *Journal,* 103.

46. Smith, "Time and Qualitative," 15.

47. Raymie E. McKerrow, "Rationality and Reasonableness in a Theory of Argument," in *Advances in Argumentation Theory and Research,* ed. J. Robert Cox and Charles A. Willard (Carbondale: Southern Illinois University Press, 1982). See also William D. Harpine, "The Appeal to Tradition: Cultural Evolution and Logical Soundness," *Informal Logic* 15 (1993): 109–19.

48. See, e.g., David A. McKay, "Food, Illness, and Folk Medicine: Insights from Ulu Trengganu, West Malaysia," in *Food, Ecology and Culture: Readings in the Anthropology of Dietary Practices,* ed. J. R. K. Robson (New York: Gordon and Breach Science Publishers, 1980), 65.

49. Celeste M. Condit, "The Functions of Epideictic: The Boston Massacre Orations as Exemplar," *Communication Quarterly* 33 (1985): 289; Dale L. Sullivan, "A Closer Look at Education as Epideictic Rhetoric," *Rhetoric Society Quarterly* 23 (1993): 72; Dale L. Sullivan, "The Ethos of Epideictic Encounter," *Philosophy and Rhetoric* 26 (1993): 116; Scott Consigny, "Gorgias's Use of the Epideictic," *Philosophy and Rhetoric* 25 (1992): 281; J. R. Chase, "The Classical Conception of Epideictic," *Quarterly Journal of Speech* 47 (1961): 300; c.f. D. Jaehne, "Arguers as Value Adjusters: Epideictic Discourse in the Environmental Movement," in *Argument and Critical Practices: Proceedings of the Fifth SCA/AFA Conference on Argumentation,* ed. Joseph W. Wenzel (Annandale, Va.: Speech Communication Association, 1987); Theodore Chalon Burgess, *Epideictic Literature,* preprint from Studies in Classical Philology 3 (Chicago: University of Chicago Press, 1902), 93–94.

50. Lawrence W. Rosenfield, "The Practical Celebration of Epideictic," in *Rhetoric in Transition: Studies in the Nature and Uses of Rhetoric*, ed. Eugene E. White (University Park: Pennsylvania State University Press, 1980), 131–55, quote at 139; see also Gerard A. Hauser, *Introduction to Rhetorical Theory* (New York: Harper and Row, 1986), 66.

51. Rosenfield, "Practical Celebration," 135.

52. Chaim Perelman, "The New Rhetoric," 116.

53. Charles U. Larson, *Persuasion: Reception and Responsibility*, 9th ed. (Belmont, CA: Wadsworth–Thomson Learning, 2001), 115–16.

54. "Doctrine of Hate Not Taught," *Canton Repository*, 25 October 1896, 6.

Chapter 10

1. "Pointers on the Handshake," Editorial, *Chicago Evening Post*, 12 July 1896, 4.

2. Oliver, *History*, 479; Wood, "William Jennings Bryan, Crusader," 158; Springen, *William Jennings Bryan: Orator*, 19.

3. David D. Anderson, *William Jennings Bryan* (Boston: Hall-Twayne, 1981), 189.

4. Edwin Black, *Rhetorical Criticism: A Study in Method* (Madison: University of Wisconsin Press, 1978), 150.

5. See Douglas Ehninger, "Debate as Method: Limitations and Values," *Speech Teacher* 15 (1966): 180–85; Douglas Ehninger, "Decision by Debate: A Re-Examination," *Quarterly Journal of Speech* 45 (1959): 282–87; Douglas Ehninger, "Argument as Method: Its Nature, Its Limitations and Its Uses," *Speech Monographs* 37 (1970): 101–10. See also Douglas Ehninger and Wayne Brockriede, *Decision by Debate* (New York: Dodd, Mead and Company, 1970), 15, for a summary of these ideas.

6. E.g., Joseph W. Wenzel, "Jurgen Habermas and the Dialectical Perspective on Argumentation," *Journal of the American Forensic Association* 16 (1979): 83–94; Joseph W. Wenzel, "Perspectives on Argument," in *Proceedings of the Summer Conference on Argumentation*, ed. J. Rhodes and Sara Newell (Falls Church, Va.: Speech Communication Association, 1980), 112–33; Jurgen Habermas, *Knowledge and Human Interests*, trans. J. J. Shapiro (Boston: Beacon Press, 1968); Ehninger, "Decision by Debate," 282–87.

7. Ehninger and Brockriede, *Decision by Debate*, 15

8. Ehninger, "Decision by Debate," 283.

9. "A Joint Debate," *Washington Evening Star*, 13 August 1896, 1.

10. "To the Polish Club of Cleveland," *Canton Repository*, 11 October 1896, 2.

11. "A Warning to the Banks," *Cleveland Plain Dealer*, 3 October 1896, 8.

12. This was the same statistic that Bryan quoted in 1895; see "Seems to Lack Vitality," *New York Times*, 5 May 1895, 1.

13. "On to St. Louis," *Cleveland Plain Dealer*, 4 October 1896, 1.

14. Ibid.

15. Ibid., 1–2.

16. Bryan was presumably referring to William McKinley's speech of August 18, 1986: "I do not know what you think about it, but I believe it is a good deal better to open the mills of the United States to the labor of America than to open the mints of the United States to the silver of the world." William McKinley, "Comrades of the Twenty-Third Ohio: Major McKinley's Response," in *McKinley's Speeches in August,* comp. Joseph P. Smith (Canton, Ohio: Republican National Committee, 1896), 83.

17. "Great Speech at East St. Louis," *Cleveland Plain Dealer,* 4 October 1896, 5.

18. Ehninger and Brockriede, *Decision by Debate,* 15.

19. Wenzel, "Perspectives."

20. "Bryan in Dixie," *Cleveland Plain Dealer,* 6 October 1896, 7.

21. "Biggest but One," *Cleveland Plain Dealer,* 7 October 1896, 2.

22. Ibid., 1.

23. "A Plea for Farmers," *Cleveland Plain Dealer,* 7 October 1896, 2.

24. "Two M'Kinley's," *Cleveland Plain Dealer,* 9 October 1896, 6.

25. "Talks to Farmers," *Cleveland Plain Dealer,* 10 October 1896, 1.

26. "At Peep O'Day," *Cleveland Plain Dealer,* 11 October 1896, 3.

27. "A Well Earned Rest," *Cleveland Plain Dealer,* 12 October 1896, 1.

28. "Progress of the Campaign," *New York Evening Post,* 12 October 1896, 5.

29. "Four in One Night," *Cleveland Plain Dealer,* 13 October 1896, 1.

30. "A Bottle of Ink," *Cleveland Plain Dealer,* 14 October 1896, 1.

31. "Through Minnesota Towns," *Cleveland Plain Dealer,* 14 October 1896, 3.

32. Ibid.

33. "Address to Women," *Washington Evening Star,* 13 October 1896, 2.

34. "Many Women," *Canton Repository,* 16 July 1896, 1.

35. "Up in Michigan," *Cleveland Plain Dealer,* 15 October 1896, 1.

36. Ibid.

37. "Up at Daybreak," *Cleveland Plain Dealer,* 16 October 1896, 2.

38. Ibid.

39. "The Whirlwind Campaign," *New York Herald,* 2 October 1896, 3. Includes sketches of campaign events.

40. E. R. Hull and Dutton, Advertisement, *Cleveland Plain Dealer,* 18 October 1896, 3.

41. "Partisan Flag Desecration," Editorial, *Cleveland Plain Dealer,* 18 October 1896, 6. See "Republican Flag Day," *New York Herald,* 27 October 1896, 5.

42. "Wakes 'Em," *Cleveland Plain Dealer,* 20 October 1896, 2.

43. Ibid.

44. "Bryan Shows a Bit of Temper," *New York Herald,* 21 October 1896, 6.

45. "A Royal Welcome to Bryan," *Cleveland Plain Dealer,* 17 October 1896, 2.

46. W. S. Lloyd, "Bryan Crosses Ohio," *Cleveland Plain Dealer,* 21 October 1896, 1.

47. "A Great Triumph in Ohio," *Cleveland Plain Dealer,* 21 October 1896, 1.

48. "At Boiling Point," *Cleveland Plain Dealer,* 22 October 1896, 1–2.

49. "On the Offensive," *Cleveland Plain Dealer,* 23 October 1896, 6.

50. "Bryan's Rebuke," *Cleveland Plain Dealer,* 24 October 1896, 1; "Threw an Egg at Carlisle," *New York Herald,* 23 October 1896, 3.

51. "Bryan's Rebuke."

52. "Eggs for Bryan," *Cleveland Plain Dealer,* 18 October 1896, 6.

53. "Bryan's Great Day," *Cleveland Plain Dealer,* 29 October 1896, 1.

54. Ibid., 2

55. Ibid.

56. "Back in Chicago," *Cleveland Plain Dealer,* 30 October 1896, 1.

57. Bryan's reference is presumably to Michel Chevalier, *On the Probable Fall in the Value of Gold: The Commercial and Social Consequences Which May Ensue, and the Measures Which It Invites,* trans. Richard Cobden (New York: Greenbook Press, 1868). Chevalier's book appears to advocate a version of bimetallism.

58. "Back in Chicago," 2.

59. Ibid.

60. Ibid., 1.

61. Bryan, *First Battle,* 602.

62. "Methods and Tactics of the Campaign," *Review of Reviews* 4 (1896): 553–55.

63. Bryan, *First Battle,* 592–93.

64. Ibid., 608.

65. Richard Whately, *Elements of Rhetoric: Comprising an Analysis of the Laws of Moral Evidence and of Persuasion, with Rules for Argumentative Composition and Elocution,* ed. Douglas Ehninger (Carbondale: Southern Illinois University Press, 1963), 112–32, esp. 115.

66. Larson, *Persuasion,* 116.

Conclusion

1. "McKinley's Opportunity," Editorial, *Kansas City Star,* 4 November 1896, 4.

2. James L. Kinneavy, "*Kairos:* A Neglected Concept in Classical Rhetoric," in *Rhetoric and Praxis: The Contribution of Classical Rhetoric to Practical Reasoning,* ed. Jean Dietz Moss (Washington: Catholic University Press of America), 82–84. B. Lee Artz and Mark A. Pollock, "The Rhetoric of Unconditional Surrender: Locating the Necessary Moment for Coercion," *Communication Studies* 48 (1997): 159–73, esp. 162. James L. Kinneavy and Catherine R. Eskin, "'Kairos' in Aristotle's 'Rhetoric,'" *Written Communication* 11 (1994): 137.

3. "It's an Honest Nation," *Canton Repository,* 24 September 1896, 5.

4. "Conservatism Wins," Editorial, *Kansas City Star,* 4 November 1896, 4.

5. Ibid.

6. "Bryan's Unprecedented Canvass," *Review of Reviews* 14 (1896): 519.

7. "Methods and Tactics of the Campaign," *Review of Reviews* 14 (1896): 558.

8. "Bryan's Unprecedented Canvass," 519.

9. E.g., "Rainy Weather," *Akron Beacon and Republican,* 16 September 1896, 3; "In the South," *Akron Beacon and Republican,* 17 September 1896, 3; "Yale Would Not Listen," *New York Times,* 25 September 1896, pt. 1, p. 5; "Bryan in the Darkness," *New York Times,* 29 September 1896, pt. 1, p. 3.

10. "The Pivotal States," *Washington Evening Star,* 12 October 1896, 1.

11. Coletta, *William Jennings Bryan,* 1:191; Diamond, "Urban and Rural Voting."

12. Coletta, *William Jennings Bryan,* 1:191; Diamond, "Urban and Rural Voting," 291–92.

13. "Up at Daybreak," *Cleveland Plain Dealer,* 16 October 1896, 2.

14. Ibid.

15. W. J. Stone, Missouri, to Hon. W. J. Bryan, Omaha, 14 July 1896, MS, William Jennings Bryan Papers, Manuscript Division, Library of Congress, Washington, D.C., box 4.

16. Bryan, *First Battle,* 233ff., 300–301, 597–604

17. Trent and Friedenberg, *Political Campaign Communication,* 70.

18. Lewis L. Gould, *American in the Progressive Era, 1890–1914* (Harlow, England: Longman, 2001), 16.

19. E.g., "Employment and Prosperity," *Canton Repository,* 4 October 1896, 6.

20. "The Victory—Elements and Meaning," Editorial, *Washington Evening Star,* 4 November 1896, 6.

21. "Brotherhood of Man," *Canton Repository,* 1 October 1896, 5.

22. "Presidential Motives for War," *Quarterly Journal of Speech* 60 (1974): 343.

23. Glad, *McKinley, Bryan,* 167–88; Trent and Friedenberg, *Political Campaign Communication,* 78; Leech, *Days of McKinley,* 66–96.

24. "McKinley's Opportunity," Editorial, *Kansas City Star,* 4 November 1896, 4.

25. Harold Barrett, "Scott of the *Oregonian* vs. William Jennings Bryan," *Quarterly Journal of Speech* 48 (1962): 169–73.

26. Glad, *McKinley, Bryan,* 203–204.

27. Coletta, *William Jennings Bryan,* 1:189–92.

28. Springen, *William Jennings Bryan: Orator,* 19; Jones, *Presidential Election,* 345; Diamond, "Urban and Rural Voting," 281–305, esp. 284, 291–92.

29. Bryan College, "William Jennings Bryan and the Scopes Trial," http://www.bryan.edu/historical/wjbryan_trial/index.html, accessed 18 September 2002.

Index

studies of his speaking, 7; parallel language, 93, 122; public speaking style of, 2, 5–6; rhetoric of, 7, 90, 92, 108–10

McKinley, William, speeches: acceptance speech, 45–46; after nomination, 42; of August and September 1896, 10; at campaign opening, 98–99; to Civil War veterans from Cuyahoga, County, Ohio, 48; to Civil War Veterans, 98; to Cleveland Foraker Club, 46–47; to commercial travelers, 152; to Democrats from Chicago, 97; 1890 tariff speech, 35; to Elroy M. Avery Drill Corps, 104–105; to Garfield club of Louisville Ky., 154; to glass workers, 49–50; to Goodland, Ind., 151; to group from African-American Episcopal Church, 181; to group from Alliance, Ohio, 40; to group from Duquesne, Pa., 106; to group from East Liverpool, Ohio, 50–51; to group from Edgar Thomas Steel Works, 101–102; to group from Geurnsey County, Ohio, 49; to group from Grand Rapids, Minn., 154; to group from Homestead, Pa, 111–27, 120–22, 124–25; to group from Jamestown, N.Y., 102–103; to group from Lawrence County, 52; on Labor Day, 95–96; lack of refutation in, 162–63; to group from McDonald, Pa., 152–53; to group from McKeesport Pa., 97; to group from Niles, Ohio, 35, 43; to group from Peoria, Ill., 104–105; to group from Pittsburgh, 52, 152; to group from Portage County, Ohio, 149; to group from Wheeling, W.Va., 44; to group of women from Cleveland, 47–48; to L'Ouverture Rifles, 50; to McKinley League of New York State, 42; to Ohio farmers, 104; to Ohio Republican editors, 96; to oil workers from Pennsylvania, 104; to Pennsylvania farmers, 150; to Pittsburgh Commercial travelers, 100; to Pittsburgh group, 95–96; to Polish Club of Cleveland, 152; to railroad workers, 100–101; to Republican Hungarian-American National Committee, 99–100; to Republican Press Association of West Virginia, 93; to steelworkers from Cleveland, 152; to Syracuse N.Y., 150; to tin workers, 103–104; to Tippecanoe Club of Cleveland, 46; to union veterans, 149; to Vermonters, 96–97; to women's suffrage group from Cleveland, 105; to woolgrowers, 97–98

McKinley League of New York State, 42

Madison, Wis., 174

Madison Square Garden, 76–77, 84–85, 87

marching bands, 53–53, 93, 102, 104, 117, 182

Market Street, 117, 150

Massillon, Ohio, 74

Medhurst, Martin J., 114

Memphis, Tenn., 164–65

Methodist Episcopal Church, 154–55

Mexican system of finance, 149. *See also* silver

Michigan State Party Committee, 16

Milford, Va., 139

Milholland, John E., 42–43

Milwaukee, 134

Minneapolis, Minn., 166–67

Mississippi Valley states, 135

Missouri, 136

Missouri Democratic Party State Committee, 16

moderation, 177

Molamphy, J. M. *See* Molanthy, J. M.

Molanthy, J. M., 118, 123

money-changers. *See* financiers

money issue, 59, 163–64

money standard, 26

money supply, 29, 137–38

Monroe Doctrine, 135

Morgan, John Pierpont, 65